Julia for Data Science

Explore the world of data science from scratch with Julia by your side

Anshul Joshi

BIRMINGHAM - MUMBAI

Julia for Data Science

First published: September 2016

Production reference: 1260916

Published by Packt Publishing Ltd.
Livery Place
35 Livery Street
Birmingham
B3 2PB, UK.
ISBN 978-1-78528-969-9

www.packtpub.com

Credits

Author

Anshul Joshi

Reviewer

Sébastien Celles

Commissioning Editor

Akram Hussain

Acquisition Editor

Sonali Vernekar

Content Development Editor

Aishwarya Pandere

Technical Editor

Vivek Arora

Copy Editor

Safis Editing

Project Coordinator

Nidhi Joshi

Proofreader

Safis Editing

Indexer

Mariammal Chettiyar

Graphics

Disha Haria

Production Coordinator

Arvindkumar Gupta

About the Author

Anshul Joshi is a data science professional with more than 2 years of experience primarily in data munging, recommendation systems, predictive modeling, and distributed computing. He is a deep learning and AI enthusiast. Most of the time, he can be caught exploring GitHub or trying anything new on which he can get his hands on. He blogs on anshuljoshi.xyz.

I'd like to thank my parents, who have been really supportive throughout, my professors, who helped me during my days at university and got me where I am, and my friends, who were very understanding. A big thanks to the Julia community. These people are amazing and are the rockstars of our generation.

I would also like to thank Packt Publishing and the editors for helping me throughout. A special thanks to Sébastien Celles; his expertise and reviews really helped me improve the book.

About the Reviewer

Sébastien Celles is a professor of applied physics at Poitiers Institute of Technology (Université de Poitiers—IUT de Poitiers—thermal science department). He teaches physics and computer sciences (data processing).

He has used Python for numerical simulations, data plotting, data predicting, and various other tasks since the early 2000s. He is a member of PyData and was granted commit rights to the pandas DataReader project. He is also involved in several open source projects about the scientific Python ecosystem.

He is also author of some Python packages available on PyPi:

- `openweathermap_requests`: A package to fetch data from `http://openweathermap.org/` using requests and requests-cache and get pandas DataFrames with weather history
- `pandas_degreedays`: A package to calculate degree days (a measure of heating or cooling) from a pandas time series of temperature
- `pandas_confusion`: A package to manage confusion matrices, plot them, binarize them, calculate overall statistics, and class statistics

He made some contributions (unit testing, continuous integration, Python 3 port...) too:

- `python-constraint`: A Constraint Solving Problem (CSP) resolver for Python

He was a technical reviewer of *Mastering Python for Data Science* explores the world of data science through Python and learn how to make sense of data. Samir Madhavan. Birmingham, UK, Packt Publishing, August 2015.

Two years ago, he started to learn Julia, with which he has performed various tasks about data mining, machine learning, forecasting, and so he's a user of (and sometimes a contributor too) some Julia packages (`DataStructures.jl`, `CSV.jl`, `DataFrames.jl`, `TimeSeries.jl`, `NDSparseData.jl`, `JuliaTS.jl`, `MLBase.jl`, `Mocha.jl`, and so on)

He is also author of some Julia packages:

- `Pushover.jl`: A package to send notifications using the Pushover Notification Service
- `BulkSMS.jl`: A Julia package to send SMS (Short Message Service) using BulkSMS API
- `DataReaders.jl`: A package to get remote data via `Requests.jl` and get DataFrames thanks to `DataFrames.jl`
- `RequestsCache.jl`: A transparent persistent cache using the `Requests.jl` library to perform requests and using `JLD.jl` library as a storage backend
- `PubSub.jl`: A very basic implementation of the publish-subscribe pattern
- `SignalSlot.jl`: A very basic implementation of the signal-slot pattern
- `TALib.jl`: A Julia wrapper for TA-Lib (Technical Analysis Library)

He has a keen interest in open data and he is a contributor of some projects of the Open Knowledge Foundation (especially around the DataPackage format).

You can find more information about him at `http://www.celles.net/wiki/Contact`.

www.PacktPub.com

For support files and downloads related to your book, please visit www.PacktPub.com.

Did you know that Packt offers eBook versions of every book published, with PDF and ePub files available? You can upgrade to the eBook version at www.PacktPub.com and as a print book customer, you are entitled to a discount on the eBook copy. Get in touch with us at service@packtpub.com for more details.

At www.PacktPub.com, you can also read a collection of free technical articles, sign up for a range of free newsletters and receive exclusive discounts and offers on Packt books and eBooks.

https://www.packtpub.com/mapt

Get the most in-demand software skills with Mapt. Mapt gives you full access to all Packt books and video courses, as well as industry-leading tools to help you plan your personal development and advance your career.

Why subscribe?

- Fully searchable across every book published by Packt
- Copy and paste, print, and bookmark content
- On demand and accessible via a web browser

To my sister — I hope I made you a little proud.

Table of Contents

Preface

Data Scientist: The Sexiest Job of the 21st Century, Harvard Business Review. And why Julia? A high level language with large scientific community and performance comparable to C, it is touted as next best language for data science. Using Julia, we can create statistical models, highly performant machine learning systems, and beautiful and attractive visualizations.

What this book covers

Chapter 1, *The Groundwork – Julia's Environment*, explains how to set up the Julia's environment (Command Line(REPL) and Jupyter Notebook) and explains Julia's ecosystem, why Julia is special, and package management. It also gives an introduction to parallel processing and multiple dispatch and explains how Julia is suited for data science.

Chapter 2, *Data Munging*, explains the need for and process of data preparation, also called data munging. Data munging refers to changing data from one state to other, in well-defined reversible steps. It is preparing data to be used for analytics and visualizations.

Chapter 3, *Data Exploration*, explains that statistics is the core of data science, shows that Julia provides various statistical functions. This chapter will give a high-level overview of statistics and will explain the techniques required to apply those statistical concepts to general problems using Julia's statistical packages, such as Stats.jl and Distributions.jl.

Chapter 4, *Deep Dive into Inferential Statistics*, continues statistics is the core of the data science and is Julia provides various statistical functions. This chapter will give high level overview of advance statistics and then will explain the techniques to apply those statistical concepts on general problems using Julia's statistical packages such as Stats.jl and Distributions.jl.

Chapter 5, *Making Sense of Data Using Visualization*, explains why data visualization is essential part of data science and how it makes communicating the results more effective and reaches out to larger audience. This chapter will go through the Vega, Asciiplot, and Gadfly packages of Julia, which are used for data visualization.

`Chapter 6`, *Supervised Machine Learning*, says *"A computer program is said to learn from experience E with respect to some class of tasks T and performance measure P if its performance at tasks in T, as measured by P, improves with experience E"* – Tom M. Mitchell. Machine learning is a field of study that gives computers the ability to learn and enhance without being explicitly programmed. This chapter will explain that Julia is a high-level language with a great performance, and is nicely suited for machine learning. This chapter will focus on supervised machine learning algorithms such as Naive Bayes, regression, and decision trees.

`Chapter 7`, *Unsupervised Machine Learning*, explains that unsupervised learning is a little bit different and harder than supervised learning. The aim is to get the system to learn something but we don't know what it will learn. This chapter will focus on unsupervised learning algorithms such as clustering.

`Chapter 8`, *Creating Ensemble Models*, explains that a group of people has the ability to take better decisions than a single individual, especially when each group member comes in with their own biases. This is also true for machine learning. This chapter will focus on a machine learning technique called ensemble learning, an example being random forest.

`Chapter 9`, *Time Series*, shows the capacity to demonstrate and perform decision modeling, and explains that examination is a crucial component of some real-world applications running from emergency medical treatment in intensive care units to military command and control frameworks. This chapter focuses on time series data and forecasting using Julia.

`Chapter 10`, *Collaborative Filtering and Recommendation System*, explains that every day we are confronted with decisions and choices. These can range from our clothes to the movies we watch or what to eat when we order online. We take decisions in business too. For instance, which stock should we invest in? What if decision making could be automated, and suitable recommendations could be given to us. This chapter focuses on recommendation systems and techniques such as collaborative filtering and association rule mining.

`Chapter 11`, *Introduction to Deep Learning*, explains that deep learning refers to a class of machine learning techniques that do unsupervised or supervised feature extraction and pattern analysis or classification by exploiting multiple layers of non-linear information processing. This chapter will introduce us to deep learning in Julia. Deep learning is a new branch of machine learning with one goal – Artificial Intelligence. We will also learn about Julia's framework, Julia's, Mocha.jl, with which we can implement deep learning.

What you need for this book

The reader will requires a system (64-bit recommended) having a fairly recent operating system (Linux, Windows 7+, and Mac OS) with a working Internet connection and privileges to install Julia, Git and various packages used in the book.

Who this book is for

The standard demographic is data analysts and aspiring data scientists with little to no grounding in the fundamentals of the Julia language, who are looking to explore how to conduct data science with Julia's ecosystem of packages. On top of this are competent Python or R users looking to leverage Julia to enhance the efficiency of their ability to conduct data science. A good background in statistics and computational mathematics is expected.

Conventions

In this book, you will find a number of text styles that distinguish between different kinds of information. Here are some examples of these styles and an explanation of their meaning.

Code words in text, database table names, folder names, filenames, file extensions, pathnames, dummy URLs, user input, and Twitter handles are shown as follows: "Julia also provides another function, summarystats()."

A block of code is set as follows:

```
ci(x::HypothesisTests.FisherExactTest)
ci(x::HypothesisTests.FisherExactTest, alpha::Float64)
ci(x::HypothesisTests.TTest)
ci(x::HypothesisTests.TTest, alpha::Float64)
```

Any command-line input or output is written as follows:

```
julia> Pkg.update()
julia> Pkg.add("StatsBase")
```

New terms and **important words** are shown in bold.

Warnings or important notes appear in a box like this.

 Tips and tricks appear like this.

Reader feedback

Feedback from our readers is always welcome. Let us know what you think about this book-what you liked or disliked. Reader feedback is important for us as it helps us develop titles that you will really get the most out of.

To send us general feedback, simply e-mail feedback@packtpub.com, and mention the book's title in the subject of your message.

If there is a topic that you have expertise in and you are interested in either writing or contributing to a book, see our author guide at www.packtpub.com/authors.

Customer support

Now that you are the proud owner of a Packt book, we have a number of things to help you to get the most from your purchase.

Downloading the example code

You can download the example code files for this book from your account at http://www.packtpub.com. If you purchased this book elsewhere, you can visit http://www.packtpub.com/support and register to have the files e-mailed directly to you.

You can download the code files by following these steps:

1. Log in or register to our website using your e-mail address and password.
2. Hover the mouse pointer on the **SUPPORT** tab at the top.
3. Click on **Code Downloads & Errata**.
4. Enter the name of the book in the **Search** box.
5. Select the book for which you're looking to download the code files.

6. Choose from the drop-down menu where you purchased this book from.
7. Click on **Code Download**.

Once the file is downloaded, please make sure that you unzip or extract the folder using the latest version of:

- WinRAR / 7-Zip for Windows
- Zipeg / iZip / UnRarX for Mac
- 7-Zip / PeaZip for Linux

The code bundle for the book is also hosted on GitHub at `https://github.com/PacktPublishing/Julia-for-data-science`. We also have other code bundles from our rich catalog of books and videos available at `https://github.com/PacktPublishing/`. Check them out!

Downloading the color images of this book

We also provide you with a PDF file that has color images of the screenshots/diagrams used in this book. The color images will help you better understand the changes in the output. You can download this file from `http://www.packtpub.com/sites/default/files/downloads/JuliaforDataScience_ColorImages.pdf`.

Errata

Although we have taken every care to ensure the accuracy of our content, mistakes do happen. If you find a mistake in one of our books-maybe a mistake in the text or the code-we would be grateful if you could report this to us. By doing so, you can save other readers from frustration and help us improve subsequent versions of this book. If you find any errata, please report them by visiting `http://www.packtpub.com/submit-errata`, selecting your book, clicking on the **Errata Submission Form** link, and entering the details of your errata. Once your errata are verified, your submission will be accepted and the errata will be uploaded to our website or added to any list of existing errata under the Errata section of that title.

To view the previously submitted errata, go to `https://www.packtpub.com/books/content/support` and enter the name of the book in the search field. The required information will appear under the **Errata** section.

Piracy

Piracy of copyrighted material on the Internet is an ongoing problem across all media. At Packt, we take the protection of our copyright and licenses very seriously. If you come across any illegal copies of our works in any form on the Internet, please provide us with the location address or website name immediately so that we can pursue a remedy.

Please contact us at `copyright@packtpub.com` with a link to the suspected pirated material.

We appreciate your help in protecting our authors and our ability to bring you valuable content.

Questions

If you have a problem with any aspect of this book, you can contact us at `questions@packtpub.com`, and we will do our best to address the problem.

The Groundwork – Julia's Environment

Julia is a fairly young programming language. In 2009, three developers (Stefan Karpinski, Jeff Bezanson, and Viral Shah) at MIT in the Applied Computing group under the supervision of Prof. Alan Edelman started working on a project that lead to Julia. In February 2012, Julia was presented publicly and became open source. The source code is available on GitHub (`https://github.com/JuliaLang/julia`). The source of the registered packages can also be found on GitHub. Currently, all four of the initial creators, along with developers from around the world, actively contribute to Julia.

 The current release is 0.4 and is still away from its 1.0 release candidate.

Based on solid principles, its popularity is steadily increasing in the field of scientific computing, data science, and high-performance computing.

This chapter will guide you through the download and installation of all the necessary components of Julia. This chapter covers the following topics:

- How is Julia different?
- Setting up Julia's environment.
- Using Julia's shell and REPL.
- Using Jupyter notebooks

- Package management
- Parallel computation
- Multiple dispatch
- Language interoperability

Traditionally, the scientific community has used slower dynamic languages to build their applications, although they have required the highest computing performance. Domain experts who had experience with programming, but were not generally seasoned developers, always preferred dynamic languages over statically typed languages.

Julia is different

Over the years, with the advancement in compiler techniques and language design, it is possible to eliminate the trade-off between performance and dynamic prototyping. So, the scientific computing required was a good dynamic language like Python together with performance like C. And then came Julia, a general purpose programming language designed according to the requirements of scientific and technical computing, providing performance comparable to C/C++, and with an environment productive enough for prototyping like the high-level dynamic language of Python. The key to Julia's performance is its design and **Low Level Virtual Machine** (LLVM) based Just-in-Time compiler which enables it to approach the performance of C and Fortran.

The key features offered by Julia are:

- A general purpose high-level dynamic programming language designed to be effective for numerical and scientific computing
- A **Low-Level Virtual Machine** (**LLVM**) based **Just-in-Time** (**JIT**) compiler that enables Julia to approach the performance of statically-compiled languages like C/C++

The following quote is from the development team of Julia—Jeff Bezanson, Stefan Karpinski, Viral Shah, and Alan Edelman:

> **We are greedy: we want more.**
>
> We want a language that's open source, with a liberal license. We want the speed of C with the dynamism of Ruby. We want a language that's homoiconic, with true macros like Lisp, but with obvious, familiar mathematical notation like Matlab. We want something as usable for general programming as Python, as easy for statistics as R, as natural for string processing as Perl, as powerful for linear algebra as Matlab, as good at gluing programs together as the shell. Something that is dirt simple to learn, yet keeps the most serious hackers happy. We want it interactive and we want it compiled.
>
> (Did we mention it should be as fast as C?)

It is quite often compared with Python, R, MATLAB, and Octave. These have been around for quite some time and Julia is highly influenced by them, especially when it comes to numerical and scientific computing. Although Julia is really good at it, it is not restricted to just scientific computing as it can also be used for web and general purpose programming.

The development team of Julia aims to create a remarkable and never done before combination of power and efficiency without compromising the ease of use in one single language. Most of Julia's core is implemented in C/C++. Julia's parser is written in Scheme. Julia's efficient and cross-platform I/O is provided by the Node.js's libuv.

Features and advantages of Julia can be summarized as follows:

- It's designed for distributed and parallel computation.
- Julia provides an extensive library of mathematical functions with great numerical accuracy.
- Julia gives the functionality of multiple dispatch. Multiple dispatch refers to using many combinations of argument types to define function behaviors.
- The Pycall package enables Julia to call Python functions in its code and Matlab packages using Matlab.jl. Functions and libraries written in C can also be called directly without any need for APIs or wrappers.
- Julia provides powerful shell-like capabilities for managing other processes in the system.

- Unlike other languages, user-defined types in Julia are compact and quite fast as built-ins.
- Data analysis makes great use of vectorized code to gain performance benefits. Julia eliminates the need to vectorize code to gain performance. De-vectorized code written in Julia can be as fast as vectorized code.
- It uses lightweight "green" threading also known as tasks or coroutines, cooperative multitasking, or one-shot continuations.
- Julia has a powerful type system. The conversions provided are elegant and extensible.
- It has efficient support for Unicode.
- It has facilities for metaprogramming and Lisp-like macros.
- It has a built-in package manager. (Pkg)
- Julia provides efficient, specialized and automatic generation of code for different argument types.
- It's free and open source with an MIT license.

Setting up the environment

Julia is available free. It can be downloaded from its website at the following address: `http://julialang.org/downloads/`. The website also has exhaustive documentation, examples, and links to tutorials and community. The documentation can be downloaded in popular formats.

Installing Julia (Linux)

Ubuntu/Linux Mint is one of the most famous Linux distros, and their deb packages of Julia are also provided. These are available for both 32-bit and 64-bit distributions.

To install Julia, add the **PPA** (**personal package archive**). Ubuntu users are privileged enough to have PPA. It is treated as an apt repository to build and publish Ubuntu source packages. In the terminal, type the following:

```
sudo apt-get add-repository ppa:staticfloat/juliareleases
sudo apt-get update
```

This adds the PPA and updates the package index in the repository.

Now install Julia:

```
sudo apt-get install Julia
```

The installation is complete. To check if the installation is successful in the Terminal type in the following:

```
julia --version
```

This gives the installed Julia's version.

To open the Julia's interactive shell, type `julia` into the Terminal. To uninstall Julia, simply use `apt` to remove it:

```
sudo apt-get remove julia
```

For Fedora/RHEL/CentOS or distributions based on them, enable the EPEL repository for your distribution version. Then, click on the link provided. Enable Julia's repository using the following:

```
dnf copr enable nalimilan/julia
```

Or copy the relevant `.repo` file available as follows:

```
/etc/yum.repos.d/
```

Finally, in the Terminal type the following:

```
yum install julia
```

Installing Julia (Mac)

Users with Mac OS X need to click on the downloaded `.dmg` file to run the disk image. After that, drag the app icon into the **Applications** folder. It may prompt you to ask if you want to continue as the source has been downloaded from the Internet and so is not considered secure. Click on continue if it is downloaded for the Julia language official website.

Julia can also be installed using homebrew on the Mac as follows:

```
brew update
brew tap staticfloat/julia
brew install julia
```

The installation is complete. To check if the installation is successful in the Terminal, type the following:

```
julia --version
```

This gives you the installed Julia version.

Installing Julia (Windows)

Download the `.exe` file provided on the download page according to your system's configuration (32-bit/64-bit). Julia is installed on Windows by running the downloaded `.exe` file, which will extract Julia into a folder. Inside this folder is a batch file called `julia.bat`, which can be used to start the Julia console.

To uninstall, delete the `Julia` folder.

Exploring the source code

For enthusiasts, Julia's source code is available and users are encouraged to contribute by adding features or by bug fixing. This is the directory structure of the tree:

base/	**Source code for Julia's standard library**
contrib/	Editor support for Julia source, miscellaneous scripts
deps/	External dependencies
doc/manual	Source for the user manual
doc/stdlib	Source for standard library function help text
examples/	Example Julia programs
src/	Source for Julia language core
test/	Test suites
test/perf	Benchmark suites
ui/	Source for various frontends
usr/	Binaries and shared libraries loaded by Julia's standard libraries

Using REPL

Read-Eval-Print-Loop is an interactive shell or the language shell that provides the functionality to test out pieces of code. Julia provides an interactive shell with a Just-in-Time compiler at the backend. We can give inputs in a line, it is compiled and evaluated, and the result is given in the next line.

```
julia> a=10; b=20
20

julia> a+b
30

julia> function hello()
           println("Hello World!")
       end
hello (generic function with 1 method)

julia> hello()
Hello World!

julia>
```

The benefit of using the REPL is that we can test out our code for possible errors. Also, it is a good environment for beginners. We can type in the expressions and press *Enter* to evaluate.

A Julia library, or custom-written Julia program, can be included in the REPL using `include`. For example, I have a file called `hello.jl`, which I will include in the REPL by doing the following:

```
julia> include ("hello.jl")
```

Julia also stores all the commands written in the REPL in the `.julia_history`. This file is located at `/home/$USER` on Ubuntu, `C:\Users\username` on Windows, or `~/.julia_history` on OS X.

As with a Linux Terminal, we can reverse-search using *Ctrl + R* in Julia's shell. This is a really nice feature as we can go back in the history of typed commands.

Typing `?` in the language shell will change the prompt to:

```
help?>
```

```
help?> +
search: + .+

  +(x, y...)

  Addition operator. x+y+z+... calls this function with all arguments, i.e.
  +(x, y, z, ...).

julia>
```

To clear the screen, press *Ctrl + L*. To come out of the REPL press *Ctrl + D* or type the following:

```
julia> exit().
```

Using Jupyter Notebook

Data science and scientific computing are privileged to have an amazing interactive tool called Jupyter Notebook. With Jupyter Notebook you can to write and run code in an interactive web environment, which also has the capability to have visualizations, images, and videos. It makes testing of equations and prototyping a lot easier. It has the support of over 40 programming languages and is completely open source.

GitHub supports Jupyter notebooks. The notebook with the record of computation can be shared via the Jupyter notebook viewer or other cloud storage. Jupyter notebooks are extensively used for coding machine-learning algorithms, statistical modeling and numerical simulation, and data munging.

Jupyter Notebook is implemented in Python but you can run the code in any of the 40 languages provided you have their kernel. You can check if Python is installed on your system or not by typing the following into the Terminal:

```
python —version
```

This will give the version of Python if it is there on the system. It is best to have Python 2.7.x or 3.5.x or a later version.

If Python is not installed then you can install it by downloading it from the official website for Windows. For Linux, typing the following should work:

```
sudo apt-get install python
```

It is highly recommended to install Anaconda if you are new to Python and data science. Commonly used packages for data science, numerical, and scientific computing including Jupyter notebook come bundled with Anaconda making it the preferred way to set up the environment. Instructions can be found at https://www.continuum.io/downloads.

Jupyter is present in the Anaconda package, but you can check if the Jupyter package is up to date by typing in the following:

```
conda install jupyter
```

Another way to install Jupyter is by using pip:

```
pip install jupyter
```

To check if Jupyter is installed properly, type the following in the Terminal:

```
jupyter -version
```

It should give the version of the Jupyter if it is installed.

Now, to use Julia with Jupyter we need the `IJulia` package. This can be installed using Julia's package manager.

After installing IJulia, we can create a new notebook by selecting Julia under the **Notebooks** section in Jupyter.

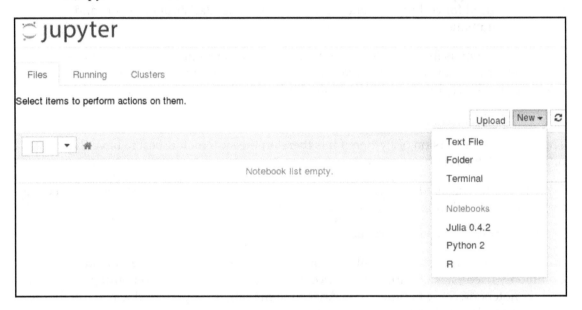

To get the latest version of all your packages, in Julia's shell type the following:

```
julia> Pkg.update()
```

After that add the IJulia package by typing the following:

```
julia> Pkg.add("IJulia")
```

In Linux, you may face some warnings, so it's better to build the package:

```
julia> Pkg.build("IJulia")
```

After IJulia is installed, come back to the Terminal and start the Jupyter notebook:

```
jupyter notebook
```

A browser window will open. Under **New**, you will find options to create new notebooks with the kernels already installed. As we want to start a Julia notebook we will select **Julia 0.4.2**. This will start a new Julia notebook. You can try out a simple example.

In this example, we are creating a histogram of random numbers. This is just an example we will be studying the components used in detail in coming chapters.

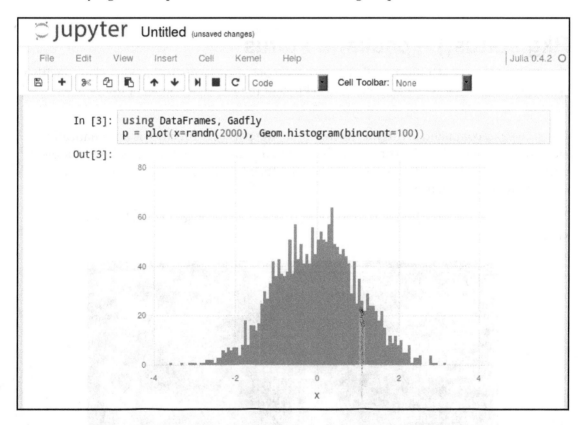

Popular editors such as Atom and Sublime have a plugin for Julia. Atom has language—julia and Sublime has Sublime—IJulia, both of which can be downloaded from their package managers.

Package management

Julia provides a built-in package manager. Using Pkg we can install libraries written in Julia. For external libraries, we can also compile them from their source or use the standard package manager of the operating system. A list of registered packages is maintained at htt p://pkg.julialang.org.

Pkg is provided in the base installation. The Pkg module contains all the package manager commands.

Pkg.status() – package status

The Pkg.status() is a function that prints out a list of currently installed packages with a summary. This is handy when you need to know if the package you want to use is installed or not.

When the Pkg command is run for the first time, the package directory is automatically created. It is required by the command that the Pkg.status() returns a valid list of the packages installed. The list of packages given by the Pkg.status() are of registered versions which are managed by Pkg.

Pkg.installed() can also be used to return a list of all the installed packages with their versions.

```
julia> Pkg.installed()
Dict{ASCIIString,VersionNumber} with 43 entries:
  "ImmutableArrays"   => v"0.0.11"
  "ZMQ"               => v"0.3.1"
  "ArrayViews"        => v"0.6.4"
  "DataStructures"    => v"0.4.0"
  "Compat"            => v"0.7.8"
  "Calculus"          => v"0.1.14"
  "GZip"              => v"0.2.18"
  "Measures"          => v"0.0.1"
  "StatsFuns"         => v"0.2.0"
  "DataFrames"        => v"0.6.10"
```

Pkg.add() – adding packages

Julia's package manager is declarative and intelligent. You only have to tell it what you want and it will figure out what version to install and will resolve dependencies if there are any. Therefore, we only need to add the list of requirements that we want and it resolves which packages and their versions to install.

The ~/.julia/v0.4/REQUIRE file contains the package requirements. We can open it using a text editor such as vi or atom, or use Pkg.edit() in Julia's shell to edit this file. After editing the file, run Pkg.resolve() to install or remove the packages.

We can also use Pkg.add(package_name) to add packages and Pkg.rm(package_name) to remove packages. Earlier, we used Pkg.add("IJulia") to install the IJulia package.

When we don't want to have a package installed on our system anymore, Pkg.rm() is used for removing the requirement from the REQUIRE file. Similar to Pkg.add(), Pkg.rm() first removes the requirement of the package from the REQUIRE file and then updates the list of installed packages by running Pkg.resolve() to match.

Working with unregistered packages

Frequently, we would like to be able to use packages created by our team members or someone who has published on Git but they are not in the registered packages of Pkg. Julia allows us to do that by using a clone. Julia packages are hosted on Git repositories and can be cloned using mechanisms supported by Git. The index of registered packages is maintained at METADATA.jl. For unofficial packages, we can use the following:

```
Pkg.clone("git://example.com/path/unofficialPackage/Package.jl.git")
```

Sometimes unregistered packages have dependencies that require fulfilling before use. If that is the scenario, a REQUIRE file is needed at the top of the source tree of the unregistered package. The dependencies of the unregistered packages on the registered packages are determined by this REQUIRE file. When we run Pkg.clone(url), these dependencies are automatically installed.

Pkg.update() – package update

It's good to have updated packages. Julia, which is under active development, has its packages frequently updated and new functionalities are added.

To update all of the packages, type the following:

```
Pkg.update()
```

Under the hood, new changes are pulled into the METADATA file in the directory located at `~/.julia/v0.4/` and it checks for any new registered package versions which may have been published since the last update. If there are new registered package versions, `Pkg.update()` attempts to update the packages which are not dirty and are checked out on a branch. This update process satisfies the top-level requirements by computing the optimal set of package versions to be installed. The packages with specific versions that must be installed are defined in the REQUIRE file in Julia's directory (`~/.julia/v0.4/`).

METADATA repository

Registered packages are downloaded and installed using the official `METADATA.jl` repository. A different `METADATA` repository location can also be provided if required:

```
julia> Pkg.init("https://julia.customrepo.com/METADATA.jl.git", "branch")
```

Developing packages

Julia allows us to view the source code and as it is tracked by Git, the full development history of all the installed packages is available. We can also make our desired changes and commit to our own repository, or do bug fixes and contribute enhancements upstream.

You may also want to create your own packages and publish them at some point in time. Julia's package manager allows you to do that too.

It is a requirement that Git is installed on the system and the developer needs an account at their hosting provider of choice (GitHub, Bitbucket, and so on). Having the ability to communicate over SSH is preferred—to enable that, upload your public ssh-key to your hosting provider.

Creating a new package

It is preferable to have the REQUIRE file in the package repository. This should have the bare minimum of a description of the Julia version.

For example, if we would like to create a new Julia package called HelloWorld we would have the following:

```
Pkg.generate("HelloWorld", "MIT")
```

Here, HelloWorld is the package that we want to create and MIT is the license that our package will have. The license should be known to the package generator.

This will create a directory as follows: ~/.julia/v0.4/HelloWorld. The directory that is created is initialized as a Git repository. Also, all the files required by the package are kept in this directory. This directory is then committed to the repository.

This can now be pushed to the remote repository for the world to use.

Parallel computation using Julia

Advancement in modern computing has led to multi-core CPUs in systems and sometimes these systems are combined together in a cluster capable of performing a task which a single system might not be able to perform alone, or if it did it would take an undesirable amount of time. Julia's environment of parallel processing is based on message passing. Multiple processes are allowed for programs in separate memory domains.

Message passing is implemented differently in Julia from other popular environments such as MPI. Julia provides one-sided communication, therefore the programmer explicitly manages only one process in the two-process operation.

Julia's parallel programming paradigm is built on the following:

- Remote references
- Remote calls

A request to run a function on another process is called a remote call. The reference to an object by another object on a particular process is called a remote reference. A remote reference is a construct used in most distributed object systems. Therefore, a call which is made with some specific arguments to the objects generally on a different process by the objects of the different process is called the remote call and this will return a reference to the remote object which is called the remote reference.

The remote call returns a remote reference to its result. Remote calls return immediately. The process that made the call proceeds to its next operation. Meanwhile, the remote call happens somewhere else. A call to `wait()` on its remote reference waits for the remote call to finish. The full value of the result can be obtained using `fetch()`, and `put!()` is used to store the result to a remote reference.

Julia uses a single process default. To start Julia with multiple processors use the following:

```
julia -p n
```

where n is the number of worker processes. Alternatively, it is possible to create extra processors from a running system by using `addproc(n)`. It is advisable to put n equal to the number of the CPU cores in the system.

`pmap` and `@parallel` are the two most frequently used and useful functions.

Julia provides a *parallel for loop*, used to run a number of processes in parallel. This is used as follows.

Parallel for loop works by having multiple processes assigned iterations and then reducing the result (in this case (+)). It is somewhat similar to the map-reduce concept. Iterations will run independently over different processes and the results obtained by these processes will be combined at the end (like map-reduce). The resultant of one loop can also become the feeder for the other loop. The answer is the resultant of this whole parallel loop.

It is very different than a normal iterative loop because the iterations do not take place in a specified sequence. As the iterations run on different processes, any writes that happens on variables or arrays are not globally visible. The variables used are copied and broadcasted to each process of the parallel for loop.

For example:

```
arr = zeros(500000)
@parallel for i=1:500000
  arr[i] = i
end
```

This will not give the desired result as each process gets their own separate copy of `arr`. The vector will not be filled in with `i` as expected. We must avoid such *parallel for loops*.

`pmap` refers to parallel map. For example:

```
julia> nheads = @parallel (+) for i=1:100000000
           Int(rand(Bool))
       end
50001992
```

This code solves the problem if we have a number of large random matrices and we are required to obtain the singular values, in parallel.

Julia's `pmap()` is designed differently. It is well suited for cases where a large amount of work is done by each function call, whereas `@parallel` is suited for handling situations which involve numerous small iterations. Both `pmap()` and `@parallel` for utilize worker nodes for parallel computation. However, the node from which the calling process originated does the final reduction in `@parallel` for.

Julia's key feature – multiple dispatch

A function is an object, mapping a tuple of arguments using some expression to a return value. When this function object is unable to return a value, it throws an exception. For different types of arguments the same conceptual function can have different implementations. For example, we can have a function to add two floating point numbers and another function to add two integers. But conceptually, we are only adding two numbers. Julia provides a functionality by which different implementations of the same concept can be implemented easily. The functions don't need to be defined all at once. They are defined in small abstracts. These small abstracts are different argument type combinations and have different behaviors associated with them. The definition of one of these behaviors is called a method.

The types and the number of arguments that a method definition accepts is indicated by the annotation of its signatures. Therefore, the most suitable method is applied whenever a function is called with a certain set of arguments. To apply a method when a function is invoked is known as dispatch. Traditionally, object-oriented languages consider only the first argument in dispatch. Julia is different as all of the function's arguments are considered (not just only the first) and then it choses which method should be invoked. This is known as multiple dispatch.

Multiple dispatch is particularly useful for mathematical and scientific code. We shouldn't consider that the operations belong to one argument more than any of the others. All of the argument types are considered when implementing a mathematical operator. Multiple dispatch is not limited to mathematical expressions as it can be used in numerous real-world scenarios and is a powerful paradigm for structuring the programs.

Methods in multiple dispatch

+ is a function in Julia using multiple dispatch. Multiple dispatch is used by all of Julia's standard functions and operators. For various possible combinations of argument types and count, all of them have many methods defining their behavior. A method is restricted to take certain types of arguments using the :: type-assertion operator:

```
julia> f(x::Float64, y::Float64) = x + y
```

The function definition will only be applied for calls where x and y are both values of type Float64:

```
julia> f(10.0, 14.0)
24.0
```

If we try to apply this definition to other types of arguments, it will give a method error.

```
julia> M = {rand(500,500) for i=1:10}; pmap(svd, M)
```

The arguments must be of precisely the same type as defined in the function definition.

The function object is created in the first method definition. New method definitions add new behaviors to the existing function object. When a function is invoked, the number and types of the arguments are matched, and the most specific method definition matching will be executed.

The following example creates a function with two methods. One method definition takes two arguments of the type Float64 and adds them. The second method definition takes two arguments of the type Number, multiplies them by two and adds them. When we invoke the function with Float64 arguments, then the first method definition is applied, and when we invoke the function with Integer arguments, the second method definition is applied as the number can take any numeric values. In the following example, we are playing with floating point numbers and integers using multiple dispatch.

```julia
julia> f(x::Float64, y::Float64)= x+y
f (generic function with 1 method)

julia> f(10.0,14.0)
24.0

julia> f(2,10.0)
ERROR: MethodError: `f` has no method matching f(::Int64, ::Float64)
Closest candidates are:
  f(::Float64, ::Float64)
```

In Julia, all values are instances of the abstract type "Any". When the type declaration is not given with ::, that means it is not specifically defined as the type of the argument, therefore Any is the default type of method parameter and it doesn't have the restriction of taking any type of value. Generally, one method definition is written in such a way that it will be applied to the certain arguments to which no other method definition applies. It is one of the Julia language's most powerful features.

It is efficient with a great ease of expressiveness to generate specialized code and implement complex algorithms without caring much about the low-level implementation using Julia's multiple dispatch and flexible parametric type system.

Ambiguities – method definitions

Sometimes function behaviors are defined in such a way that there isn't a unique method to apply for a certain set of arguments. Julia throws a warning in such cases about this ambiguity, but proceeds by arbitrarily picking a method. To avoid this ambiguity we should define a method to handle such cases.

In the following example, we define a method definition with one argument of the type `Any` and another argument of the type `Float64`. In the second method definition, we just changed the order, but this doesn't differentiate it from the first definition. In this case, Julia will give a warning of ambiguous method definition but will allow us to proceed.

```
julia> f(x::Float64, y::Float64)= x+y
f (generic function with 1 method)

julia> f(x::Number, y::Number)=2x+2y
f (generic function with 2 methods)

julia> f(24.0,4.0)
28.0

julia> f(10,11)
42
```

Facilitating language interoperability

Although Julia can be used to write most kinds of code, there are mature libraries for numerical and scientific computing which we would like to exploit. These libraries can be in C, Fortran or Python. Julia allows the ease of using the existing code written in Python, C, or Fortran. This is done by making Julia perform simple and efficient-to-call C, Fortran, or Python functions.

The C/Fortran libraries should be available to Julia. An ordinary but valid call with `ccall` is made to this code. This is possible when the code is available as a shared library. Julia's JIT generates the same machine instructions as the native C call. Therefore, it is generally no different from calling through a C code with a minimal overhead.

Importing Python code can be beneficial and sometimes needed, especially for data science, because it already has an exhaustive library of implementations of machine learning and statistical functions. For example, it contains scikit-learn and pandas. To use Python in Julia, we require `PyCall.jl`. To add `PyCall.jl` do the following:

```
Pkg.add("PyCall")
```

PyCall contains a macro `@pyimport` that facilitates importing Python packages and provides Julia wrappers for all of the functions and constants therein, including automatic conversion of types between Julia and Python.

PyCall also provides functionalities for lower-level manipulation of Python objects, including a PyObject type for opaque Python objects. It also has a `pycall` function (similar to Julia's `ccall` function), which can be used in Julia to call Python functions with type conversions. PyCall does not use the Python program but links directly to the `libpython` library. During the `Pkg.build`, it finds the location of the `libpython` by Punning python.

Calling Python code in Julia

The `@pyimport` macro automatically makes the appropriate type conversions to Julia types in most of the scenarios based on a runtime inspection of the Python objects. It achieves better control over these type conversions by using lower-level functions. Using PyCall in scenarios where the return type is known can help in improving the performance, both by eliminating the overhead of runtime type inference, and also by providing more type information to the Julia compiler:

- `pycall(function::PyObject, returntype::Type, args...)`: This calls the given Python function (typically looked up from a module) with the given `args...` (of standard Julia types which are converted automatically to the corresponding Python types if possible), converting the return value to `returntype` (use a `returntype` of PyObject to return the unconverted Python object reference, or PyAny to request an automated conversion).
- `pyimport(s)`: This imports the Python modules (a string or symbol) and returns a pointer to it (a PyObject). Functions or other symbols in the module may then be looked up by s[name] where the name is a string (for the raw PyObject) or a symbol (for automatic type conversion). Unlike the `@pyimport` macro, this does not define a Julia module and members cannot be accessed with an s.name.

Summary

In this chapter, we learned how Julia is different and how an LLVM-based JIT compiler enables Julia to approach the performance of C/C++. We introduced you to how to download Julia, install it, and build it from source. The notable features that we found were that the language is elegant, concise, and powerful and it has amazing capabilities for numeric and scientific computing.

We worked on some examples of working with Julia via the command line (REPL) and saw how full of features the language shell is. The features found were tab-completion, reverse-search, and help functions. We also discussed why should we use Jupyter Notebook and went on to set up Jupyter with the IJulia package. We worked on a simple example to use the Jupyter Notebook and Julia's visualization package, Gadfly.

In addition, we learned about Julia's powerful built-in package management and how to add, update, and remove modules. Also, we went through the process of creating our own package and publishing it to the community. We also introduced you to one of the most powerful features of Julia—multiple dispatch—and worked on some basic examples of how to create method definitions to implement multiple dispatch.

In addition, we introduced you to the parallel computation, explaining how it is different from conventional message passing and how to make use of all the compute resources available. We also learned Julia's feature of language interoperability and how we can call a Python module or a library from the Julia program.

References

- http://julialang.org/
- https://github.com/JuliaLang
- https://github.com/JuliaStats

2
Data Munging

It is said that around 50% of the data scientist's time goes into transforming raw data into a usable format. Raw data can be in any format or size. It can be structured like RDBMS, semi-structured like CSV, or unstructured like regular text files. These contain some valuable information. And to extract that information, it has to be converted into a data structure or a usable format from which an algorithm can find valuable insights. Therefore, usable format refers to the data in a model that can be consumed in the data science process. This usable format differs from use case to use case.

This chapter will guide you through data munging, or the process of preparing the data. It covers the following topics:

- What is data munging?
- DataFrames.jl
- Uploading data from a file
- Finding the required data
- Joins and indexing
- Split-Apply-Combine strategy
- Reshaping the data
- Formula (ModelFrame and ModelMatrix)
- PooledDataArray
- Web scraping

What is data munging?

Munging comes from the term "munge," which was coined by some students of Massachusetts Institute of Technology, USA. It is considered one of the most essential parts of the data science process; it involves collecting, aggregating, cleaning, and organizing the data to be consumed by the algorithms designed to make discoveries or to create models. This involves numerous steps, including extracting data from the data source and then parsing or transforming the data into a predefined data structure. Data munging is also referred to as data wrangling.

The data munging process

So what's the data munging process? As mentioned, data can be in any format and the data science process may require data from multiple sources. This data aggregation phase includes scraping it from websites, downloading thousands of `.txt` or `.log` files, or gathering the data from RDBMS or NoSQL data stores.

It is very rare to find data in a format that can be used directly by the data science process. The data received is generally in a format unsuitable for modeling and analysis. Generally, algorithms require data to be stored in a tabular format or in matrices. This phase of converting the gathered raw data into the required format can get very complex and time consuming. But this phase creates the foundation of the sophisticated data analysis that can now be done.

It is good to define the structure of the data that you will be feeding the algorithms in advance. This data structure is defined according to the nature of the problem. The algorithms that you have designed or will be designing should not just be able to accept this format of data, but they should also be able to easily identify the patterns, find the outliers, make discoveries, or meet whatever the desired outcomes are.

After defining how the data will be structured, you define the process to achieve that. This is like a pipeline that will accept some forms of data and will give out meaningful data in a predefined format. This phase consists of various steps. These steps include converting data from one form to another, which may or may not require string operations or regular expressions, and finding the missing values and outliers.

Generally, data science problems revolve around two kinds of data. These two kinds of data will be either categorical or numerical. Categorical data comes with labels. These labels are formed by some group of values. For example, we can treat weather with categorical features. Weather can be sunny, cloudy, rainy, foggy, or snowy. These labels are formed when the underlying values are associated with one of the groups of the data (which comes under a label). These labels have some unique characteristics and we may not be able to apply arithmetic operations on them.

Numerical data is much more common, for example, temperature. Temperature will be in floating-point numbers and we can certainly apply mathematical operations on it. Every value is comparable with other values in the dataset, so we can say that they have a direct relation with each other.

What is a DataFrame?

A DataFrame is a data structure that has labeled columns, which individually may have different data types. Like a SQL table or a spreadsheet, it has two dimensions. It can also be thought of as a list of dictionaries, but fundamentally, it is different.

DataFrames are the recommended data structure for statistical analysis. Julia provides a package called `DataFrames.jl`, which have all necessary functions to work with DataFrames.

Julia's package, DataFrames, provides three data types:

- `NA`: A missing value in Julia is represented by a specific data type, `NA`.
- `DataArray`: The array type defined in the standard Julia library, though it has many features, doesn't provide any specific functionalities for data analysis. DataArray provided in `DataFrames.jl` provides such features (for example, if we required to store in an array some missing values).
- `DataFrame`: DataFrame is 2-D data structure, like spreadsheets. It is much like R or pandas's DataFrames, and provides many functionalities to represent and analyze data.

The NA data type and its importance

In the real world, we come across data with missing values. It is very common but it's not provided in Julia by default. This functionality is added using the `DataFrames.jl` package. The DataFrames package brings with it DataArray packages, which provide NA data type. Multiple dispatch is one of the most powerful features of Julia and NA is one such example. Julia has NA type, which provides the singleton object NA that we are using to represent missing values.

Why is the NA data type needed?

Suppose, for example, we have a dataset having floating-point numbers:

```
julia> x = [1.1, 2.2, 3.3, 4.4, 5.5, 6.6]
```

This will create a six-element `Array{Float64,1}`.

Now, suppose this dataset has a missing value at position [1]. That means instead of 1.1, there is no value. This cannot be represented by the array type in Julia. When we try to assign an NA value, we get this error:

```
julia> x[1] = NA
LoadError: UndefVarError: NA not defined
while loading In[2], in expression starting on line 1
```

Therefore, right now we cannot add NA values to the array that we have created.

So, to load the data into an array that does have NA values, we use `DataArray`. This enables us to have NA values in our dataset:

```
julia> using DataArrays
julia> x = DataArray([1.1, 2.2, 3.3, 4.4, 5.5, 6.6])
```

This will create a six-element `DataArrays.DataArray{Float64,1}`.

So, when we try to have an NA value, it gives us:

```
julia> X[1] = NA
NA
julia> x
6-element DataArrays.DataArray{Float64,1}:
 1.1
 2.2
 3.3
 4.4
 5.5
 6.6
```

Therefore, by using DataArrays, we can handle missing data. One more feature provided is that NA doesn't always affect functions applied on the particular dataset. So, the method that doesn't involve an NA value or is not affected by it can be applied on the dataset. If it does involve the NA value, then it will give NA as the result.

In the following example, we are applying the mean function and `true || x`. The mean function doesn't work as it involves an NA value, but `true || x` works as expected:

```
julia> true || x
True

julia> true && x[1]
NA

julia> mean(x)
NA

julia> mean(x[2:6])
4.4
```

DataArray – a series-like data structure

In the previous section, we discussed how DataArrays are used to store datasets containing missing (NA) values, as Julia's standard Array type cannot do so.

There are other features similar to Julia's Array type. Type aliases of Vector (one-dimensional Array type) and Matrix (two-dimensional Array type) are DataVector and DataMatrix provided by DataArray.

Creating a 1-D DataArray is similar to creating an Array:

```
julia> using DataArrays
julia> dvector = data([10,20,30,40,50])
5-element DataArrays.DataArray{Int64,1}:
10
20
30
40
50
```

Here, we have NA values, unlike in Arrays. Similarly, we can create a 2-D DataArray, which will be a DataMatrix:

```julia
julia> dmatrix = data([10 20 30; 40 50 60])
2x3 DataArrays.DataArray{Int64,2}:
10 20 30
40 50 60
julia> dmatrix[2,3]
60
```

In the previous example, to the calculate mean, we used slicing. This is not a convenient method to remove or not to consider the NA values while applying a function. A much better way is to use dropna:

```julia
julia> dropna(x)
5-element Array{Float64,1}:
2.2
3.3
4.4
5.5
6.6
```

DataFrames – tabular data structures

Arguably, this is the most important and commonly used data type in statistical computing, whether it is in R (data.frame) or Python (Pandas). This is due to the fact that all the real-world data is mostly in tabular or spreadsheet-like format. This cannot be represented by a simple DataArray:

```julia
julia> df = DataFrame(Name = ["Ajava Rhodiumhi", "Las Hushjoin"],
           Count = [14.04, 17.3],
           OS = ["Ubuntu", "Mint"])
```

```
julia> df
2x3 DataFrames.DataFrame
| Row | Name              | Count | OS       |
|-----|-------------------|-------|----------|
| 1   | "Ajava Rhodiumhi" | 14.04 | "Ubuntu" |
| 2   | "Las Hushjoin"    | 17.3  | "Mint"   |
```

This dataset, for example, can't be represented using DataArray. The given dataset has the following features because it cannot be represented by DataArray:

- This dataset has different types of data in different columns. These different data types in different columns cannot be represented using a matrix. Matrix can only contain values of one type.
- It is a tabular data structure and records have relations with other records in the same row of different columns. Therefore, it is a must that all the columns are of the same length. Vectors cannot be used because same-length columns cannot be enforced using them. Therefore, a column in DataFrame is represented by DataArray.
- In the preceding example, we can see that the columns are labeled. This labeling helps us to easily become familiar with the data and access it without the need to remember its exact positions. So, the columns are accessible using numerical indices and also by their label.

Therefore, due to these reasons, the DataFrames package is used. So, DataFrames are used to represent tabular data having DataArrays as columns.

In the given example, we constructed a DataFrame by:

```julia
julia> df = DataFrame(Name = ["Ajava Rhodiumhi", "Las Hushjoin"],
Count = [14.04, 17.3],
OS = ["Ubuntu", "Mint"])
```

Using the keyword arguments, column names can be defined.

Let's take another example by constructing a new DataFrame:

```julia
julia> df2 = DataFrame()

julia> df2[:X] = 1:10

julia> df2[:Y] = ["Head", "Tail",
"Head", "Head",
"Tail", "Head",
"Tail", "Tail",
"Head", "Tail"]
julia> df2
```

To find out the size of the DataFrame created, we use the size function:

```
julia> size(df2)
(10, 2)
```

Here, 10 refers to the number of rows and 2 refers to the number of columns.

To view the first few lines of the dataset, we use head(), and for the last few lines, we use the tail() function:

```
Julia> head(df2)
```

```
julia> head(df2)
6x2 DataFrames.DataFrame
| Row | X | Y        |
|-----|---|----------|
| 1   | 1 | "Head"   |
| 2   | 2 | "Tail"   |
| 3   | 3 | "Head"   |
| 4   | 4 | "Head"   |
| 5   | 5 | "Tail"   |
| 6   | 6 | "Head"   |
```

As we have given names to the columns of the DataFrame, these can be accessed using these names.

For example:

```
julia> df2[:X]
10-element DataArrays.DataArray{Int64,1}:
 1
 2
 3
 4
 5
 6
 ...
```

This simplifies access to the columns as we can give meaningful names to real-world datasets that have numerous columns without the need to remember their numeric indices.

If needed, we can also rename using these columns by using the rename function:

```
Julia> rename!(df2, :X, :newX)
```

If there is a need to rename multiple columns, then it is done by using this:

```
julia> rename!(df2, {:X => :newX, :Y => :newY})
```

But right now, we are sticking to old column names for ease of use.

Julia also provides a function called `describe()`, which summarizes the entire dataset. For a dataset with many columns, it can turn out to be very useful:

```
julia> describe(df2) X
Min 1.0
1st Qu. 3.25
Median 5.5
Mean 5.5
3rd Qu. 7.75
Max 10.0
NAs 0
NA% 0.0%


Y
Length 10
Type ASCIIString
NAs 0
NA% 0.0%
Unique 2
```

Installation and using DataFrames.jl

Installation is quite straightforward as it is a registered Julia package:

```
Julia> Pkg.update()
julia> Pkg.add("DataFrames")
```

This adds all the required packages to the current namespace. To use the `DataFrames` package:

```
julia> using DataFrames
```

It is also good to have classical datasets that are common for learning purposes. These datasets can be found in the `RDatasets` package:

```
Julia> Pkg.add("RDatasets")
```

The list of the R packages available can be found using:

```
julia> Rdatasets.packages()
```

Here, you can see this:

```
datasets - The R Datasets Package
```

It contains datasets available to R. To use this `dataset`, simply use the following:

```
using RDatasets
iris_dataset = dataset("datasets", "iris")
```

Here, dataset is the function that takes two arguments.

The first argument is the name of the package and the second is the name of the dataset that we want to load.

In the following example, we loaded the famous iris dataset into the memory. You can see that the `dataset()` function has returned a DataFrame. The dataset contains five columns: `SepalLength`, `SepalWidth`, `PetalLength`, `PetalWidth`, and `Species`. It is quite easy to understand the data. A large number of samples have been taken for every species, and the length and width of sepal and petal have been measured, which can be used later to distinguish between them:

```
julia> head(iris_dataset)
6x5 DataFrames.DataFrame
| Row | SepalLength | SepalWidth | PetalLength | PetalWidth |
|-----|-------------|------------|-------------|------------|
| 1   | 5.1         | 3.5        | 1.4         | 0.2        |
| 2   | 4.9         | 3.0        | 1.4         | 0.2        |
| 3   | 4.7         | 3.2        | 1.3         | 0.2        |
| 4   | 4.6         | 3.1        | 1.5         | 0.2        |
| 5   | 5.0         | 3.6        | 1.4         | 0.2        |
| 6   | 5.4         | 3.9        | 1.7         | 0.4        |

| Row | Species   |
|-----|-----------|
| 1   | "setosa"  |
| 2   | "setosa"  |
| 3   | "setosa"  |
| 4   | "setosa"  |
| 5   | "setosa"  |
| 6   | "setosa"  |
```

Actual data science problems generally do not deal with the artificial randomly generated data or data read through the command line. But they work on data that is loaded from files or any other external source. These files can have data in any format and we may have to process it before loading it to the dataframe.

Julia provides a `readtable()` function that can be used to read a tabular file in a dataframe. Generally, we come across datasets in comma-separated or tab-separated formats (CSV or TSV). The `readtable()` works perfectly with them.

We can give the location of the file as UTF8String and the separator type to the readtable() function as arguments. The default separator type is comma (',') for CSV, tab ('\t') for TSV, and whitespace (' ') for WSV.

In the following example, we load the sample iris dataset into a dataframe using the `readtable()` function.

Although the iris dataset is available in the RDatasets package, we will download the CSV to work with the external datasets. The iris CSV can be downloaded from `https://github.com/scikit-learn/scikit-learn/blob/master/sklearn/datasets/data/iris.csv`.

Remember to put the downloaded CSV into the current working directory (from where the REPL was started—generally it is the `~/home/<username>` directory):

```
julia> using DataFramesjulia> df_iris_sample =
  readtable("iris_sample.csv",
  separator = ',')
julia> df_iris_sample
```

It is the same dataset that we used in the previous example, but now we are loading the data from a CSV file.

The `readtable()` is used in a similar way for other text-based datasets such as TSV, WSV, or TXT. Suppose the same iris dataset is in TSV, WSV, or TXT format. It will be used in a similar way:

```
julia> df_iris_sample = readtable("iris_dataset.tsv",
separator='\t')
```

And for example, if we have a dataset without a header and separated by `;`, we would use `readtable()` as follows:

```
julia> df_random_dataset = readtable("random_dataset.txt",
header=false, separator=';')
```

The `readtable()` exploits Julia's functionality of multiple dispatch and has been implemented with different method behaviors:

```
julia> methods(readtable)
3 methods for generic function readtable:
readtable(io::IO) at
/home/anshul/.julia/v0.4/DataFrames/src/dataframe/io.jl:820
readtable(io::IO, nbytes::Integer) at
/home/anshul/.julia/v0.4/DataFrames/src/dataframe/io.jl:820
readtable(pathname::AbstractString) at
/home/anshul/.julia/v0.4/DataFrames/src/dataframe/io.jl:930
```

We can see that there are three methods for the `readtable()` function.

These methods implement some of the advanced options to ease the loading and to support various kinds of data formats:

- `header::Bool`: In the iris example we used, we had headers such as Sepal Length, Sepal Width, and so on, which makes it easier to describe the data. But headers are not always available in the dataset. The default value of `header` is `true`; therefore, whenever headers are not available, we pass the argument as false.

- `separator::Char`: Data in a file must have been organized in the file in a way to form a tabular structure. This is generally by using `,`, `\t`, `;`, or combinations of these sometimes. The `readtable()` guesses the separator type by the extension of the file, but it is a good practice to provide it manually.

- `nastrings::Vector{ASCIIString}`: Suppose there are missing values or some other values and we want NA to replace them. This is done using nastrings. By default, it takes empty records and replaces them with NA.

- `truestrings::Vector{ASCIIString}`: This transforms the strings to Boolean, true. It is used when we want a set of strings to be treated as true in the dataset. By default, `True`, `true`, `T`, and `t` are transformed if no argument is given.

  - `falsestrings::Vector{ASCIIString}`: This works just like truestrings but transforms the strings to Boolean, false. By default, `False`, `false`, `F`, and `f` are transformed if no argument is given.

- `nrows::Int`: If we want only a specific number of rows to be read by `readtable()`, we use nrows as the argument. By default, it is `-1`, which means that `readtable()` will read the whole file.

- `names::Vector{Symbol}`: If we want some specific names for our columns, different from what is mentioned in the header, then we use names. Here, we pass a vector having the names of the columns that we want to use. By default, it is `[]`, which means the names in the headers should be used if they are there; otherwise, the numeric indices must be used.

- `eltypes::Vector{DataType}`: We can specify the column types by passing a vector, by using eltypes. It is an empty vector (`[]`) by default if nothing is passed.

- `allowcomments::Bool`: In the dataset, we may have records having comments with them. These comments can be ignored. By default, it is `false`.

- `commentmark::Char`: If we are using allowcomments, we will also have to mention the character (symbol) where the comment starts. By default, it is `#`.

- `ignorepadding::Bool`: Our dataset might not be as perfect as we want. The records may contain whitespace characters on either side. This can be ignored using ignorepadding. By default, it is true.

- `skipstart::Int`: Our dataset can have some rows describing the data with the header that we might not want, or we just want to skip the first few rows. This is done by skipstart, by specifying the number of rows to skip. By default, it is 0 and will read the entire file.

- `skiprows::Vector{Int}`: If want to skip some specific rows in the data then skiprows is used. We only need to specify the indices of the rows in a vector that we want to skip. By default, it is `[]` and will read the entire file.

- `skipblanks::Bool`: As mentioned earlier, our dataset may not be perfect. There can be some blank lines if we have scraped the data from the Web or extracted the data from other sources. We can skip these blank lines by using skipblanks. By default it is true, but we can choose otherwise if we do not want it.

- `encoding::Symbol`: We can specify the encoding of the file if it is other than UTF8.

Writing the data to a file

We may also want to output our results or transform a dataset and store it in a file. In Julia we do this by using the `writetable()` function. It is very similar to the `readtable()` function that we discussed in the last section.

For example, we want to write the `df_iris_sample` dataframe into a CSV file:

```
julia> writetable("output_df_iris.csv", df_iris_sample)
```

This is the way of writing to a file with the default set of arguments. One visible difference is that we are passing the dataframe that we want to write with the name of the file that we want to write to.

`writetable()` also accepts various arguments such as `readtable()`.

We could have also written the previous statement like this with the separator defined:

```
julia> writetable("output_df_iris.csv", df_iris_sample, separator = ',')
```

Similarly, we can have a header and quote marks in the arguments.

Working with DataFrames

We will follow or inherit some of the traditional strategies to manipulate the data. We will go through these strategies and methods in this section and discuss how and why they are important to data science.

Understanding DataFrames joins

While working with multiple datasets, we often need to merge the datasets in a particular fashion to make the analysis easier or to use it with a particular function.

We will be using the *Road Safety Data* published by the Department for Transport, UK, and it is open under the OGL-Open Government Licence.

The datasets can be found here: `https://data.gov.uk/dataset/road-accidents-safety-data`.

We will be using two datasets:

- Road Safety: Accidents 2015
- Road Safety: Vehicles 2015

`DfTRoadSafety_Accidents_2015` contains columns such as `Accident_Index`, `Location_Easting_OSGR`, `Location_Northing_OSGR`, `Longitude`, `Latitude`, `Police_Force`, `Accident_Severity`, `Number_of_Vehicles`, `Number_of_Casualties`, `Date`, `Day_of_Week`, `Time`, and so on. `DfTRoadSafety_Vehicles_2015` contains columns such as `Accident_Index`, `Vehicle_Reference`, `Vehicle_Type`, `Towing_and_Articulation`, `Vehicle_Manoeuvre`, `Vehicle_Location-Restricted_Lane`, `Junction_Location`, `Skidding_and_Overturning`, `Hit_Object_in_Carriageway`, and so on.

We can see that `Accident_Index` is a common field and is unique. It is used as the index in the dataset.

First we will be making the DataFrames package available and then we will load the data. We load the data into two different dataframes using the readtable function that we discussed earlier:

```julia
julia> using DataFrames

julia> DfTRoadSafety_Accidents_2015 =
readtable("DfTRoadSafety_Accidents_2015.csv")

julia> head(DfTRoadSafety_Accidents_2015)
```

head(DfTRoadSafety_Accidents_2015)				
	_Accident_Index	Location_Easting_OSGR	Location_Northing_OSGR	Longitude	Latitt
1	201501BS70001	525130	180050	-0.198465	51.50
2	201501BS70002	526530	178560	-0.178838	51.49
3	201501BS70004	524610	181080	-0.20559	51.51
4	201501BS70005	524420	181080	-0.208327	51.51
5	201501BS70008	524630	179040	-0.206022	51.49
6	201501BS70009	525480	179530	-0.19361	51.50

The first dataset is loaded into the DataFrame and we try getting information about the dataset using `head`. It gives a few starting columns.

If we are more interested in knowing the names of the columns, we can use the `names` function:

```
julia> names(DfTRoadSafety_Accidents_2015)
32-element Array{Symbol,1}:
 :_Accident_Index
 :Location_Easting_OSGR
 :Location_Northing_OSGR
 :Longitude
 :Latitude
 :Police_Force
 :Accident_Severity
 :Number_of_Vehicles
 :Number_of_Casualties
 :Date
 :Day_of_Week
 :Time
 :Local_Authority_District_
 :x2nd_Road_Class
 :x2nd_Road_Number
 :Pedestrian_Crossing_Human_Control
 :Pedestrian_Crossing_Physical_Facilities
 :Light_Conditions
 :Weather_Conditions
 :Road_Surface_Conditions
 :Special_Conditions_at_Site
 :Carriageway_Hazards
 :Urban_or_Rural_Area
 :Did_Police_Officer_Attend_Scene_of_Accident
 :LSOA_of_Accident_Location
```

Similarly, we will be loading the second dataset in a dataframe:

```
julia> DfTRoadSafety_Vehicles_2015 =
readtable("DfTRoadSafety_Vehicles_2015.csv")
```

The second dataset is loaded into the memory.

Later we will delve deeper, but for now let's do a full join between the two datasets. A join between these two datasets will tell us which accident involved which vehicles:

```julia
julia> DfTRoadSafety_Vehicles_2015 =
readtable("DfTRoadSafety_Vehicles_2015.csv")

julia> full_DfTRoadSafety_2015 =
join(DfTRoadSafety_Accidents_2015,
DfTRoadSafety_Vehicles_2015,
on = :_Accident_Index)
```

```
head(full_DfTRoadSafety_2015)
```

	_Accident_Index	Location_Easting_OSGR	Location_Northing_OSGR	Longitude	Latitu
1	201501BS70001	525130	180050	-0.198465	51.50
2	201501BS70002	526530	178560	-0.178838	51.49
3	201501BS70004	524610	181080	-0.20559	51.51
4	201501BS70005	524420	181080	-0.208327	51.51
5	201501BS70008	524630	179040	-0.206022	51.49
6	201501BS70008	524630	179040	-0.206022	51.49

We can see that the full join has worked. Now we have the data, which can tell us the time of the accident, the location of the vehicle, and many more details.

The benefit is that the join is really easy to do and is really quick, even over large datasets.

We have read about other joins available in relation databases. Julia's DataFrames package provides these joins too:

- **Inner join**: The output, which is the DataFrame, contains only those rows that have keys in both the dataframes.
- **Left join**: The output DataFrame has the rows for keys that are present in the first (left) DataFrame, irrespective of them being present in the second (right) DataFrame.
- **Right join**: The output DataFrame has the rows for keys that are present in the second (right) DataFrame, irrespective of them being present in the first (left) DataFrame.
- **Outer join**: The output DataFrame has the rows for the keys that are present in the first or second DataFrame, which we are joining.

- **Semi join**: The output DataFrame has only the rows from the first (left) DataFrame for the keys that are present in both the first (left) and second (right) DataFrames. The output contains only rows from the first DataFrame.
- **Anti join**: The output DataFrame has the rows for keys that are present in the first (left) DataFrame but rows for the same keys are not present in the second (right) DataFrame. The output contains only rows from the first DataFrame.
- **Cross join**: The output DataFrame has the rows that are the Cartesian product of the rows from the first DataFrame (left) and the second DataFrame (right).

Cross join doesn't involve a key; therefore it is used like this:

```julia
julia> cross_DfTRoadSafety_2014 = join(DfTRoadSafety_Accidents_2014,
DfTRoadSafety_Vehicles_2014, kind = :cross)
```

Here we have used the `kind` argument to pass the type of join that we want. Other joins are also done using this argument.

The kind of join that we want to use is done using the `kind` argument.

Let's understand this using a simpler dataset. We will create a dataframe and will apply different joins on it:

```julia
julia> left_DfTRoadSafety_2014 = join(DfTRoadSafety_Accidents_2014,
DfTRoadSafety_Vehicles_2014, on = :_Accident_Index, kind = :left)
```

For left join, we can use:

```julia
julia> Cities = ["Delhi","Amsterdam","Hamburg"][rand(1:3, 10)]

julia> df1 = DataFrame(Any[[1:10], Cities,
        rand(10)], [:ID, :City, :RandomValue1])

julia> df2 = DataFrame(ID = 1:10, City = Cities,
        RandomValue2 = rand(100:110, 10))
```

This created two dataframes having 10 rows. The first dataframe, df1, has three columns: ID, City, and RandomValue1. The second dataframe has df2 with three columns: ID, City, and RandomValue2.

Applying full join, we can use:

```julia
julia> full_df1_df2 = join(df1,df2,
            on = [:ID, :City])
```

We have used two columns to apply the join.

This will generate:

	ID	City	RandomValue1	RandomValue2
1	2	Amsterdam	0.45225250816056284	100
2	3	Amsterdam	0.45097306910048696	107
3	8	Amsterdam	0.5567617467537034	102
4	9	Amsterdam	0.29952715400087837	107
5	4	Delhi	0.9703172728242426	106
6	5	Delhi	0.7235992085381457	100
7	6	Delhi	0.9517456514707969	101
8	7	Delhi	0.32919783621458265	103
9	10	Delhi	0.5552632497124872	101
10	1	Hamburg	0.2965785054730816	110

Other joins can also be applied using the `kind` argument. Let's go through our old dataset of accidents and vehicles.

The different joins using `kind` are:

```
julia> right_DfTRoadSafety_2014 = join(DfTRoadSafety_Accidents_2014,
DfTRoadSafety_Vehicles_2014, on = :_Accident_Index, kind = :right)

julia> inner_DfTRoadSafety_2014 = join(DfTRoadSafety_Accidents_2014,
DfTRoadSafety_Vehicles_2014, on = :_Accident_Index, kind = :inner)

julia> outer_DfTRoadSafety_2014 = join(DfTRoadSafety_Accidents_2014,
DfTRoadSafety_Vehicles_2014, on = :_Accident_Index, kind = :outer)

julia> semi_DfTRoadSafety_2014 = join(DfTRoadSafety_Accidents_2014,
DfTRoadSafety_Vehicles_2014, on = :_Accident_Index, kind = :semi)

julia> anti_DfTRoadSafety_2014 = join(DfTRoadSafety_Accidents_2014,
DfTRoadSafety_Vehicles_2014, on = :_Accident_Index, kind = :anti)
```

The Split-Apply-Combine strategy

A paper was published by Hadley Wickham (Wickham, Hadley. "The split-apply-combine strategy for data analysis." *Journal of Statistical Software* 40.1 (2011): 1-29), defining the Split-Apply-Combine strategy for data analysis. In this paper, he explained why it is good to break up a big problem into manageable pieces, independently operate on each piece, obtain the necessary results, and then put all the pieces back together.

This is needed when a dataset contains a large number of columns and for some operations all the columns are not necessary. It is better to split the dataset and then apply the necessary functions; and we can always put the dataset back together.

This is done using the by function by takes three arguments:

- DataFrame (this is the dataframe that we would be splitting)
- The column name (or numerical index) on which the DataFrame would be split
- A function that can be applied on every subset of the DataFrame

Let's try to apply by to our same dataset:

```
julia> by(DfTRoadSafety_Accidents_2014, :Location_Northing_OSGR, size)
96296x2 DataFrames.DataFrame
| Row | Location_Northing_OSGR | x1      |
|-----|------------------------|---------|
| 1   | 10304                  | (1,32)  |
| 2   | 10620                  | (1,32)  |
| 3   | 13264                  | (1,32)  |
| 4   | 16554                  | (1,32)  |
| 5   | 17181                  | (1,32)  |
| 6   | 19800                  | (1,32)  |
| 7   | 21245                  | (1,32)  |
| 8   | 22410                  | (1,32)  |
  :
```

The aggregate() function provides an alternative to apply the Split-Apply-Combine strategy. The aggregate() function uses the same three arguments:

- DataFrame (this is the DataFrame that we would be splitting)
- The column name (or numerical index) on which the DataFrame would be split
- A function that can be applied on the every subset of the DataFrame

The function provided in the third argument is applied to every column, which wasn't used in splitting up the DataFrame.

Reshaping the data

The use case may require data to be in a different shape than we currently have. To facilitate this, Julia provides reshaping of the data.

Let's use the same dataset that we were using, but before that let's check the size of the dataset:

```julia
julia> size(DfTRoadSafety_Accidents_2014)
(146322,32)
```

We can see that there are greater than 100,000 rows. Although we can work on this data, for simplicity of understanding, let's take a smaller dataset.

Datasets provided in RDataset are always good to start with. We will use the tried and tested iris dataset for this.

We will import RDatasets and DataFrames (if we have started a new terminal session):

```julia
julia> using RDatasets, DataFrames
```

Then, we will load the iris dataset into a DataFrame. We can see that the dataset has 150 rows and 5 columns:

```
julia> iris_dataframe = dataset("datasets", "iris")
150x5 DataFrames.DataFrame
| Row | SepalLength | SepalWidth | PetalLength | PetalWidth | Species   |
|-----|-------------|------------|-------------|------------|-----------|
| 1   | 5.1         | 3.5        | 1.4         | 0.2        | "setosa"  |
| 2   | 4.9         | 3.0        | 1.4         | 0.2        | "setosa"  |
| 3   | 4.7         | 3.2        | 1.3         | 0.2        | "setosa"  |
| 4   | 4.6         | 3.1        | 1.5         | 0.2        | "setosa"  |
| 5   | 5.0         | 3.6        | 1.4         | 0.2        | "setosa"  |
| 6   | 5.4         | 3.9        | 1.7         | 0.4        | "setosa"  |
| 7   | 4.6         | 3.4        | 1.4         | 0.3        | "setosa"  |
| 8   | 5.0         | 3.4        | 1.5         | 0.2        | "setosa"  |
⋮
```

Now we use the `stack()` function to reshape the dataset. Let's use it without any arguments except the DataFrame.

Stack works by creating a dataframe for categorical variables with all of the information one by one:

```
julia> iris_stackdf = stackdf(iris_dataframe)
600x3 DataFrames.DataFrame
| Row | variable     | value | Species      |
|-----|--------------|-------|--------------|
| 1   | SepalLength  | 5.1   | "setosa"     |
| 2   | SepalLength  | 4.9   | "setosa"     |
| 3   | SepalLength  | 4.7   | "setosa"     |
| 4   | SepalLength  | 4.6   | "setosa"     |
| 5   | SepalLength  | 5.0   | "setosa"     |
| 6   | SepalLength  | 5.4   | "setosa"     |
| 7   | SepalLength  | 4.6   | "setosa"     |
| 8   | SepalLength  | 5.0   | "setosa"     |
:
```

We can see that our dataset has been stacked. Here we have stacked all the columns. We can also provide specific columns to stack:

```
Julia> iris_dataframe [:id] = 1:size(iris_dataframe, 1)
# create a new column to track the id of the row

Julia> iris_stack = (iris_dataframe,  [1:4])
```

The second argument depicts the columns that we want to stack. We can see in the result that column 1 to 4 have been stacked, which means we have reshaped the dataset into a new dataframe:

```
Julia> iris_stack = stack(iris_dataframe,  [1:4])

Julia> size(iris_stack)
(600,4)
Julia> head(iris_stack)
```

	variable	value	Species	id
1	SepalLength	5.1	setosa	1
2	SepalLength	4.9	setosa	2
3	SepalLength	4.7	setosa	3
4	SepalLength	4.6	setosa	4
5	SepalLength	5.0	setosa	5
6	SepalLength	5.4	setosa	6

We can see that there is a new column `:id`. That's the identifier of the stacked dataframe. Its value is repeated the number of times the rows are repeated.

As all the columns are included in the resultant DataFrame, there is repetition for some columns. These columns are actually the identifiers for this DataFrame and are denoted by the column (`id`). Other than the identifiers column (`:id`), there are two more columns, `:variable` and `:values`. These are the columns that actually contain the stacked values.

```
| Row | variable    | value |
|-----|-------------|-------|
| 1   | SepalLength | 5.1   |
| 2   | SepalLength | 4.9   |
| 3   | SepalLength | 4.7   |
```

We can also provide a third argument (optional). This is the column whose values are repeated. Using this, we can specify which column to include and which not to include.

```
julia> iris_dataframe = stack(iris, [:PetalLength, :PetalWidth], :Species)
300x3 DataFrames.DataFrame
| Row | variable    | value | Species    |
|-----|-------------|-------|------------|
| 1   | PetalLength | 1.4   | "setosa"   |
| 2   | PetalLength | 1.4   | "setosa"   |
| 3   | PetalLength | 1.3   | "setosa"   |
| 4   | PetalLength | 1.5   | "setosa"   |
| 5   | PetalLength | 1.4   | "setosa"   |
| 6   | PetalLength | 1.7   | "setosa"   |
| 7   | PetalLength | 1.4   | "setosa"   |
| 8   | PetalLength | 1.5   | "setosa"   |
⋮
```

The `melt()` function is similar to the stack function but has some special features. Here we need to specify the identifier columns and the rest are stacked:

```
Julia> iris_melt = stack(iris_dataframe, [1:4])
```

```
600x4 DataFrames.DataFrame
| Row | variable    | value | Species     | id  |
|-----|-------------|-------|-------------|-----|
| 1   | SepalLength | 5.1   | "setosa"    | 1   |
| 2   | SepalLength | 4.9   | "setosa"    | 2   |
| 3   | SepalLength | 4.7   | "setosa"    | 3   |
| 4   | SepalLength | 4.6   | "setosa"    | 4   |
| 5   | SepalLength | 5.0   | "setosa"    | 5   |
| 6   | SepalLength | 5.4   | "setosa"    | 6   |
| 7   | SepalLength | 4.6   | "setosa"    | 7   |
| 8   | SepalLength | 5.0   | "setosa"    | 8   |
⋮
| 592 | PetalWidth  | 2.3   | "virginica" | 142 |
| 593 | PetalWidth  | 1.9   | "virginica" | 143 |
```

The remaining columns are stacked with the assumption that they contain measured variables.

Opposite to stack and melt is unstack, which is used to convert from a long format to wide format. We need to specify the identifier columns and variable/value columns to the unstack function:

```julia
julia> unstack(iris_melt, :id, :variable, :value)
```

```
julia> unstack(iris_melt, :id, :variable, :value)
150x5 DataFrames.DataFrame
| Row | variable | PetalLength | PetalWidth | SepalLength | SepalWidth |
|-----|----------|-------------|------------|-------------|------------|
| 1   | 1        | 1.4         | 0.2        | 5.1         | 3.5        |
| 2   | 2        | 1.4         | 0.2        | 4.9         | 3.0        |
| 3   | 3        | 1.3         | 0.2        | 4.7         | 3.2        |
| 4   | 4        | 1.5         | 0.2        | 4.6         | 3.1        |
| 5   | 5        | 1.4         | 0.2        | 5.0         | 3.6        |
| 6   | 6        | 1.7         | 0.4        | 5.4         | 3.9        |
| 7   | 7        | 1.4         | 0.3        | 4.6         | 3.4        |
| 8   | 8        | 1.5         | 0.2        | 5.0         | 3.4        |
⋮
```

:id (identifier) in the arguments of the unstack can be skipped if the remaining columns are unique:

```julia
julia> unstack(iris_melt, :variable, :value)
```

meltdf and stackdf are two additional functions that work like melt and stack but also provide a view into the original wide DataFrame:

```julia
Julia> iris_stackdf = stackdf(iris_dataframe)
```

```
julia> iris_stackdf = stackdf(iris_dataframe)
600x3 DataFrames.DataFrame
| Row | variable    | value | Species    |
|-----|-------------|-------|------------|
| 1   | SepalLength | 5.1   | "setosa"   |
| 2   | SepalLength | 4.9   | "setosa"   |
| 3   | SepalLength | 4.7   | "setosa"   |
| 4   | SepalLength | 4.6   | "setosa"   |
| 5   | SepalLength | 5.0   | "setosa"   |
| 6   | SepalLength | 5.4   | "setosa"   |
| 7   | SepalLength | 4.6   | "setosa"   |
| 8   | SepalLength | 5.0   | "setosa"   |
⋮
```

This seems exactly similar to the stack function, but we can see the difference by looking at their storage representation.

To look at the storage representation, dump is used. Let's apply it to the stack function:

```
julia> dump(stack(iris_dataframe))
DataFrames.DataFrame  600 observations of 3 variables
  variable: Array(Symbol,(600,)) [:SepalLength,:SepalLength,:Sep
alLength,:SepalLength,:SepalLength,:SepalLength,:SepalLength,:Se
palLength,:SepalLength,:SepalLength  …  :PetalWidth,:PetalWidth,
:PetalWidth,:PetalWidth,:PetalWidth,:PetalWidth,:PetalWidth,:Pet
alWidth,:PetalWidth,:PetalWidth]
  value: DataArrays.DataArray{Float64,1}(600) [5.1,4.9,4.7,4.6]
  Species: DataArrays.PooledDataArray{ASCIIString,UInt8,1}(600)
ASCIIString["setosa","setosa","setosa","setosa"]
```

- Here, we can see that `:variable` is of type `Array(Symbol,(600,))`
- `:value` is of type `DataArrays.DataArray{Float64,1}(600)`
- Identifier (`:Species`) is of type `DataArrays.PooledDataArray{ASCIIString,UInt8,1}(600)`

Now, we will look at the storage representation of `stackdf`:

```
julia> dump(stackdf(iris_dataframe))
DataFrames.DataFrame  600 observations of 3 variables
  variable: DataFrames.RepeatedVector{Symbol}
    parent: Array(Symbol,(4,)) [:SepalLength,:SepalWidth,:Peta
lLength,:PetalWidth]
    inner: Int64 150
    outer: Int64 1
  value: DataFrames.StackedVector
    components: Array(Any,(4,))
      1: DataArrays.DataArray{Float64,1}(150) [5.1,4.9,4.7,4.6
]
      2: DataArrays.DataArray{Float64,1}(150) [3.5,3.0,3.2,3.1
]
      3: DataArrays.DataArray{Float64,1}(150) [1.4,1.4,1.3,1.5
]
      4: DataArrays.DataArray{Float64,1}(150) [0.2,0.2,0.2,0.2
]
  Species: DataFrames.RepeatedVector{ASCIIString}
    parent: DataArrays.PooledDataArray{ASCIIString,UInt8,1}(15
0) ASCIIString["setosa","setosa","setosa","setosa"]
    inner: Int64 1
    outer: Int64 4
```

Here, we can see that:

- `:variable` is of type `DataFrames.RepeatedVector{Symbol}`. Variable is repeated n times, where n refers to the number of rows in the original `AbstractDataFrame`.
- `:value` is of type `DataFrames.StackedVector`. This facilitates the view of the columns stacked together as in the original DataFrame.
- Identifier (`:Species`) is of type `Species`: `DataFrames.RepeatedVector{ASCIIString}`. The original column is repeated n times where n is the number of the columns stacked.

Using these AbstractVectors, we are now able to create views, thus saving memory by using this implementation.

Reshaping functions don't provide the capabilities to perform aggregation. So to perform aggregation, a combination of the Split-Apply-Combine strategy with reshaping is used.

We will use `iris_stack`:

```julia
julia> iris_stack = stack(iris_dataframe)
```

```julia
julia> iris_mean_stack = by(iris_stack, [:variable, :Species],
 df -> DataFrame(iris_mean = mean(df[:value])))
12x3 DataFrames.DataFrame
| Row | variable    | Species      | iris_mean |
|-----|-------------|--------------|-----------|
| 1   | PetalLength | "setosa"     | 1.462     |
| 2   | PetalLength | "versicolor" | 4.26      |
| 3   | PetalLength | "virginica"  | 5.552     |
| 4   | PetalWidth  | "setosa"     | 0.246     |
| 5   | PetalWidth  | "versicolor" | 1.326     |
| 6   | PetalWidth  | "virginica"  | 2.026     |
| 7   | SepalLength | "setosa"     | 5.006     |
| 8   | SepalLength | "versicolor" | 5.936     |
| 9   | SepalLength | "virginica"  | 6.588     |
| 10  | SepalWidth  | "setosa"     | 3.428     |
| 11  | SepalWidth  | "versicolor" | 2.77      |
| 12  | SepalWidth  | "virginica"  | 2.974     |
```

Here, we created a new column having the mean values of the columns according to the species. We can now unstack this.

```
julia> unstack(iris_mean_stack, :Species, :iris_mean)
4x4 DataFrames.DataFrame
| Row | variable    | setosa | versicolor | virginica |
|-----|-------------|--------|------------|-----------|
| 1   | PetalLength | 1.462  | 4.26       | 5.552     |
| 2   | PetalWidth  | 0.246  | 1.326      | 2.026     |
| 3   | SepalLength | 5.006  | 5.936      | 6.588     |
| 4   | SepalWidth  | 3.428  | 2.77       | 2.974     |
```

Sorting a dataset

Sorting is one of the most used techniques in data analysis. Sorting is facilitated in Julia by calling the sort or sort! function.

The difference between the sort and sort! is that sort! works in-place, which sorts the actual array rather than creating a copy.

Let's use the sort! function on the iris dataset:

```
julia> sort!(iris_dataframe)
150x5 DataFrames.DataFrame
| Row | SepalLength | SepalWidth | PetalLength | PetalWidth |
|-----|-------------|------------|-------------|------------|
| 1   | 4.3         | 3.0        | 1.1         | 0.1        |
| 2   | 4.4         | 2.9        | 1.4         | 0.2        |
| 3   | 4.4         | 3.0        | 1.3         | 0.2        |
| 4   | 4.4         | 3.2        | 1.3         | 0.2        |
| 5   | 4.5         | 2.3        | 1.3         | 0.3        |
| 6   | 4.6         | 3.1        | 1.5         | 0.2        |
| 7   | 4.6         | 3.2        | 1.4         | 0.2        |
| 8   | 4.6         | 3.4        | 1.4         | 0.3        |
⋮
```

We can see that the columns are not sorted according to [:SepalLength, :SepalWidth, :PetalLength, :PetalWidth]. But these are actually sorted according to the :Species column.

The sorting function takes some arguments and provides a few features. For example, to sort in reverse, we have:

```julia
julia> sort!(iris_dataframe, rev = true)
```

To sort some specific columns, we have:

```julia
julia> sort!(iris_dataframe, cols = [:SepalLength, :PetalLength])
```

We can also use the by function with `sort!` to apply another function on the DataFrame or the single column.

```julia
julia> sort!(iris_dataframe, cols = [order(:Species, by = uppe
rcase), order(:PetalLength, rev = true)])
150x5 DataFrames.DataFrame
| Row | SepalLength | SepalWidth | PetalLength | PetalWidth |
|-----|-------------|------------|-------------|------------|
| 1   | 4.8         | 3.4        | 1.9         | 0.2        |
| 2   | 5.1         | 3.8        | 1.9         | 0.4        |
| 3   | 5.1         | 3.3        | 1.7         | 0.5        |
| 4   | 5.4         | 3.4        | 1.7         | 0.2        |
| 5   | 5.4         | 3.9        | 1.7         | 0.4        |
| 6   | 5.7         | 3.8        | 1.7         | 0.3        |
| 7   | 4.7         | 3.2        | 1.6         | 0.2        |
| 8   | 4.8         | 3.1        | 1.6         | 0.2        |
:
```

`order` is used to specify ordering a specific column amongst a set of columns.

Formula – a special data type for mathematical expressions

Data science involves various statistical formulas to get insights from data. The creation and application of these formulas is one of the core processes of data science. It maps input variables with some function and mathematical expression to an output.

Julia facilitates this by providing a formula type in the `DataFrame` package, which is used with the symbol ~. ~ is a binary operator. For example:

```julia
julia> formulaX = A ~ B + C
```

For statistical modeling, it is recommended to use ModelMatrix, which constructs a Matrix{Float64}, making it more suited to fit in a statistical model. Formula can also be used to transform to a ModelFrame object from a DataFrame, which is a wrapper over it, to meet the needs of statistical modeling.

Create a dataframe with random values:

```
julia> random_dataframe = DataFrame(A = randn(5), B = randn(5), C
 = randn(5))
5x3 DataFrames.DataFrame
| Row | A         | B        | C         |
|-----|-----------|----------|-----------|
| 1   | 0.610386  | 0.39672  | 0.843678  |
| 2   | 0.386281  | 1.53446  | -0.199888 |
| 3   | -0.118111 | -1.17061 | -1.44164  |
| 4   | 0.203097  | 1.3115   | 1.03606   |
| 5   | -0.856892 | 1.68626  | 0.149367  |
```

Use formula to transform it into a `ModelFrame` object:

```
julia> random_modelframe = ModelFrame(A ~ B + C, random_dataframe)
DataFrames.ModelFrame(5x3 DataFrames.DataFrame
| Row | A         | B         | C         |
|-----|-----------|-----------|-----------|
| 1   | 1.03875   | -0.698513 | 0.664952  |
| 2   | 0.500446  | 1.97565   | 0.43762   |
| 3   | 1.70717   | 0.424157  | -0.846524 |
| 4   | -0.869665 | 0.182574  | -0.703025 |
| 5   | 0.801253  | 0.311777  | 2.08523   |,DataFrames.Terms(Any[:B,
:C],Any[:A,:B,:C],3x3 Array{Int8,2}:
 1  0  0
 0  1  0
 0  0  1,[1,1,1],true,true),Bool[true,true,true,true,true])
```

Creating a `ModelMatrix` from a `ModelFrame` is quite easy:

```
julia> random_modelmatrix = ModelMatrix(ModelFrame(A ~ B + C, ran
dom_dataframe))
DataFrames.ModelMatrix{Float64}(5x3 Array{Float64,2}:
 1.0   0.39672    0.843678
 1.0   1.53446   -0.199888
 1.0  -1.17061   -1.44164
 1.0   1.3115     1.03606
 1.0   1.68626    0.149367,[0,1,2])
```

There is an extra column containing only `value = 1.0`. It is used in a regression model to fit an intercept term.

Pooling data

To analyze huge datasets efficiently, PooledDataArray is used. DataArray uses an encoding that represents a full string for every entry of a vector. This is not very efficient, especially for large datasets and memory-intensive algorithms.

Our use case more often deals with factors involving a small number of levels:

```
julia> datavector = @data(["A", "A", "A","B", "B", "B"])
6-element DataArrays.DataArray{ASCIIString,1}:
 "A"
 "A"
 "A"
 "B"
 "B"
 "B"
```

`PooledDataArray` uses indices in a small pool of levels instead of strings to represent data efficiently.

```
julia> pooleddatavector = @pdata(["A", "A", "A","B", "B", "B"])
6-element DataArrays.PooledDataArray{ASCIIString,UInt32,1}:
 "A"
 "A"
 "A"
 "B"
 "B"
 "B"
```

`PooledDataArray` also provides us with the functionality to find out the levels of the factor using the levels function:

```
julia> levels(pooleddatavector)
2-element Array{ASCIIString,1}:
 "A"
 "B"
```

`PooledDataArray` even provides a compact function to efficiently use memory:

```
Julia> pooleddatavector = compact (pooleddatavector)
```

Then, it provides a pool function for converting a single column when factors are encoded not in `PooledDataArray` columns but in DataArray or DataFrame:

```
Julia>  pooleddatavector = pool(datavector)
```

```
julia> dataframe_notpooled = DataFrame(A = [10, 10, 10, 20, 20, 2
0], B = ["X", "X", "X", "Y", "Y", "Y"])
6x2 DataFrames.DataFrame
| Row | A  | B   |
|-----|----|-----|
| 1   | 10 | "X" |
| 2   | 10 | "X" |
| 3   | 10 | "X" |
| 4   | 20 | "Y" |
| 5   | 20 | "Y" |
| 6   | 20 | "Y" |

julia> pooleddf = pool!(dataframe_notpooled, [:A, :B])
```

PooledDataArray facilitates the analysis of categorical data, as columns in ModelMatrix are treated as 0-1 indicator columns. Each of the levels of PooledDataArray is associated with one column.

Web scraping

Real-world use cases also include scraping data from the Web for analysis. Let's build a small web scraper to fetch Reddit posts.

For this, we will need the JSON and Requests packages:

```
julia> Pkg.add("JSON")
julia> Pkg.add("Requests")

# import the required libraries
julia> using JSON, Requests

# Use the reddit URL to fetch the data from
julia> reddit_url = https://www.reddit.com/r/Julia/

# fetch the data and store it in a variable
julia> response = get("$(reddit_url)/.json")
Response(200 OK, 21 headers, 55426 bytes in body)

# Parse the data received using JSON.parse
julia> dataReceived = JSON.parse(Requests.text(response))
# Create the required objects
julia> nextRecord = dataReceived["data"]["after"]
julia> counter = length(dataReceived["data"]["children"])
```

Here, we defined a URL from where we will be scraping the data. We are scraping from Julia's section on Reddit.

Then, we are getting the content from the defined URL using the get function from the Requests package. We can see that we've got response 200 OK with the data:

```
julia> statuscode(response)
200

julia> HttpCommon.STATUS_CODES[200]
"OK"
```

We then parse the JSON data received using the JSON parser provided by the JSON package of Julia. We can now start reading the record.

```
julia> allPosts = []
0-element Array{Any,1}

julia> for record in 1:counter
julia> for record in 1:counter
       url = dataReceived["data"]["children"][record]["data"]["url"]
       redditrecord_id  = dataReceived["data"]["children"][record]["data"]
["id"]
       redditrecord_title  = dataReceived["data"]["children"][record]["dat
a"]["title"]
       author  = dataReceived["data"]["children"][record]["data"]["author"
]
       created = dataReceived["data"]["children"][record]["data"]["created
"]
       push!(allPosts, (url, redditrecord_id, redditrecord_title, author,
created))
       end
```

We can store the data received in an Array or DataFrame (depending on the use case and ease of use). Here, we are using an Array to store the parsed data. We can check the data stored in an Array.

```
julia> allPosts
26-element Array{Any,1}:
 ("http://juliacon.org/","3ztvre","SAVE THE DATE: JuliaCon 2016 - Boston, MA
","Mr_You",1.452170599e9)


 ("https://www.reddit.com/r/Julia/comments/41iz6o/native_plotting_function_i
n_julia/","41iz6o","Native plotting function in Julia","shivaramkrs",1.45315
3237e9)
```

Suppose we only need to see the title of these posts and know what we have scraped; we just need to know in which column they are.

```
julia> for post in allPosts
           println(post[3])
       end
SAVE THE DATE: JuliaCon 2016 - Boston, MA
Native plotting function in Julia
A Speed Comparison Of C, Julia, Python, Numba, and Cython on LU Factorizatio
n
Julia 0.4.3 released
Julia IDE work in Atom
RBM written from scratch in Julia and trained with persistent states -- 98%
on MNIST without fine-tuning
Looking for a couple people to test my Julia editor
Vetting of a package
How to initialize columns of a matrix with a function?
Gave these as Christmas presents this year
RStudio equivalent for Julia
Julia for robotics programming
PyData Amsterdam CFP, we'd love to have somebody talk about Julia!
Why is this loop in Julia slower than the Python equivalent? What am I doing
 wrong?
Deep neural network written from scratch in Julia
```

We can now see the title of the Reddit posts. But what if we had too many columns or we had some missing values? DataFrames would definitely be a better option.

Summary

In this chapter, we learned what data munging is and why it is necessary for data science. Julia provides functionalities to facilitate data munging with the DataFrames.jl package, with features such as these:

- `NA`: A missing value in Julia is represented by a specific data type, NA.
- `DataArray`: DataArray provided in the `DataFrames.jl` provides features such as allowing us to store some missing values in an array.
- `DataFrame`: DataFrame is 2-D data structure like spreadsheets. It is very similar to R or pandas's dataframes, and provides many functionalities to represent and analyze data. DataFrames has many features well suited for data analysis and statistical modeling.
- A dataset can have different types of data in different columns.
- Records have a relation with other records in the same row of different columns of the same length.
- Columns can be labeled. Labeling helps us to easily become familiar with the data and access it without the need to remember their numerical indices.

We learned about importing data from a file using the `readtable()` function and exporting data to a file. The `readtable()` function provides flexibility when using many arguments.

We also explored joining of datasets, such as RDBMS tables. Julia provides various joins that we can exploit according to our use case.

We discussed the Split-Apply-Combine Strategy, one of the most widely used techniques deployed by data scientists, and why it is needed. We went through reshaping or pivoting data using stack and melt (stackdf, meltdf) functions and explored the various possibilities involved. We were also introduced to `PooledDataArray` and learned why it is required for efficient memory management.

We were introduced to web scraping, which is sometimes a must for a data scientist to gather data. We also used the Requests package to fetch an HTTP response.

References

- http://julia.readthedocs.org/en/latest/manual/
- http://dataframesjl.readthedocs.io/en/latest/
- https://data.gov.uk/dataset/road-accidents-safety-data
- Wickham, Hadley. "The split-apply-combine strategy for data analysis." *Journal of Statistical Software* 40.1 (2011): 1-29

3
Data Exploration

When we first receive a dataset, most of the times we only know what it is related to—an overview that is not enough to start applying algorithms or create models on it. Data exploration is of paramount importance in data science. It is the necessary process prior to creating a model because it gives a highlight of the dataset and definitely makes clear the path to achieving our objectives. Data exploration familiarizes the data scientist with the data and helps to know what general hypothesis we can infer from the dataset. So, we can say it is a process of extracting some information from the dataset, not knowing beforehand what to look for.

In this chapter, we will study:

- Sampling, population, and weight vectors
- Inferring column types
- Summary of a dataset
- Scalar statistics
- Measures of variation
- Data exploration using visualizations

Data exploration involves descriptive statistics. Descriptive statistics is a field of data analysis that finds out patterns by meaningfully summarizing data. This may not lead to the exact results or the model that we intend to build, but it definitely helps to understand the data. Suppose there are 10 million people in New Delhi and if we calculate the mean of the heights of 1,000 people taken at random living there, it wouldn't be the average height of the people of New Delhi, but it would definitely give an idea.

Julia can effectively be used for data exploration. Julia provides a package called StatsBase.jl, which contains the necessary functions for statistics. We would presume throughout the chapter that you have added the package:

```
julia> Pkg.update()
julia> Pkg.add("StatsBase")
```

Sampling

In the previous example, we spoke about calculating the mean height of 1,000 people out of the 10 million people living in New Delhi. While gathering the data of these 10 million people, let's say we started from a particular age or community, or in any sequential manner. Now, if we take 1,000 people who are consecutive in the dataset, there is a high probability that they would have similarities among them. This similarity would not give us the actual highlight of the dataset that we are trying to achieve. So, taking a small chunk of consecutive data points from the dataset wouldn't give us the insight that we want to gain. To overcome this, we use sampling.

Sampling is a technique to randomly select data from the given dataset such that they are not related to each other, and therefore we can generalize the results that we generate on this selected data over the complete dataset. Sampling is done over a population.

Population

A population in statistics refers to the set of all the data points that are there in the dataset and which have at least one common property. In the previous example, the people have the common property of being from the same geographic region.

Let's take the example of the iris dataset. Although it has just 150 records, it would give us an idea on how to take a sample from the dataset:

```
julia> using RDatasets

julia> iris_dataframe = dataset("datasets", "iris")
```

We will use the RDatasets package, which contains the iris dataset, and will load it into a DataFrame. So, this DataFrame contains the "population" and we want to take a sample from it:

```
julia> sample(iris_dataframe[:SepalLength])
6.6
```

```
julia> sample(iris_dataframe[:SepalLength], 5)
5-element Array{Float64,1}:
  4.8
  5.4
  5.0
  5.2
  4.3
```

The `sample()` function can be used to return a random value from the dataset or an array of randomly chosen values:

```
Julia> sample(x, num_of_elements[; replace=true, ordered=false])
```

The `replace` and `ordered` arguments are used in specific cases:

- `replace`: This is used if the replacement is done when a same value is returned (default=true)
- `ordered`: This is used when the values returned are in ascending order (default=false)

Ideally, the sample taken from the given dataset should represent the population. But mostly, it under—or over—represents many groups present in the dataset. Let's take the earlier example, what if we were unable to gather the complete data for ages between 50-70 and from community X? Therefore, our dataset doesn't represent the exact population. Something has to be done to correct the observed dataset.

Weighting adjustment is one of the very common correction techniques. In this technique, an adjustment weight is assigned to each record. The record or group that we think is under-represented gets a weight larger than 1 and the record or group that we think is over-represented gets a weight smaller than 1.

Weight vectors

Julia has a type, WeightVec, to represent weight vectors to facilitate the assignment of weights to samples. The need for a specialized data type for weight vectors was:

- To explicitly distinguish the role of this particular vector from other data vectors
- To save computation cycles by storing the sum of the weights and avoiding recomputing the sum of the weights again

Weight vectors can be constructed like this:

```
julia> wv = WeightVec([1., 2., 3.], 6.)
StatsBase.WeightVec{Float64,Array{Float64,1}}([1.0,2.0,3.0],6.0)
```

We have provided the sum of the weights as the second argument. It is optional and is done to save computation time.

For simplicity, WeightVec supports a few general methods. Let wv be of the type WeightVec:

```
julia> eltype(wv)
Float64
```

eltype is used to get the type of the values in WeightVec:

```
julia> length(wv)
3

julia> isempty(wv)
false

julia> values(wv)
3-element Array{Float64,1}:
 1.0
 2.0
 3.0

julia> sum(wv)
6.0

# Applying eltypes to iris_dataframe
# this method is of DataFrames.jl
julia> eltypes(iris_dataframe)
5-element Array{Type{T},1}:
 Float64
 Float64
 Float64
 Float64
 Union{ASCIIString,UTF8String}
```

Other methods are self-explanatory. As the sum is already stored by WeightVec, it is returned instantaneously without any computation.

Inferring column types

To understand the dataset and move any further, we need to first understand what type of data we have. As our data is stored in columns, we should know their type before performing any operations. This is also called creating a data dictionary:

```julia
julia> typeof(iris_dataframe[1, :SepalLength])
Float64

julia> typeof(iris_dataframe[1, :Species])
ASCIIString
```

We have used the classic dataset of iris here. We already know the type of the data in these columns. We can apply the same function to any similar dataset. Suppose we were only given columns without labels; then it would have been hard to determine the type of data these columns contain. Sometimes, the dataset looks as if it contains numeric digits but their data type is ASCIIString. These can lead to errors in further steps. These errors are avoidable.

Basic statistical summaries

Although, we are currently using RDatasets, about which we have sufficient details and documentation, these methods and techniques can be extended to other datasets.

Let's use a different dataset:

```
julia> exam = dataset("mlmRev", "Exam")
4059x10 DataFrames.DataFrame
| Row | School | NormExam  | SchGend | SchAvg   | VR        | Intake     |
|-----|--------|-----------|---------|----------|-----------|------------|
| 1   | "1"    | 0.261324  | "mixed" | 0.166175 | "mid 50%" | "bottom 2  |
| 2   | "1"    | 0.134067  | "mixed" | 0.166175 | "mid 50%" | "mid 50%"  |
| 3   | "1"    | -1.72388  | "mixed" | 0.166175 | "mid 50%" | "top 25%"  |
| 4   | "1"    | 0.967586  | "mixed" | 0.166175 | "mid 50%" | "mid 50%"  |
| 5   | "1"    | 0.544341  | "mixed" | 0.166175 | "mid 50%" | "mid 50%"  |
| 6   | "1"    | 1.7349    | "mixed" | 0.166175 | "mid 50%" | "bottom 2  |
| 7   | "1"    | 1.03961   | "mixed" | 0.166175 | "mid 50%" | "top 25%"  |
| 8   | "1"    | -0.129085 | "mixed" | 0.166175 | "mid 50%" | "mid 50%"  |
| 9   | "1"    | -0.939378 | "mixed" | 0.166175 | "mid 50%" | "mid 50%"  |
⋮
```

We are using another dataset from the RDatasets package. These are exam scores from Inner London. To get some information about the dataset, we will use the `describe()` function, which we have already discussed in previous chapters:

```
julia> describe(exam)
School
Length   4059
Type     Pooled ASCIIString
NAs      0
NA%      0.0%
Unique   65

NormExam
Min       -3.666072
1st Qu.   -0.699505
Median    0.0043222
Mean      -0.00011380542005424873
3rd Qu.   0.6787592
Max       3.6660912
NAs       0
NA%       0.0%
```

The columns are described as follows:

- `Length` refers to the number of records (rows).
- `Type` refers to the data type of the column. Therefore, `School` is of the `Pooled ASCIIString` data type.
- `NA` and `NA%` refer to the number and percentage of the `NA` values present in the column. This is really helpful as you don't need to manually check for missing records now.
- `Unique` refers to the number of unique records present in the column.
- `Min` and `Max` are the minimum and maximum values present in the column (this does not apply to columns having `ASCIIstrings`). These are the values at the 0% and 100% of the data points. `Min` and `Max` define the range of data.
- 1st quantile and 3rd quantile refer to the value at 25% and 75% of the data points respectively. Similarly, median refers to the value at the 50% of the data points.

Calculating the mean of the array or dataframe

Julia provides different kinds of mean functions. Each has its own use case:

- geomean(arr): This computes the geometric mean of arr:

```
julia> a = [123,4234,23423,1231231,1432432423,1341413413]
6-element Array{Int64,1}:
        123
       4234
      23423
    1231231
 1432432423
 1341413413

julia> geomean(a)
553833.3901002567
```

- harmmean(arr): This computes the harmonic mean of arr:

```
julia> harmmean(a)
713.4557870657444
```

- trimmean(arr, fraction): This is used to compute the mean of the trimmed dataset. The second argument is used to provide the fraction over which the dataset will be trimmed. For example, if the value provided in fraction is 0.3, the mean will be computed by neglecting the top 30% and bottom 30% values. It's generally used to remove outliers:

```
julia> a = [123,4234,23423,1231231,1432432423,1341413413]
6-element Array{Int64,1}:
        123
       4234
      23423
    1231231
 1432432423
 1341413413

julia> trimmean(a,0.1)
2.685344848e8
```

The mean function is also extended. It can take a weighted vector as an argument to compute the weighted mean:

```julia
julia> a
6-element Array{Int64,1}:
        123
       4234
      23423
    1231231
 1432432423
 1341413413

julia> wv = rand(6)
6-element Array{Float64,1}:
 0.79903
 0.131471
 0.951132
 0.248691
 0.631604
 0.186289

julia> mean(a, weights(wv))
3.917448913086356e8
```

Scalar statistics

Various functions are provided by Julia's package to compute various statistics. These functions are used to describe data in different ways as required.

Standard deviations and variances

The mean and median we earlier computed (in the `describe()` function) are measures of central tendency. Mean refers to the center computed after applying weights to all the values and median refers to the center of the list.

This is only one piece of information and we would like to know more about the dataset. It would be good to have knowledge about the spread of data points across the dataset. We cannot use just the min and max functions as we can have outliers in the dataset. Therefore, these min and max functions will lead to incorrect results.

Variance is a measurement of the spread between data points in a dataset. It is computed by calculating the distance of numbers from the mean. Variance measures how far each number in the set is from the mean.

The following is the formula for variance:

$$\text{var}_x = \frac{\sum_{i=1}^{n} (x_i - x)^2}{n}$$

```
julia> a
6-element Array{Int64,1}:
           123
          4234
         23423
       1231231
    1432432423
    1341413413

julia> var(a)
5.1354392444543296e17
```

We can also have a variance along a specific dimension, which is useful for DataFrames:

```julia
julia> a = [1 2;3 4;5 6;7 8;9 10]
5x2 Array{Int64,2}:
 1   2
 3   4
 5   6
 7   8
 9  10

julia> var(a, 2)
5x1 Array{Float64,2}:
 0.5
 0.5
 0.5
 0.5
 0.5
```

Here, the second argument is the dimension along which we want to compute the variance.

Standard deviation is the measurement of the spread or dispersion of the values in the dataset. It is square root of the variance. If it is close to 0, that means the dataset has very little dispersion from the mean. And greater values define high dispersion of the values from the mean. Standard deviation is different from variance as it has the same units as the mean:

```julia
julia> std(a)
3.0276503540974917
```

We can also calculate the standard deviation along a dimension such as variance.

Julia provides a function to calculate mean and variance, and also mean and standard deviation together:

```julia
julia> mean_and_var(a)
(5.5,9.166666666666666)

julia> mean_and_std(a)
(5.5,3.0276503540974917)
```

Statistical analysis involves characterization of data based on skewness and kurtosis. Skewness is the measure of the lack of symmetry from the center point of the dataset or the distribution. So, a distribution can be skewed to the left or it can be skewed to the right.

Kurtosis is the measure of the flatness of the distribution or the dataset as compared to a normal distribution. So, a distribution with a high peak at the center (mean) and a sharp decline to both the sides is said to have high kurtosis, and a distribution with a flatter peak at the mean is said to have low kurtosis:

```julia
julia> a = [12,234,567,1234,535,335,19]
7-element Array{Int64,1}:
     12
    234
    567
   1234
    535
    335
     19

julia> skewness(a)
0.9763073577410081

julia> kurtosis(a)
0.04885930438714192
```

A moment in statistics is:

- 0th moment is the total probability
- 1st moment is the mean
- 2nd central moment is the variance
- 3rd moment is the skewness
- 4th moment is the kurtosis (with shift and normalization)

```julia
julia> moment(a,3)
5.80616226472303e7
```

Here we are calculating the k-th order central moment. It is defined as:

```
(a - mean(a)).^k
```

Measures of variation

It is good to have knowledge of the variation of values in the dataset. Various statistical functions facilitate:

- `span(arr)`: span is used to calculate the total spread of the dataset, which is `maximum(arr)` to `minimum(arr)`:

```
julia> a
7-element Array{Int64,1}:
     12
    234
    567
   1234
    535
    335
     19

julia> span(a)
12:1234
```

- `variation(arr)`: Also called the coefficient of variance. It is the ratio of the standard deviation to the mean of the dataset. In relation to the mean of the population, CV denotes the extent of variability. Its advantage is that it is a dimensionless number and can be used to compare different datasets.

```
julia> variation(a)
1.0051933013705867
```

Standard error of mean: We work on different samples drawn from the population. We compute the means of these samples and call them sample means. For different samples, we wouldn't be having the same sample mean but a distribution of sample means. The standard deviation of the distribution of these sample means is called standard error of mean.

In Julia, we can compute standard error of mean using `sem(arr)`.

Mean absolute deviation is a robust measure of central tendency. Robustness refers to not being affected by outliers.

```
julia> a = [12,23,45,68,99,72,61,39,21,71]
10-element Array{Int64,1}:
 12
 23
 45
 68
 99
 72
 61
 39
 21
 71

julia> mad(a)
27.428099999999997

julia> mad(a,5)
71.1648
```

We can provide the center as a second argument.

Z-scores

A z-score refers to the relationship with the mean of the scores. It is calculated by how many standard deviations an element is above or below the mean. A 0 z-score means it is the same as the mean.

It is given by the formula $z = (X - \mu) / \sigma$:

```
julia> a = [12,23,45,68,99,72,61,39,21,71]
```

On this dataset, we can calculate the z-score like this:

```julia
julia> zscore(a)
10-element Array{Float64,1}:
 -1.4102
 -1.01347
 -0.220005
  0.609522
  1.72758
  0.753788
  0.357057
 -0.436403
 -1.0856
  0.717721
```

The mean and the standard deviation are calculated by themselves.

Entropy

Entropy is the measure of disorder in the dataset and provides the approximate measure of randomness in the system. It increases with randomness.

Let's create a probability vector:

```julia
julia> using Distributions

julia> d = Dirichlet([1.0, 3.0, 5.0])
Distributions.Dirichlet(alpha=[1.0,3.0,5.0])
```

We have created a rather small array:

```julia
julia> arr=rand(d)
3-element Array{Float64,1}:
 0.190511
 0.80904
 0.000449442
```

The sum of the elements of the probability vector is 1. It is tending to 1 here. We now calculate the entropy:

```
julia> sum(arr)
1.0000000000000002

julia> entropy(arr)
0.4907814135561367
```

The entropy computation is done using natural logarithms. We can also provide the base of the logarithm if needed.

```
julia> entropy(arr,2)
0.7080479114979139
```

The second argument that we have provided is for the base of the logarithm. We can also compute cross-entropy, which is considered an effective alternative to a squared error:

```
Julia> crossentropy(ProbabilityVector1, ProbabilityVector2)
```

Quantiles

To understand the dataset better, we want to know the lowest and highest points in the dataset. We can use min and max functions for that. So, we can also say that the min and max data points are at 0% and at 100%. If we want to find out any data point at n% of the dataset we use the `quantile` function.

Quantiles can be very useful in scenarios where there are outliers. For example, for a we are analyzing the response times of various browsers for a website: 98% of the traffic comes from the desktop and it is able to load the page in less than a second; 2% of the remaining traffic is from mobile, where it takes 5 seconds to load the page. Here, we might want to ignore this 2% (if the use case allows us) to analyze the actual traffic of the website.

```
julia> a = rand(10)
10-element Array{Float64,1}:
 0.256684
 0.0760744
 0.959692
 0.933633
 0.170989
 0.371441
 0.123852
 0.959958
 0.552251
 0.999725
```

Now, to compute the quantile:

```
julia> quantile(a)
5-element Array{Float64,1}:
 0.0760744
 0.192413
 0.461846
 0.953178
 0.999725
```

Here, we have received five values. These five values represent data points at 0%, 25%, 50%, 75%, and 100% of the dataset.

Interquartile range is the measure of the variability and is calculated by having the difference of the upper and lower quartiles, which is Q3-Q1. It is computed as:

```
julia> iqr(a)
0.7607643393430641
```

Percentile is a common term in statistics and is used to represent where the data point falls in the dataset. It can be calculated as:

```
julia> percentile(a,0.5)
0.07822436710303723
```

We have used the same dataset and calculated where 0.5 would lie in the dataset.

There is another important function, nquantile. It is used to create a vector of quantiles defined by us:

```
julia> nquantile(a,2)
3-element Array{Float64,1}:
 0.0760744
 0.461846
 0.999725
```

Modes

While exploring the dataset, we would want to know which data is frequently repeated in the dataset. This is the value that has the maximum probability to come in the sample. Julia provides a function to calculate the mode:

```
julia> mode(a)
0.2566843440628257
```

We calculated the mode on the same dataset that we used in the previous example. So, 0.2566 appears most often in the dataset.

Summary of datasets

Earlier we discussed the `describe()` function, which prints the summary of the dataset. Julia also provides another function, `summarystats()`.

Using `summarystats(a)` on the same dataset of the previous example, we get the following result. So, we now don't have to calculate them individually and it gives an idea of what kind of dataset we have.

```
julia> summarystats(a)
Summary Stats:
Mean:           0.540430
Minimum:        0.076074
1st Quartile:   0.192413
Median:         0.461846
3rd Quartile:   0.953178
Maximum:        0.999725
```

Scatter matrix and covariance

Covariance is used very often by data scientists to find out how two ordered sets of data follow in the same direction. It can very easily define whether the variables are correlated or not. To best represent this behavior, we create a covariance matrix. The unnormalized version of the covariance matrix is the scatter matrix.

To create a scatter matrix, we use the `scattermat(arr)` function.

The default behavior is to treat each row as an observation and column as a variable. This can be changed by providing the keyword arguments `vardim` and `mean`:

- `Vardim`: `vardim=1` (default) means each column is a variable and each row is an observation. `vardim=2` is the reverse.
- `mean`: The mean is computed by `scattermat`. We can use a predefined mean to save compute cycles.

We can also create a weighted covariance matrix using the `cov` function. It also takes vardim and mean as optional arguments for the same purpose.

Computing deviations

StatsBase.jl provides various functions to compute deviations between two datasets. This can be calculated using other functions, but to facilitate and for ease of use, StatsBase provides these efficiently implemented functions:

- **Mean absolute deviation**: For two datasets, a and b, it is calculated as `meanad(x,y)` which is a wrapper over `mean(abs(x-y))`.
- **Maximum absolute deviation**: For two datasets, a and b, it is calculated as `maxad(x,y)`, which is a wrapper over `maximum(abs(x-y))`.
- **Mean squared deviation**: For two datasets, a and b, it is calculated as `msd(x,y)`, which is a wrapper over `mean(abs2(x-y))`.
- **Root mean squared deviation**: For two datasets, a and b, it is calculated as `rmsd(a,b)`, which is a wrapper over `sqrt(msd(a, b))`.

Rankings

When a dataset is sorted in ascending order, a rank is assigned to each value. Ranking is a process where the dataset is transformed and values are replaced by their ranks. Julia provides functions for various types of rankings.

In ordinal ranking, all items in the dataset are assigned a distinct value. Items that have equal values are assigned a ranking arbitrarily. In Julia, this is done using the `ordinalrank` function.

```
julia> a = rand(4)
4-element Array{Float64,1}:
 0.462513
 0.340506
 0.269411
 0.283305
```

Suppose this is our dataset and we want to do ordinal ranking:

```
julia> ordinalrank(a)
4-element Array{Int64,1}:
 4
 3
 1
 2
```

Using the `ordinalrank(arr)` function, we've got the ordinal ranking. Similarly, StatsBase also provides functions to find other types of rankings, such as `competerank()`, `denserank()`, and `tiedrank()`.

Counting functions

In data exploration, counting over a range is often done. It helps to find out the most/least occurring value. Julia provides the counts function to count over a range. Let's say we have an array of values. For our convenience, we will now use the random function to create an array:

```
julia> a = rand([1:5],30)
30-element Array{Int64,1}:
 4
 1
 3
 1
 1
 4
```

We have created an array of 30 values ranging from 1 to 5. Now we want to know how many times they occur in the dataset:

```
julia> counts(a)
5-element Array{Int64,1}:
  7
  1
  5
 11
  6
```

Using the `count` function, we found that 1(7), 2(1), 3(5), 4(11), and 5(6). counts take different arguments to suit the use case.

The `proportions()` function is used to compute the proportions of the values in the dataset and Julia provides the function:

```
julia> proportions(a,1:3)
3-element Array{Float64,1}:
 0.233333
 0.0333333
 0.166667
```

We calculated proportions on the same dataset that we used in the previous examples. It shows that the ratio of value 1 in the dataset is `0.23333`. This can also be seen as the probability of finding the value in the dataset.

Other count functions include:

- `countmap(arr)`: This is a map function that maps the values to the number of occurrences (or total weights) in the dataset:

```
julia> countmap(a)
Dict{Int64,Int64} with 5 entries:
  4 => 11
  2 => 1
  3 => 5
  5 => 6
  1 => 7
```

- `proportionmap(arr)`: This is a map function similar to `countmap(arr)` but maps values to their proportions:

```
julia> proportionmap(a)
Dict{Int64,Float64} with 5 entries:
  4 => 0.36666666666666664
  2 => 0.03333333333333333
  3 => 0.16666666666666666
  5 => 0.2
  1 => 0.23333333333333334
```

Applying `countmap` and `proportionmap` to our dataset gave these values. Both these functions return a dictionary.

Histograms

Data exploration after a basic understanding can also be done with the aid of visualizations. Plotting a histogram is one of the most common ways of data exploration through visualization. A histogram type is used to tabulate data over a real plane separated into regular intervals.

A histogram is created using the fit method:

```
julia> fit(Histogram, data[, weight][, edges])
```

`fit` takes the following arguments:

- `data`: Data is passed to the `fit` function in the form of a vector, which can either be one-dimensional or n-dimensional (tuple of vectors of equal length).
- `weight`: This is the optional argument. A `WeightVec` type can be passed as an argument if values have different weights. The default weight of values is 1.
- `edges`: This is a vector used to give the edges of the bins along each dimension.

It also takes a keyword argument, `nbins`, which is used to define the number of bins that the histogram should use along each side:

```
h = fit(Histogram, (rand(100),rand(100)),nbins=10)

StatsBase.Histogram{Int64,2,Tuple{FloatRange{Float64},FloatRange{Float64}}}
edges:
  0.0:0.1:1.0
  0.0:0.1:1.0
weights: 10x10 Array{Int64,2}:
 1  1  0  1  1  0  0  0  0  1
 1  0  2  0  3  1  0  1  0  0
 1  1  3  0  2  3  0  1  1  0
 1  1  2  1  3  1  3  0  0  2
 1  1  0  2  0  0  1  1  1  0
 1  1  2  1  1  1  1  2  2  1
 0  1  1  2  0  1  1  0  0  3
 0  1  2  0  3  0  2  1  0  3
 2  0  0  1  2  0  2  2  1  0
 1  0  1  3  1  1  0  2  1  0
closed: right
```

In this example, we used two random value generators and `nbins` to define the number of bins. We created a histogram on the randomly generated data. Let's try this on a dataset from the `RDatasets` package. This package is explained here: `https://stat.ethz.ch/R-m anual/R-devel/library/datasets/html/sleep.html`.

```
In [2]: using RDatasets
        using Distributions
        using StatsBase
        using Gadfly

In [3]: sleep = dataset("lme4","sleepstudy")
```

Out[3]:

	Reaction	Days	Subject
1	249.56	0	308
2	258.7047	1	308
3	250.8006	2	308
4	321.4398	3	308

We are using a dataset called `sleepstudy` from the `RDatasets` package. It contains three columns: `Reaction` (`Float64`), `Days` (`Integer`), and `Subject` (`Integer`). We will create a histogram on this data.

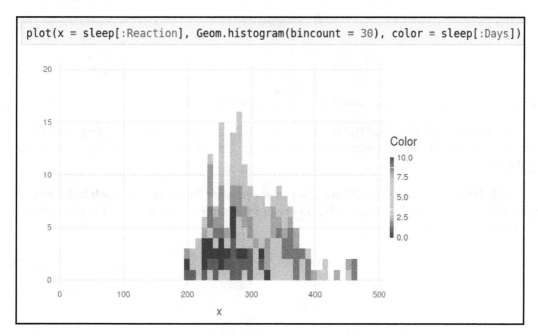

We can now realize that it is easier to understand the data through visualizations. Visualization is an important part of data exploration. To be actually able to visualize data, the necessary data munging and some understanding of variables are required. In this particular visualization, we can observe which areas are denser and the reaction times.

We discussed the scatter matrix earlier. We can create a scatter plot and will try to find out if it helps us.

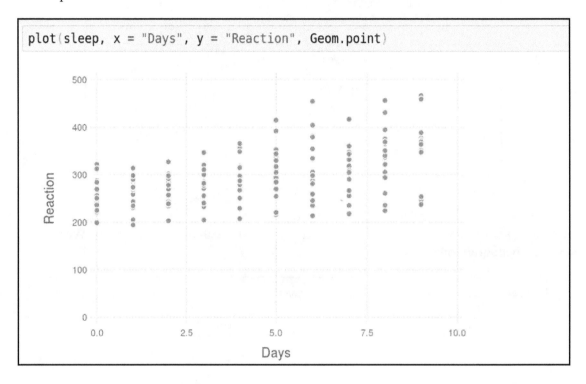

We can very well observe that the reaction times of the subjects are increasing day by day. We were able to get to this conclusion very quickly; otherwise, it would have taken some significant amount of time.

Let's drill down more into this dataset. Suppose we want to know how each individual subject has performed. As all the subjects are not the same, some might have performed quite differently from others.

On a large dataset, we can do a grouping or clustering; but here, as have a small dataset, we can individually analyze subjects.

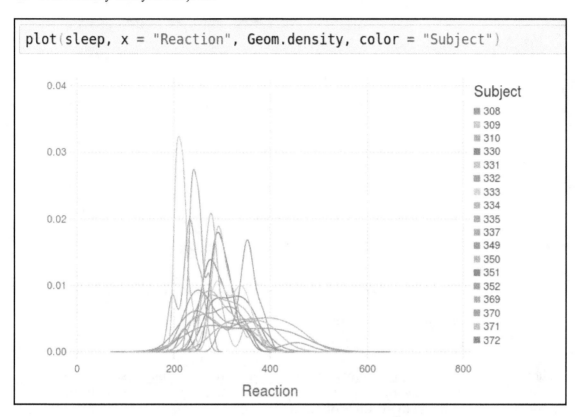

```
plot(sleep, x = "Reaction", Geom.density, color = "Subject")
```

It is evident that subject 309, even after being deprived of sleep for many days, had a very low reaction time. These are small insights that we sometimes miss through analyzing a dataset that is exposed through visualizations.

We will discuss visualizations in detail in Chapter 5, *Making Sense of Data Using Visualization*. We will explore various packages available with Julia for visualization and also how can we call R and Python's packages if needed for visualizations. We will also go through some basic D3.js examples.

It is easy to create basic plots in Julia, for example:

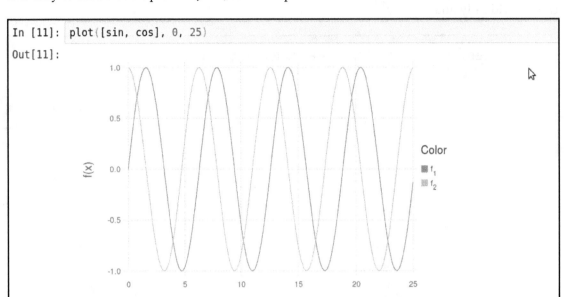

```
In [11]: plot([sin, cos], 0, 25)
Out[11]:
```

Let's now try some visualizations on the iris dataset:

```julia
julia> x=:SepalLength, y=:SepalWidth, color=:Species)
```

Although it is not completely visible now, we can see there are visible clusters. Maybe, we can differentiate between various species using these clusters. Therefore, visualizations can be very helpful in finding these kinds of insights.

Correlation analysis

Julia provides some functions to facilitate correlation analysis. Correlation and dependence are two common terms in statistics. Dependence refers to one variable having a statistical relationship with another variable, whereas correlation is one variable having a much wider class of relationship with the other variable, which may also include dependence.

The `autocov(x)` function is used to compute auto-covariance of x. It returns a vector of the same size as x.

```julia
julia> a = rand(6)
6-element Array{Float64,1}:
 0.167763
 0.015309
 0.681381
 0.842937
 0.894316
 0.432843
```

This is a dataset we generated. We can apply `autocov` on this dataset:

```julia
julia> autocov(a)
6-element Array{Float64,1}:
  0.109268
  0.0402556
 -0.0301791
 -0.0528897
 -0.0159282
  0.00410752
```

To compute auto-correlation, we use the `autocor` function:

```julia
julia> autocor(a)
6-element Array{Float64,1}:
  1.0
  0.368411
 -0.276194
 -0.484037
 -0.145772
  0.0375912
```

Similarly, we can also compute cross-covariance and cross-correlation. For that, we will generate another random array of the same size:

```
julia> crosscor(a,b)
11-element Array{Float64,1}:
   0.0637495
  -0.324786
  -0.391401
  -0.160508
   0.576313
```

Cross-covariance and cross-correlation of 2 arrays of length=6 results in arrays of lengths=11.

Summary

In this chapter, we discussed why data exploration is important and how can we perform exploratory analysis on datasets.

These are the various important techniques and concepts that we discussed:

- Sampling is a technique to randomly select unrelated data from the given dataset so that we can generalize the results that we generate on this selected data over the complete dataset.
- Weight vectors are important when the dataset that we have or gather doesn't represent the actual data.
- Why it is necessary to know the column types and how summary functions can be really helpful in getting the gist of the dataset.
- Mean, median, mode, standard deviation, variance, and scalar statistics, and how they are implemented in Julia.
- Measuring the variations in a dataset is really important and z-scores and entropy can be really useful.
- After some basic data cleaning and some understanding, visualization can be very beneficial and insightful.

References

- http://julia.readthedocs.io/en/latest/manual/
- https://dataframesjl.readthedocs.io/en/latest/
- https://github.com/JuliaStats/StatsBase.jl
- http://dcjones.github.io/Gadfly.jl/

4
Deep Dive into Inferential Statistics

Our world is a big data generating machine. These day-to-day activities consist of random and complex events that can be used to better understandUnivariate distributions: Normal, gamma, binomial the world. To achieve this, we will try to gain a deeper understanding of the processes.

Inferential statistics is to reach to a conclusion on the basis of evidence and reasoning gained from the sample data that is generalized for the population. Inferential statistics considers that there will be some sampling errors, which means the sample that we have drawn from the population may not be perfectly representing the population.

Inferential statistics include:

- Estimation
- Hypothesis testing

What is the difference between a sample and population? A population is a collection of all the events or observations about which we want want to gain knowledge. But its size can be so huge that it is not always convenient or feasible to analyze every event of this observation. In such a scenario, we take a subset that well defines the population that we want to analyze. We refer to this subset as a sample of the population.

In the last chapter, we discussed descriptive statistics. Although inferential and descriptive statistics are both done on the same set of data, they are quite different. We may apply descriptive statistics only on this sample data, but inferential statistics make use of this sample data with others to make generalizations that are valid for the larger population.

Therefore, descriptive statistics provide the summary of the data numerically or graphically. It only helps us to understand the data that we have, but we cannot use these results to form a conclusion that is generalized for the whole population.

With inferential statistics, we try to build a conclusion that is applicable for the whole population. But inferential statistics is limited by two main conditions:

- Whether the sample data that we have actually represents the population or not
- Whether the calculated assumptions that we form to make the sample data represent the population are correct or not

There is always a degree of uncertainty that the sample data taken from the population may or may not represent the population perfectly. Therefore, we make some estimations or assumptions to handle this uncertainty that again can have consequences on the results that we generate.

In Julia, we have various packages, which are used for inferential statistics. One such package is `Distributions.jl`, which provides functions related to probabilistic distributions. `Distributions.jl` covers the following statistical methods:

- Properties of distribution – mean, variance, skewness, and kurtosis (moment) and entropy
- Probability density/mass functions
- Characteristic functions
- Maximum likelihood estimation
- **Maximum-A-Posteriori (MAP)** probability estimate

Installation

`Distributions.jl` is a registered Julia package so it can be added using:

```
julia> Pkg.add("Distributions")
```

Further sections would require the package to be installed. So, we would assume you have added the package now.

Understanding the sampling distribution

The sampling distribution is the likelihood of gathering every possible statistic from a sample of a population that is taken randomly. Useful information can be derived using the sampling distribution without the complete knowledge of the population. Suppose we are calculating the sample mean but we don't know the population. Still, we can assume that the sample mean is within a certain number of standard deviations of the population mean.

Understanding the normal distribution

The normal distribution is the core of inferential statistics. It is like a bell curve (also called a Gaussian curve). Most of the complex processes can be defined by the normal distribution.

Let's see what a normal distribution looks like. First, we will import the necessary packages. We are including RDatasets now, but will be using it later:

```
using DataFrames
using RDatasets
using Distributions
using Gadfly

In [22]:

srand(619)
```

We first set the seed and then explore the normal function:

```
super(Normal)

Distributions.Distribution{Distributions.Univariate,Distributi
ons.Continuous}

names(Normal)

WARNING: names(t::DataType) is deprecated, use fieldnames(t) i
nstead.

2-element Array{Symbol,1}:
 :μ
 :σ
```

As per the warning given, we can also use `fieldnames` instead of `names`. It is recommended to use `fieldnames` only from the newer versions of Julia.

Here, we can see that the Normal function is in the Distributions package and has the features Univariate and Continuous. The constructor of the `normal()` function accepts two parameters:

- Mean (μ)
- Standard deviation (σ)

Let's instantiate a normal distribution. We will keep the mean (μ) as 1.0 and the standard deviation (σ) as `3.0`:

```
dist1 = Normal(1.0, 3.0)

Distributions.Normal(μ=1.0, σ=3.0)

params(dist1)

(1.0,3.0)
```

We can check the mean and standard deviation that we have kept:

```
dist1.μ

1.0

dist1.σ

3.0
```

Using this normal distribution object, we can now create a distribution using a random function:

```
x = rand(dist1, 1000)

1000-element Array{Float64,1}:
   7.53922
  -4.27887
   1.54685
  -1.3515
  -2.68357
   3.62544
```

To better understand the function, let's plot a histogram using Gadfly:

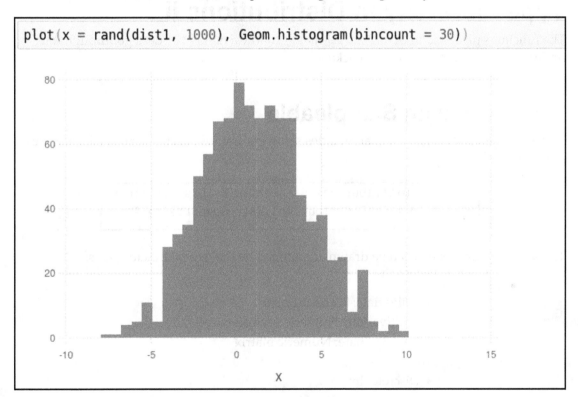

```
plot(x = rand(dist1, 1000), Geom.histogram(bincount = 30))
```

Parameter estimation

This is used to find out by what kind of distribution it is best described. We can use the `fit` function for this:

```
fit(Normal, x)
Distributions.Normal(μ=1.0038374150247216, σ=2.99929
17508924752)
```

We used `[1.0, 3.0]` to create the x and we can see that the estimates are quite close.

Type hierarchy in Distributions.jl

The functions provided in `Distributions.jl` follow a hierarchy. Let's go through it to understand the capabilities of the package.

Understanding Sampleable

Sampleable is an abstract type that includes samplers and distributions from which one can draw samples. It is defined as follows:

```
abstract Distributions.Sampleable{F<:Distributions.
VariateForm,S<:Distributions.ValueSupport} <: Any
```

The kinds of samples that can be drawn are defined by the two parameter types:

- VariateForm:
    - Univariate: Scalar number
    - Multivariate: Numeric vector
    - Matrixvariate: Numeric matrix
- ValueSupport:
    - Discrete: Int
    - Continuous: Float64

We can extract the information about the sample that the Sampleable object generates. An array can contain multiple samples depending on the variate form. We can use various functions to get the information (let's assume `sampobj` is the sampleable object):

- `length(sampobj)`: As the name suggests, it gives the length of the sample, which is 1 when the object is Univariate
- `size(sampobj)`: This returns the shape of the sample
- `nsamples(sampobj, X)`: This returns the number of samples that are in X
- `eltype(sampobj)`: This returns the default type of elements in the sample
- `rand(sampobj, x)`: This returns x number of samples taken from the sample:
  - For `sampobj=univariate`, a vector of length x is returned
  - For `sampobj=multivariate`, a matrix of x columns is returned
  - For `sampobj=matrix-variate`, an array of a sample matrix is returned

Representing probabilistic distributions

To better represent probabilistic distributions, Distribution, which is a subtype of Sampleable, is used:

```
abstract Distributions.Distribution{F<:Distributions
.VariateForm,S<:Distributions.ValueSupport} <: Distr
ibutions.Sampleable{F<:Distributions.VariateForm,S<:
Distributions.ValueSupport}
```

For ease of use, we generally use `typealias` for commonly used distributions :

```
julia> typealias UnivariateDistribution{S<:ValueSupport}
Distribution{Univariate,S}

julia> typealias MultivariateDistribution{S<:ValueSupport}
Distribution{Multivariate,S}

julia> typealias MatrixDistribution{S<:ValueSupport}
Distribution{Matrixvariate,S}
```

Univariate distributions

The distributions where each sample is scalar are Univariate distributions. We can categorize them further into two distributions based on the values they support:

- Univariate Continuous Distribution
- Univariate Discrete Distribution

Abstract types:

```julia
julia> typealias UnivariateDistribution{S<:ValueSupport}
Distribution{Univariate,S}

julia> typealias DiscreteUnivariateDistribution    Distribution{Univariate,
Discrete}
julia> typealias ContinuousUnivariateDistribution Distribution{Univariate,
Continuous}
```

Many methods are implemented for Univariate distributions in the package, which provides necessary functionalities.

Retrieving parameters

- `params(distributionX)`: This will return a tuple of parameters
- `succprob(distributionX)`: This returns the probability of success
- `failprob(distributionX)`: This returns the probability of failure
- `dof(distributionX)` : This returns the degree of freedom
- `ncategories(distributionX)`: This returns the number of categories
- `ntrials(distributionX)`: This returns the number of trials

Statistical functions

Common statistical functions such as `mean()`, `median()`, `mode()`, `std()`, `var()`, and so on, are applicable on these distributions.

Evaluation of probability

In addition to various statistical functions, Julia also provides functions for evaluating probability:

- pdf(distributionX): pdf refers to the probability density function. It returns the probability vector of distributionX. A range of values can also be provided as the second argument to the function in the form of a:b.
- cdf(distributionX): cdf refers to the cumulative distribution function.
- insupport(distributionX, x): This supports function returns if the distributionX, x is in support or not.

Sampling in Univariate distributions

We have previously discussed random number generation. It can also be used to draw a sample from a distribution:

```julia
julia> rand(distributionX)
```

This will draw a single sample from distributionX. It uses multiple dispatch and we can provide other arguments depending on our needs:

```julia
Julia> rand(distributionX, n)
```

This will return from the distributionX a vector of n independent samples.

Understanding Discrete Univariate distributions and types

Discrete Univariate Distribution is the super type of these distributions and the sample drawn from such distributions is an integer.

Bernoulli distribution

Bernoulli distribution is a discrete distribution. It has two possible outcomes, let's say these are $n=0$ and $n=1$. Here, if we take $n=1$ as success and its probability as p, then $n=0$ is failure and has the probability $q=1-p$ where $0<p<1$.

In Julia, Bernoulli distribution is implemented as follows:

```julia
julia> Bernoulli(p)
```

Here, p is the success rate (probability).

Binomial distribution

Binomial distribution is another discrete probability distribution. It is given by $P_p(n \mid N)$, which is obtaining n number of successes out of N Bernoulli trials. After a sequence of independent trials, the number of successes obtained is the binomial distribution:

```julia
julia> using Distributions

julia> Binomial()
Distributions.Binomial(n=1, p=0.5)
```

This is a Binomial distribution with number of trials=1 and success rate, p=0.5:

```julia
julia> n=5
5

julia> Binomial(n)
Distributions.Binomial(n=5, p=0.5)
```

Here we have specified the number of trials=5. The success rate remains as default:

```julia
julia> p=0.3
0.3

julia> Binomial(n,p)
Distributions.Binomial(n=5, p=0.3)
```

We can also define the success rate. So, this will return a distribution with the number of trials=5 and success rate, p=0.3.

Continuous distributions

Continuous Univariate Distribution is the super type of all the continuous univariate distributions, and each sample drawn from a continuous univariate distribution is of type `Float64`.

Cauchy distribution

Cauchy distribution is also called Lorentz distribution. It is a continuous distribution that describes the resonance behavior:

```julia
julia> Cauchy()
Distributions.Cauchy(μ=0.0, σ=1.0)
```

This gives the standard Cauchy distribution (location = 0.0, scale = 1.0):

```julia
julia> Cauchy(u,s)
Distributions.Cauchy(μ=0.2, σ=1.5)
```

We can pass parameters. This one gives us the Cauchy distribution with location `u` and scale `s`.

Chi distribution

Chi distribution with k degrees of freedom is the distribution formed by the square root of a chi-squared random variable, which is the sum of squares of k independent variables that are normally distributed.

In Julia, it is implemented as follows:

```julia
julia> Chi(k)
```

This will form a Chi distribution with k degrees of freedom.

It is used to yield the correction factor in the unbiased estimation of the standard deviation of the normal distribution by dividing by the mean of the chi distribution.

Chi-square distribution

Chi-square distribution with k degrees of freedom is the distribution of a sum of the squares of k independent standard normal random variables.

In Julia, it is implemented as follows:

```
julia> Chisq(k)
```

Here, k is the degree of freedom.

The significance of Chi-square distribution commonly used in chi-squared tests is:

- It is used to get the goodness of fit of an observed distribution
- Of a normal distribution, it is used to get the confidence interval estimation for a population standard deviation from a sample standard deviation
- It is also used to get the independence of classification criteria of qualitative data

Truncated distributions

Sometimes it is required to limit a distribution within a specific domain or range and the result from restricting a distribution is called truncated distribution. These are useful when we can only record the events in a specified range or when a threshold is given:

$$f(x|a < X <= b) = \frac{g(x)}{F(b) - F(a)} = TruncatedD(x)$$

This is the truncated distribution when it is restricted between two constants. In Julia, it is implemented as follows:

```
Summary:
immutable Distributions.Truncated{D<:Distributions
.Distribution{Distributions.Univariate,S<:Distribu
tions.ValueSupport},S<:Distributions.ValueSupport}
 <: Distributions.Distribution{Distributions.Univa
riate,S<:Distributions.ValueSupport}
```

1. The nontruncated case: $-\infty = a, b = +\infty$.

2. The lower truncated case: $-\infty < a, b = +\infty$.

3. The upper truncated case: $-\infty = a, b < +\infty$.

4. The doubly truncated case: $-\infty < a, b < +\infty$

```
Fields:
untruncated :: D<:Distributions.Distribution{Distr
ibutions.Univariate,S<:Distributions.ValueSupport}
lower        :: Float64
upper        :: Float64
lcdf         :: Float64
ucdf         :: Float64
tp           :: Float64
logtp        :: Float64

Truncated TruncatedNormal truncate
```

However, a few statistical functions that are available to Univariate Distributions are available to general Truncated distributions too. The reason for non-availability of those functions is that it gets complex to compute because of the truncation.

Truncated normal distributions

This is a special type of distribution in which the truncated distribution forms a normal distribution.

It can be made using the dedicated constructor, TruncatedNormal, or by providing the Normal constructor as an argument to the Truncated constructor:

```
Julia> TruncatedNormal(mu, sigma, l, u)
```

As this is the normal distribution, the statistical functions that are not available to general truncated distributions are available to truncated normal distributions.

Understanding multivariate distributions

A multivariate probability distribution is one containing more than one random variable. There may or may not be any correlation among these random variables. A sample drawn from this distribution is a vector. `Distributions.jl` has implementations of commonly used multivariate functions—*Multinomial*, Multivariate *Normal,* and *Dirichlet.* They are implemented as follows:

```
Distributions.MultivariateDistribution is of type
TypeConstructor:

Summary:
immutable TypeConstructor <: Type{T}

Fields:
parameters :: SimpleVector
body       :: Any

MultivariateDistribution
DiscreteMultivariateDistribution
```

Its type aliases are given as follows:

```
julia> typealias MultivariateDistribution{S<:ValueSupport}
Distribution{Multivariate,S}

julia> typealias DiscreteMultivariateDistribution
Distribution{Multivariate, Discrete}
julia> typealias ContinuousMultivariateDistribution
Distribution{Multivariate, Continuous}
```

Most of the methods available to Univariate distributions are also available to Multivariate distributions.

Multinomial distribution

This generalizes the binomial distribution. Suppose that over a finite set of size k of a categorical distribution, we take *n* independent draws.

Let's represent this as : $X = X_1, X_2, \ldots\ldots\ldots X_k$.

Then this X represents a multinomial distribution whose every sample is a k-dimensional integer vector that sums to *n*.

In Julia, it is implemented as follows:

```julia
julia> Multinomial(n, p)
```

Here, p represents the probability vector and we are creating the distribution with n trials.

Multivariate normal distribution

This is a multidimensional generalization of the normal distribution:

```
immutable Distributions.MvNormal{Cov<:PDMats.AbstractPDMat,Mean<:Uni
on{Array{Float64,1},Distributions.ZeroVector{Float64}}} <: Distributio
ns.AbstractMvNormal
```

Reasons why multivariate normal distribution is important:

- **Mathematical simplicity**: It is easier to work with this distribution
- **Multivariate version of the Central Limit Theorem**: If we have a collection of random vectors $X_1, X_2,...,X_n$ that are independent and identically distributed, then the sample mean vector, $\bar{x}$, is going to be approximately multivariate normally distributed for large samples
- It is used in the modeling of many natural phenomena

```
Fields:

μ :: Mean<:Union{Array{Float64,1},Distributions.ZeroVector{Float64}}
Σ :: Cov<:PDMats.AbstractPDMat
```

There are three types of covariances matrices that are implemented:

- Full covariance.
- Diagonal covariance.
- Isotropic covariance.

```julia
julia> typealias FullNormal MvNormal{PDMat,     Vector{Float64}}
julia> typealias DiagNormal MvNormal{PDiagMat, Vector{Float64}}
julia> typealias IsoNormal  MvNormal{ScalMat,   Vector{Float64}}

julia> typealias ZeroMeanFullNormal MvNormal{PDMat,     ZeroVector{Float64}}
julia> typealias ZeroMeanDiagNormal MvNormal{PDiagMat, ZeroVector{Float64}}
julia> typealias ZeroMeanIsoNormal  MvNormal{ScalMat,   ZeroVector{Float64}}
```

The mean vector is either of an instance of `Vector{Float64}` or `ZeroVector{Float64}`. `ZeroVector{Float64}` is a vector filled with zeros.

A multivariate normal distribution is constructed in the following ways:

- `MvNormal(mu, sig)`: mu refers to mean and sig refers to covariance
- `MvNormal(sig)`: We are not passing the mean, therefore the mean will be zero
- `MvNormal(d, sig)`: d refers to the dimension here

Dirichlet distribution

Dirichlet distribution represents the conjugate prior to the multinomial distribution. This refers to the condition that the posterior distribution is also a Dirichlet distribution if the prior distribution of the multinomial parameters is Dirichlet:

```
Summary:

 immutable Distributions.Dirichlet <: Distributions.Distribution{Distributions.
Multivariate,Distributions.Continuous}
```

This tells us that the Dirichlet is part of the Multivariate family and is a Continuous distribution:

```
Fields:

alpha  :: Array{Float64,1}
alpha0 :: Float64
lmnB   :: Float64
```

There are parameters accepted by the Dirichlet method. This is used as:

```julia
julia> Dirichlet(alpha)
```

Here alpha is a vector:

```julia
julia> Dirichlet(k, a)
```

In this, `a` is a positive scalar.

Understanding matrixvariate distributions

This is a distribution from which any sample drawn is of type matrix. Many of the methods that can be used with Univariate and Multivariate distributions can be used with Matrix-variate distributions.

Wishart distribution

This is a type of matrix-variate distribution and is a generalization of the Chi-square distribution to two or more variables. It is constructed by adding the inner products of identically distributed, independent, and zero-mean multivariate normal random vectors. It is used as a model for the distribution of the sample covariance matrix for multivariate normal random data, after scaling by the sample size:

```julia
julia> Wishart(v, S)
```

Here, `v` refers to the degrees of freedom and `S` is the base matrix.

Inverse-Wishart distribution

This is the conjugate prior to the covariance matrix of a multivariate normal distribution. In Julia, it is implemented as follows:

```julia
julia> InverseWishart(v, P)
```

This represents an Inverse-Wishart distribution with `v` degrees of freedom and base matrix `P`.

Distribution fitting

Distribution fitting is the fitting of a probability distribution to a series of data to predict the probability of variable phenomena in a certain interval. We can get good predictions from the distribution, which is a close fit to the data. Depending on the characteristics of the distribution and of the phenomenon, some can be fitted more closely with the data:

```julia
julia> d = fit(Distribution_type, dataset)
```

This fits a distribution of type `Distribution_type` to a given dataset; `dataset.x` is of the array type and comprises all the samples. The fit function finds the best way to fit the distribution.

Distribution selection

The distribution is selected by the symmetry or the skewness of the data with respect to the mean value.

Symmetrical distributions

For symmetrical distributions tending to have the bell curve, the normal distribution and the logistic distributions are most suited. When the kurtosis is higher, the values are spread far away from the center, and then one can also use Student's t-distribution.

Skew distributions to the right

Also called positive skewness, this is when the distance of the larger values from the mean is greater than the distance of the smaller values from the mean. In these scenarios, log-normal distribution, and log-logistic distribution are most suited. Also, the exponential distribution, the Weibull distribution, the Pareto distribution, and the Gumbel distribution can be suited in some of these scenarios.

Skew distributions to the left

The negative skewness or skewness to the left is when the distance of the smaller values from the mean is greater than the distance of the larger values from the mean. For such data, square-normal distribution, Gompertz distribution, and the inverted or mirrored Gumbel distributions are suited.

Maximum Likelihood Estimation

Maximum Likelihood Estimation (**MLE**) is a procedure of estimating the parameters for a given statistic, which makes the given distribution a maximum. It is an analytic maximization procedure.

For example, we have a sample from a population but for some reason we couldn't measure the whole population. We want to know some statistics of this population; this could be done by Maximum Likelihood Estimation assuming that the data is normally distributed. MLE would give the parametric values that would have the highest probability according to the data that we have and the given model.

Sample properties of MLEs:

- Unbiased minimum variance estimators (large sample size)
- Confidence bounds can be generated by calculating approximate normal distributions and approximate sample variances
- Can be used to test hypotheses about models and parameters

Drawbacks to MLEs:

- MLEs can be heavy with a small number of failures (large sample size is not able to overcome this)
- Calculating MLEs requires solving complex non-linear equations

MLE maximizes the likelihood function by selecting the set of values of the model parameters for the defined statistical model and given dataset. With large sample sizes (tending to infinity), MLEs have the following features:

- **Efficiency**: The asymptotic mean squared error of the MLE is the lowest among all the consistent estimators
- **Asymptotic normality**: The MLE distribution tends to the Gaussian distribution with increase in sample size
- **Consistency**: The probability of the sequences converges to the estimated value
- After the correction for bias, it has second-order efficiency

In Julia, we have a function for maximum likelihood estimation, `fit_mle`. This uses multiple dispatches:

```julia
julia> fit_mle(Distribution, dataset)
```

- `dataset` can be an array for univariate distribution.
- `dataset` is a matrix for multivariate distribution:

  ```julia
  julia> fit_mle(Distribution, weights, dataset)
  ```

- This includes an additional parameter, weights, which is an array of length n. n is equal to the number of samples contained in the dataset.

At the time of writing, `fit_mle` has been implemented for the following most used distributions:

- **Univariate distributions**: Normal, gamma, binomial, Bernoulli, categorical, uniform, laplace, exponential, geometric, and so on
- **Multivariate distributions**: Multinomial, multivariate normal, and Dirichlet

As mentioned, the `fit_mle` uses multiple dispatches. The implementation for some of the distributions is quite different to the others.

As for Binomial distribution:

- `fit_mle(BinomialDistribution, numOfTrials, dataset, weights)`: The number of trials is an additional parameter that represents it for each experiment. `weights` is an optional argument.

As for categorical distribution:

- `fit_mle(CategoricalDistribution, spaceSize, dataset, weights)`: `spaceSize` is an additional parameter that represents the number of distinct values. `weights` is an optional argument.

Sufficient statistics

Julia provides a function that can be used to generate the estimation and then apply the Maximum Likelihood Estimation (`fit_mle`).

Usage:

```julia
julia> gensuffstats = suffstats(Distribution, dataset, weights)
```

Here, `weights` is an optional parameter. This generates the sufficient statistics of the dataset, and now we can apply the `fit_mle`:

```julia
julia>  fit_mle(Distribution, gensuffstats)
```

The reason for using the sufficient statistics function is because it is more efficient.

Maximum-a-Posteriori estimation

This is also known as energy minimization. The parameter to be estimated, although it is unknown, is considered fixed unlike MLE, which is considered a random variable.

In Bayesian analysis, for the parameters that we want to estimate of the physical process, we may have priori information, which may have come from empirical evidence or other scientific knowledge. Such information can be encoded in the **probability distribution function (pdf)** on the parameter to be estimated:

```julia
julia> posterior(priori, suffst)
```

This returns the posterior distribution, which is based on the data provided by the sufficient statistics and is of the same type as a priori (the priori distribution).

You can generate the Maximum-a-Posteriori estimation as follows:

```julia
julia> fit_map(priori, G, dataset[, weights])
```

Here G is the likelihood model (or a distribution).

You can generate a completed distribution as follows:

```julia
julia> complete(priori, G, params)
```

This will give a completed distribution given parameter, param, and likelihood model, G.

Confidence interval

This describes the amount of uncertainty associated with the unknown population parameter in the estimated range of values of the population.

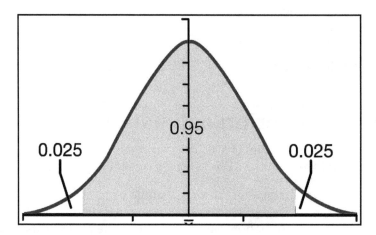

Interpreting the confidence intervals

Suppose it is given that the population mean is greater than 100 and less than 300, with a confidence interval of 95%.

General perception is that the chance of the population mean falling between 100 and 300 is 95%. This is wrong, as the population mean is not a random variable but is constant and doesn't change, and its probability of falling in any specified range is 0 to 1.

The uncertainty level associated with a sampling method is described by the confidence level. Suppose to select different samples and for each of these samples to compute a different interval estimate we used the same sampling method. The true population parameter would be included in some of these interval estimates, but not in every one.

So, the 95% confidence level means that the population parameter is included in 95% of the interval estimates.

Here are the steps to construct a confidence interval:

- A sample statistic is identified
- Select a confidence level
- Calculate the margin of error:

Margin of error = standard deviation (error) of statistic* critical value

- Describe the confidence level:

Confidence interval = margin of error + sample statistic

In Julia, a confidence interval is calculated using the `ci` function. There are 12 methods for the generic function `ci`:

```
ci(x::HypothesisTests.Btest)
ci(x::HypothesisTests.BTest, alpha::Float64)

ci(x::HypothesisTests.BinomialTest)
ci(x::HypothesisTests.BinomialTest, alpha::Float64)

ci(x::HypothesisTests.SignTest)
ci(x::HypothesisTests.SignTest, alpha::Float64)

ci(x::HypothesisTests.FisherExactTest)
ci(x::HypothesisTests.FisherExactTest, alpha::Float64)
ci(x::HypothesisTests.TTest)
ci(x::HypothesisTests.TTest, alpha::Float64)

ci(x::HypothesisTests.PowerDivergenceTest)
ci(x::HypothesisTests.PowerDivergenceTest, alpha::Float64)
```

Usage

To get the confidence interval of the Binomial proportions, it is used as follows:

```
julia> ci(test::BinomialTest,alpha=0.05;
tail=:both,method=:clopper_pearson)
```

This will compute the confidence interval that will have a coverage of 1-alpha. The method used is clopper pearson.

Other methods can also be used:

- Wald interval (`:wald`)
- Wilson score interval (`:wilson`)
- Jeffreys interval (`:jeffrey`)
- Agresti Coull interval (`:agresti_coull`)

To get the confidence interval of the multinomial proportions, it is used as follows:

```
julia> ci(test::PowerDivergenceTest, alpha=0.05; tail=:both,
method=:sison_glaz)
```

Other methods than `sison_glaz`:

- Bootstrap intervals (`:bootstrap`)
- Quesenberry, Hurst intervals (`:quesenberry_hurst`)
- Gold intervals (`:gold`)

Understanding z-score

Z-score refers to the standard deviations the element is away from the mean.

It is given by the following formula:

$$z = \frac{X - \mu}{\sigma}$$

Here X represents the value of the element, σ is the standard deviation, and μ is the population mean.

Interpreting z-scores

- `z-score<0`: The element is less than the mean
- `z-score>0`: The element is greater than the mean
- `z-score=0`: The element is equal to the mean
- `z-score=0.5`: The element is 0.5 SD greater than the mean

In Julia, it is implemented as follows:

```julia
julia> zscore(X,  μ,  σ)
```

μ and σ are optional as they can be calculated by the function.

Understanding the significance of the P-value

The probability that a null-hypothesis will be rejected even if it is proven true is the p-value. When there is no difference between two measures, then the hypothesis is said to be a null-hypothesis.

For example, if there is a hypothesis that, in the game of football, every player who plays 90 minutes will also score a goal then the null hypothesis would be that there is no relation between the number of minutes played and the goals scored.

Another example would be a hypothesis that a person with blood group A will have higher blood pressure than the person with blood group B. In a null hypothesis, there will be no difference, that is, no relation between the blood type and the pressure.

The significance level is given by (α) and if the p-value is equal or less than it, then the null hypothesis is declared inconsistent or invalid. Such a hypothesis is rejected.

One-tailed and two-tailed test

The following diagram represents the two-tails being used for a hypothesis test.

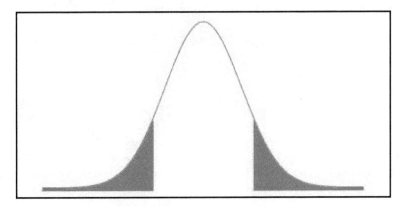

In Julia, it is calculated as follows:

```julia
julia> pvalue(test::HypothesisTest; tail=:both)
```

This will return the p-value for the two-tailed test. To get the p-value of the one-tailed test use `tail=:left` or `tail=:right`.

Summary

In this chapter, we dived deep into inferential statistics and learned about various concepts and methods in Julia to work with different kinds of datasets. We started with understanding the normal distribution, which is a must when dealing with statistics. In parallel, we started exploring Distributions.jl and various methods provided by Julia. We then moved on to Univariate distributions and understanding why they are so important. We also explored some other distributions, such as Chi, Chi-square, and Cauchy. Later in the chapter, we studied what z-score, p-value, one-tailed, and two-tailed tests are about. After studying the chapter, we should be able to understand the datasets and apply inferential statistics to gain insights as well as using the z-score and p-value to accept or reject our hypothesis.

References

- http://docs.julialang.org/en/release-.4/manual/
- https://github.com/JuliaStats/Distributions.jl
- https://people.sc.fsu.edu/~jburkardt/presentations/truncated_normal.pdf
- https://onlinecourses.science.psu.edu/

5
Making Sense of Data Using Visualization

Julia doesn't have a visualization/graphics package in the core system. Therefore, without adding and loading a package, it is not possible to create the desired visualizations on the datasets.

By not including the visualization package, Julia keeps the core system clean so that different types of backends such, as Qt and GTK on different operating systems, don't interfere with the builds.

In this chapter, we will be learning how to visualize data and how visualization helps to understand the data at a glance. We will be covering the following packages:

- PyPlot
- Unicodeplots
- Vega
- Gadfly

The `plot` function is a common function used by the packages to plot a graph. When we have loaded multiple plotting libraries, which plot function will be used?

Difference between using and importall

Suppose we want to extend a function called `bar` in the `Foo` package. When we do it by using, we need include the package name too:

```
julia> using Foo
julia> function Foo.bar(...)
```

But when we do it by `importall`, we are not required to include the package name:

```
julia> importall Foo
julia> function bar(...)
```

When we use `importall`, `function bar(...)`, and `function Foo.bar(...)` are equivalent.

This prevents us from accidentally extending a function that we didn't want to extend or didn't know about, and saves us from possibly breaking future implementations of `Foo`.

Pyplot for Julia

This package was made by Steven G. Johnson and provides Python's famous `matplotlib` library to Julia. If you have used `matplotlib`, you will be familiar with its `pyplot` module.

We learned about the Julia's Pycall package in the first chapter, and PyPlot makes use of the same package to make the call to the matplotlib plotting library directly from Julia. This call has very less (or no) overhead, and arrays are passed directly without making a copy.

Multimedia I/O

Only plaintext display is provided by the base Julia runtime. By loading external modules or by using graphical environments such as `Jupyter` notebooks, rich multimedia output can be given. Julia has a standardized mechanism to display the rich multimedia outputs (images, audio, and video). This is provided by the following:

- `display(x)` is the richest multimedia display of the Julia object
- Arbitrary multimedia representations are done by overloading the `writemime` of user-defined types
- By subclassing a generic display type, different multimedia-capable backends can be used

PyPlot makes use of this multimedia I/O API of Julia for plotting in any of the Julia graphical backends, including IJulia.

Installation

It is required to have Python with Matplotlib installed to use it in Julia. The recommended way is to have the complete package from any of the bundles of scientific Python.

Popular ones are Anaconda, provided by Continuum analytics, and Canopy, provided by Enthought.

You can also install `matplotlib` using pip:

```
$ pip install matplotlib
```

You will need to install the necessary dependencies before installing `matplotlib`.

After successful installation of `matplotlib`, we can add the Pyplot package in Julia:

```
julia> Pkg.update()
julia> Pkg.add("PyPlot")
```

It will add the dependencies by itself. We will be using inline plotting with IJulia in our examples.

Basic plotting

Now that we have added the package to the system, we can start using it. We will use IJulia (jupyter notebook) in our examples:

```
using PyPlot
PyPlot.svg(true)
```

The second line, `Pyplot.svg(true)`, will allow us to get the SVG of the plots and visualizations generated. **Scalable Vector Graphics** (**SVG**) is an XML-based markup language for a vector image format for two-dimensional graphics with interactivity and animation:

```
x = [1:100]
y = [i^2 for i in x]
p = plot(x,y)
xlabel("X")
ylabel("Y")
title("Basic plot")
grid("on")
```

- The first and second lines define the values of x and y for which we want to generate the plot.
- The third line, plot(x,y), actually generates the plot.
- For the plot that we are generating, we provide labels and change the aesthetics. With xlabel and ylabel, we are providing labels for the *x* axis and *y* axis. We will explore the other options of the plot function in the coming sections.

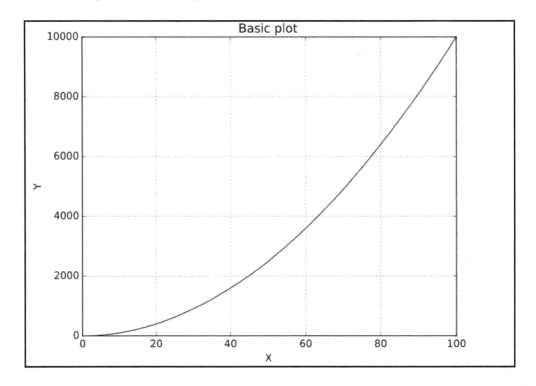

It has generated an exponential plot.

Plot using sine and cosine

In the following code, we are initializing x and y using functions:

```
x = linspace(0, 3pi, 1000)
y = cos(2*x + 3*sin(3*x));
plot(x, y, color="orange", linewidth=2.0, linestyle="--");
title("Another plot using sine and cosine");
```

Let's understand the preceding code in brief:

- In the `plot` function, we are passing the arguments for the particular plot that we want to generate
- We can change the style of the line, its width, and the color by passing the arguments.

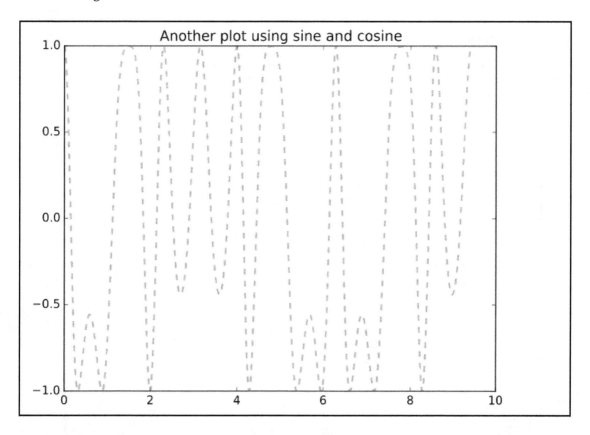

Here we can see that the line style is much different from the line style of the first figure. The default color is blue, but we have specified that the plot uses orange color for the line.

Unicode plots

Unicode plots are really useful when we want to plot on the REPL. They are extremely lightweight.

Installation

There are no dependencies, so they can be installed easily:

```
Pkg.add("UnicodePlots")
using UnicodePlots
```

Examples

Let's walk through the basic plots that can be made easily using `UnicodePlots`.

Generating Unicode scatterplots

Scatterplots are used to determine the correlation between two variables, that is, how one is affected by the other:

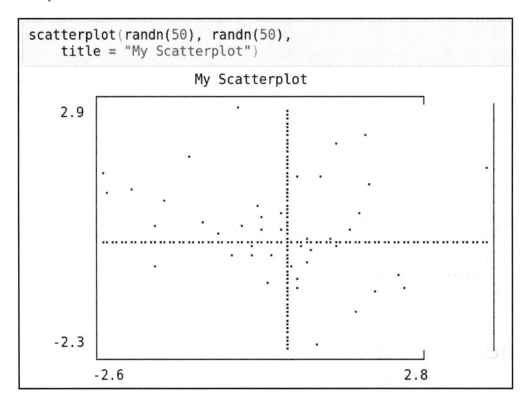

Generating Unicode line plots

A line plot displays the dataset in a series of data points:

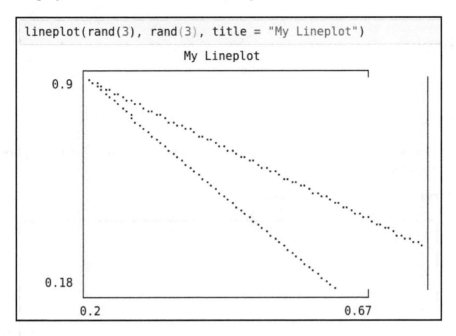

Visualizing using Vega

Vega is a beautiful visualization library provided by John Myles White. It is available as a registered Julia package, so it can be installed easily.

It is built on top of D3.js and uses JSON to create beautiful visualizations. It requires an Internet connection whenever we need to generate graphs as it doesn't store local copies of the JavaScript libraries needed.

Installation

To install Vega, use the following commands:

```
Pkg.add("Vega")
using Vega
```

Examples

Let's walk through various visualizations using Vega.

Scatterplot

Following are the arguments of a scatterplot:

- x and y: AbstractVector
- Group: AbstractVector

Scatterplots are used to determine the correlation between two variables, that is, how one is affected by the other:

```
scatterplot(x=rand(100), y=rand(100))
```

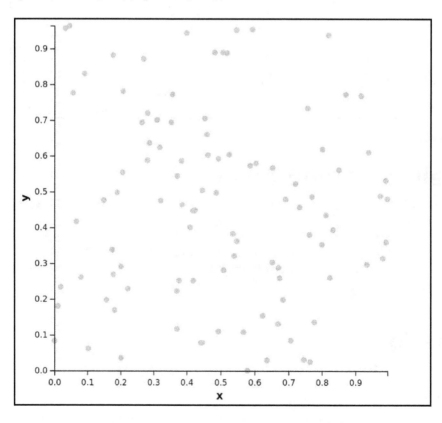

We can now move on to building a complex scatterplot:

```
using Vega, Distributions

d1 = MultivariateNormal([0.0, 0.0], [1.0 0.9; 0.9 1.0])
d2 = MultivariateNormal([10.0, 10.0], [4.0 0.5; 0.5 4.0])
points = vcat(rand(d1, 500)', rand(d2, 500)')

x = points[:, 1]
y = points[:, 2]
group = vcat(ones(Int, 500), ones(Int, 500) + 1)

scatterplot(x = x, y = y, group = group)
```

This will generate the following scatterplot. We can clearly see two clusters generated by Vega. These are d1 and d2:

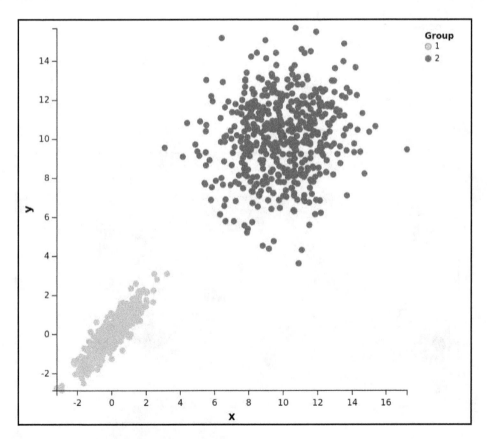

In this particular example, we grouped the data and used different colors to visualize the groups.

Heatmaps in Vega

Heatmaps in Vega are easy to generate. This helps us to easily visualize the density of data points. Arguments are as follows:

- x and y
- color

```
x = Array(Int, 900)
y = Array(Int, 900)
color = Array(Float64, 900)
tmp = 0
for counter in 1:30
    for counter2 in 1:30
        tmp += 1
        x[tmp] = counter
        y[tmp] = counter2
        color[tmp] = rand()
    end
end
hm = heatmap(x = x, y = y, color = color)
```

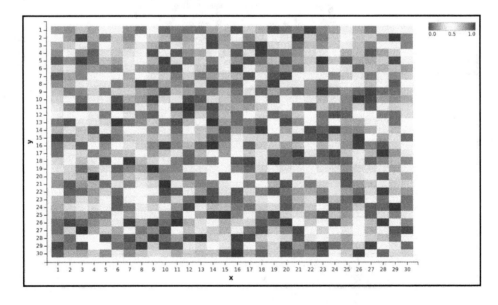

Data visualization using Gadfly

Gadfly is an exhaustive plotting and data visualization package written in Julia by Daniel Jones. It is based on the book, *The Grammar of Graphics*, by Leland Wilkinson. It is largely inspired by `ggplot2` for R, which is another amazing package for plotting and visualizations.

Installing Gadfly

Installation is straightforward as it is a registered Julia package:

```
Julia> Pkg.update()
Julia> Pkg.add("Gadfly")
```

This will also install a few other packages needed by Gadfly.

To use Gadfly, run this line:

```
Julia> using Gadfly
```

We will use IJulia (jupyter notebook) in our examples.

Gadfly has the capability to render high-quality graphics and visualizations in PNG, SVG, Postscript, and PDF. Embedded JavaScript is used by the SVG backend, which provides interactivity with the graphics such as zooming, panning, and toggling.

It is good to have Cairo installed, as it is needed by PNG, PostScript, and PDF:

```
Julia> Pkg.add("Cairo")
```

Suppose we create an `exampleplot`. To draw it on the backend, we use the draw function:

```
julia> exampleplot = plot(....)
```

- For SVG:

    ```
    julia> draw(SVG("plotinFile.svg', 4inch, 4inch), exampleplot)
    ```

- For SVG with embedded JavaScript:

    ```
    julia> draw(SVGJS("plotinFile.svg', 4inch, 4inch), exampleplot)
    ```

- For PNG:

      julia> draw(PNG("plotinFile.png', 4inch, 4inch), exampleplot)

- For PostScript:

      julia> draw(PS("plotinFile.ps', 4inch, 4inch), exampleplot)

- For PDF:

      julia> draw(PDF("plotinFile.pdf', 4inch, 4inch), exampleplot)

Interacting with Gadfly using plot function

The `plot` function is used to interact with the Gadfly package and create the desired visualizations. Aesthetics are mapped to the plot geometry and are used to specify how the `plot` function would work. They are specially named variables.

The `plot` elements can be scales, coordinates, guides, and geometries. It is defined in the grammar of graphics to avoid special cases, and aesthetics helps this by approaching the problem with well-defined inputs and outputs, which produces the desired result.

Plot can operate on the following data sources:

- Functions and expressions
- Arrays and collections
- Dataframes

Example

If we do not define the `plot` elements, then by default, point geometry is used. In point geometry, x and y inputs are taken as aesthetics.

Let's draw a scatterplot:

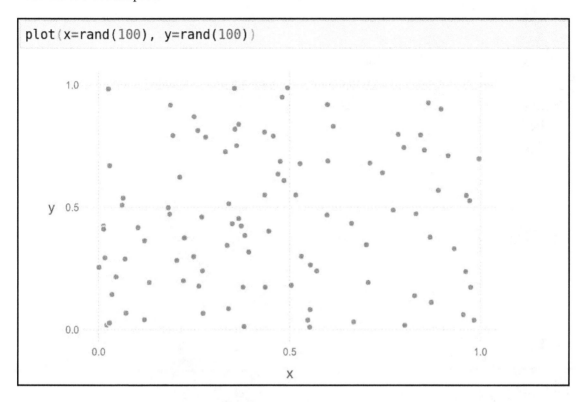

```
plot(x=rand(100), y=rand(100))
```

In the same aesthetics, we can use multiple elements to have a specific output.

For example, to have both line and point geometries on the same dataset we can make the layered plot using:

- `Geom.line`: Line plot
- `Geom.point`: Point plot

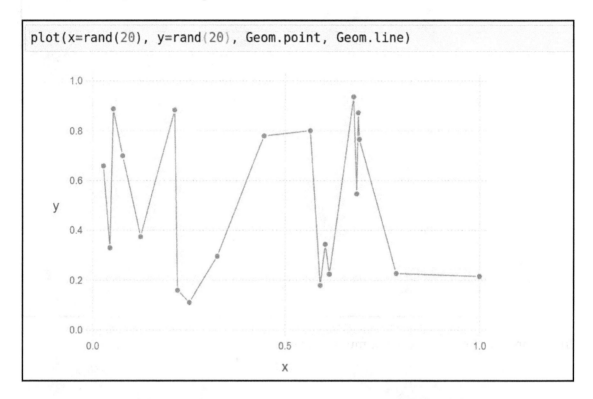

```
plot(x=rand(20), y=rand(20), Geom.point, Geom.line)
```

This generates a layered plot having both lines and points. A complex plot can be generated by combining the various elements.

Guide:

- `xlabel` and `ylabel`: Guide can be used to give the necessary labels to the plot that we use
- `title`: Use this to provide a title to the plot

Scale:

- Use this to scale up or down any desired axis of the plot

Let's create a similar plot that includes these elements. We will add x and y labels, add a title to the plot, and scale the plot:

```
plot(x=1:20, y=3.^rand(20),
    Scale.y_sqrt, Geom.point, Geom.smooth,
    Guide.xlabel("This is the X label"),
    Guide.ylabel("This is the y label"),
    Guide.title("This is the title"))
```

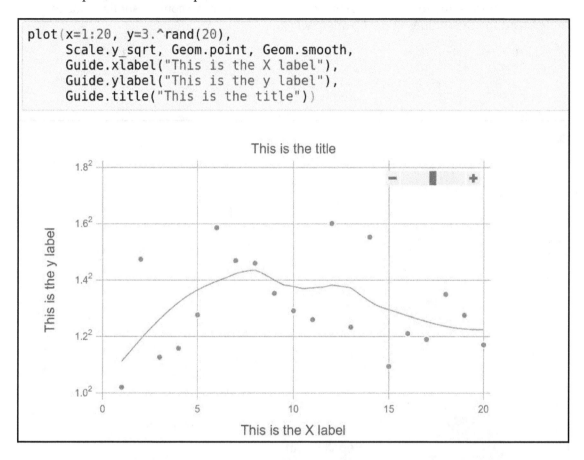

The slider in the image can be used to zoom in and out.

Using Gadfly to plot DataFrames

The capability provided by the Gadfly to work with DataFrames out of the box is really useful. We studied in previous chapters the capability of the DataFrame. It is a powerful data structure used to represent and manipulate data.

Using Gadfly, we can generate complex plots easily. DataFrame is passed to the plot function as the first argument.

The columns in the DataFrame are used by the plot function in the aesthetics by name or index. We will use RDatasets to create the DataFrame for the plot function. RDatasets provides us with some real-life datasets, on which we can make some visualizations to understand the capabilities of the Gadfly package:

```
Using Rdatasets, Gadfly
plot(iris, x=:SepalLength, y=:SepalWidth,
   color=:Species, shape=:Species, Geom.point,
   Theme(default_point_size=3pt))
```

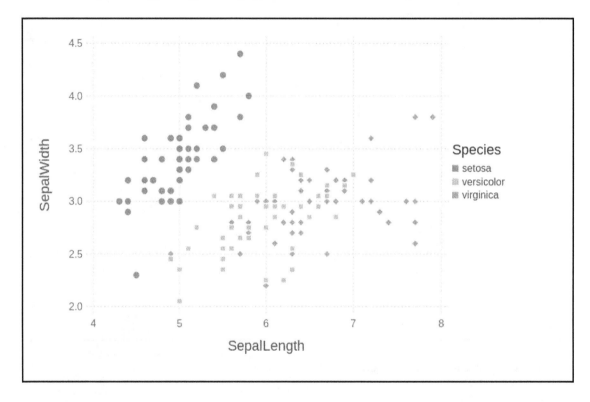

This is a very famous dataset—iris—which we also used in our previous examples. Plotting the dataset by sepal length and sepal width is easy, as we only have to pass them in x and y coordinates.

Let's now create a histogram using random number generator. We will pass the array, which we will create using a random number generator, and then we will create the histogram.

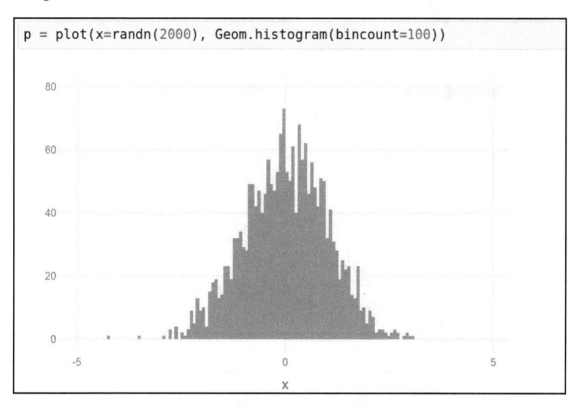

```
p = plot(x=randn(2000), Geom.histogram(bincount=100))
```

This is fairly a simple histogram. Let's use a dataset from RDataset to create a histogram:

```
plot(dataset("mlmRev","Gcsemv"),
    x="Course", color="Gender", Geom.histogram)
```

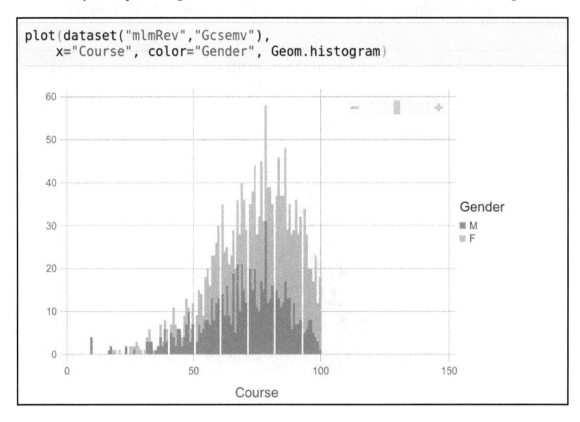

The preceding dataset is from RDatasets, and we created a histogram to see the marks secured in the course and the gender of the student.

This can be extended by creating a scatterplot:

```
set_default_plot_size(15cm, 9cm);
mlmf = dataset("mlmRev","Gcsemv")
df = mlmf[complete_cases(mlmf), :]
names(df)
plot(df, x="Course", y="Written", color="Gender")
```

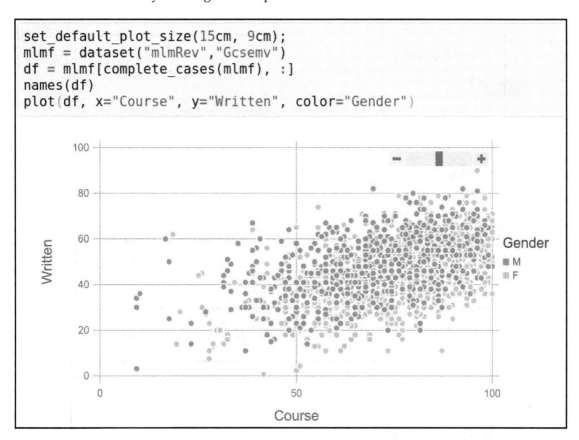

Using Gadfly to visualize functions and expressions

Plotting functions and expressions is really convenient in Gadfly.

The signatures of the plot function for functions and expressions are:

```
plot(f::Function, a, b, elements::Element...)
plot(fs::Array, a, b, elements::Element...)
```

It shows that we can pass functions or expressions as arrays with the elements that we would like to use.

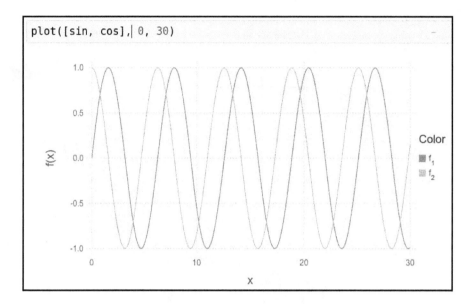

This is a plot of simple sin and cos functions. Let's create a plot from a complex expression:

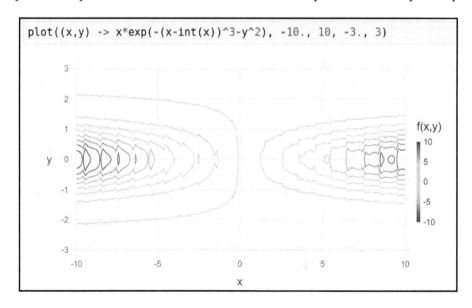

This is a random expression that we tried to plot. You can see that it is really easy to plot such a slightly complex expression. Gadfly does well even if the complexity increases.

Generating an image with multiple layers

Gadfly is able to draw multiple layers to the same plot:

```
plot(layer(x=rand(25), y=rand(25), Geom.point),
     layer(x=rand(25), y=rand(25), Geom.line))
```

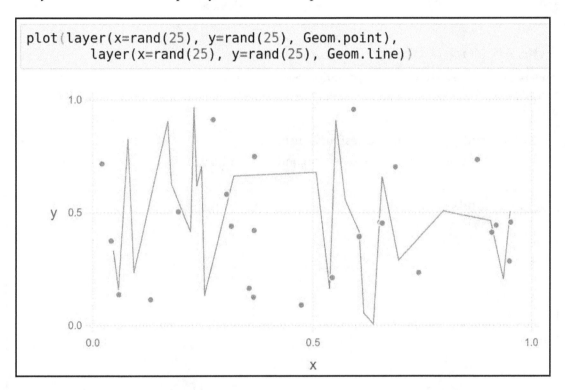

Generating plots with different aesthetics using statistics

Statistics functions in Gadfly give one or more aesthetics as output by taking one or more aesthetics as input.

Let's explore them one by one.

The step function

This is used to do a stepwise interpolation between the given points. A new point is introduced by the function between two points, which is dependent on the direction of the argument:

- x and y points are the aesthetics used
- :vh is used for vertical direction and :hv for horizontal direction

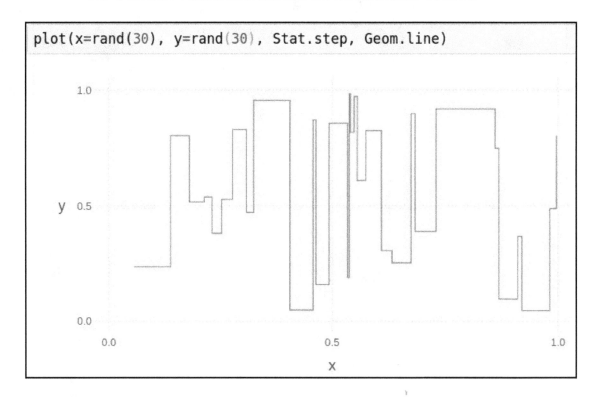

```
plot(x=rand(30), y=rand(30), Stat.step, Geom.line)
```

The quantile-quantile function

This is used to produce quantile-quantile plots. Two numeric vectors are passed to the function and a comparison of their quantiles is done.

The x and y passed to the function are the distributions or the numeric vectors:

```
using Distributions
plot(x=rand(Normal(), 150), y=rand(Normal(), 150), Stat.qq, Geom.point)
plot(x=rand(Normal(), 150), y=Normal(), Stat.qq, Geom.point)
```

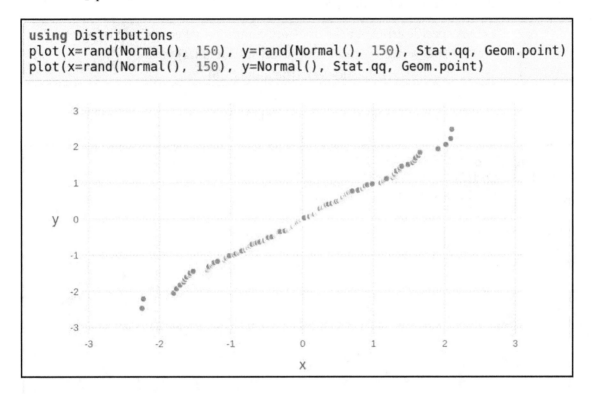

Ticks in Gadfly

Ticks are used to encompass the data between the axes.

There are two types of ticks: xticks and yticks.

Arguments taken by the ticks function are:

- ticks: A specific array of ticks (they are computed when nothing is there)
- granularity_weight: Number of ticks (default is 1/4)
- simplicity_weight: Include zero (default is 1/6)
- coverage_weight: Tightly fit the span of the data (default is 1/3)
- niceness_weight: Numbering (default is 1/4)

```
# Providing a fixed set of ticks
plot(x=rand(20), y=rand(20),
     Stat.xticks(ticks=[0.0, 0.2, 0.8, 1.0]),
     Stat.yticks(ticks=[0.0, 0.1, 0.9, 1.0]),
     Geom.point)
```

Generating plots with different aesthetics using Geometry

Geometry is responsible for the actual drawing. One or more inputs (aesthetics) are given to the function.

Boxplots

This is also known as the whisker diagram; this is a standard way of displaying data based on the quartiles:

- The first and third quartiles are represented by the bottom and top of the box
- The band inside the box is the second quartile (median)
- The bands outside the box are minimum and maximum

Aesthetics that are used directly include:

- x
- middle
- lower_hinge and upper_hinge
- lower_fence and upper_fence
- outliers

Only the dataset from which the boxplot needs to be drawn is mandatory.

```
plot(dataset("lattice", "singer"),
    x="VoicePart", y="Height", Geom.boxplot)
```

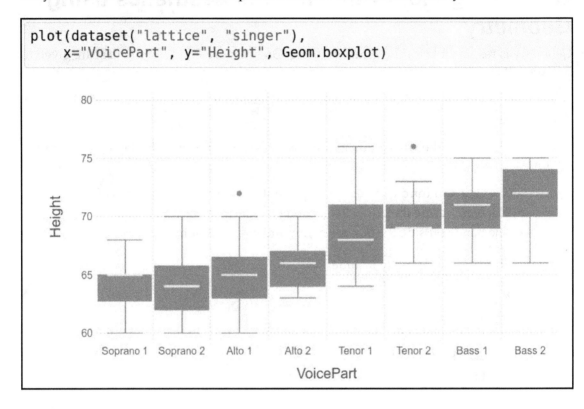

Using Geometry to create density plots

The distribution of a variable can be viewed effectively by density plots:

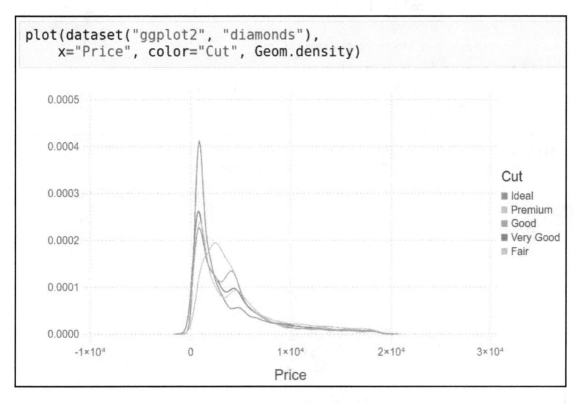

```
plot(dataset("ggplot2", "diamonds"),
    x="Price", color="Cut", Geom.density)
```

The preceding screenshot shows the density of the variables over the particular range.

Using Geometry to create histograms

A histogram helps to understand the shape of a distribution. It groups numbers into ranges.

Aesthetics are:

- x: The dataset from which the histogram will be drawn
- color (optional): Different categories can be grouped by color

Arguments are:

- `position`: There are two options, `:stack` or `:dodge`. This defines if the bars should be placed side by side or stacked on top of each other.
- `density`: Optional.
- `orientation`: Horizontal or vertical.
- `bincount`: The number of bins.
- `maxbincount` and `minbincount`: Upper and lower limits when the bin count is automatically chosen.

```
plot(dataset("mlmRev","Gcsemv"),
    x="Course", color="Gender", Geom.histogram)
```

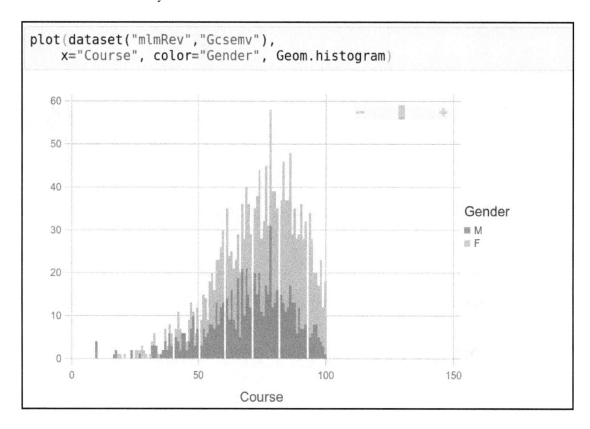

Bar plots

These consist of parallel bars that represent frequency distribution graphically.

Aesthetics are:

- y: This is required. It is the height of each bar.
- Color: This is optional. It is used to categorize the dataset with color.
- x: The position of each bar.

  xmin and xmax can also be used instead of x, which are the start and end of each bar.

Arguments are:

- position: This can be :stack or :dodge
- orientation: This can be :vertical or :horizontal

  If :horizontal is chosen, then it is required to provide y as an aesthetic (or ymin/ymax).

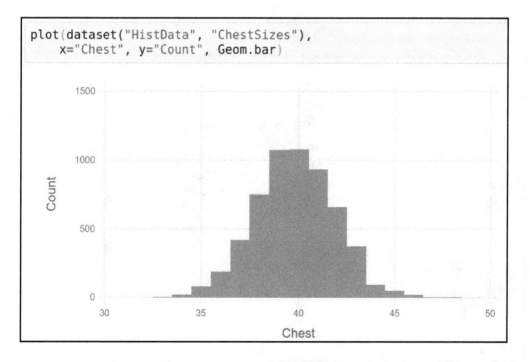

```
plot(dataset("HistData", "ChestSizes"),
    x="Chest", y="Count", Geom.bar)
```

Histogram2d – the two-dimensional histogram

This is used to create a heatmap-like histogram, where rectangular bars represent density.

Aesthetics are:

- x and y: The dataset to be plotted on the coordinates

Arguments are:

- xbincount: This specifies the number of bins in the x coordinate

    xminbincount and xmaxbincount are provided when the number of bins is determined automatically

- ybincount: This specifies the number of bins in the y coordinate

    yminbincount and ymaxbincount are provided when the number of bins is determined automatically

```
# Explicitly setting the number of bins
plot(dataset("car", "UN"), x="GDP", y="InfantMortality",
    Scale.x_log10, Scale.y_log10,
    Geom.histogram2d(xbincount=20, ybincount=20))
```

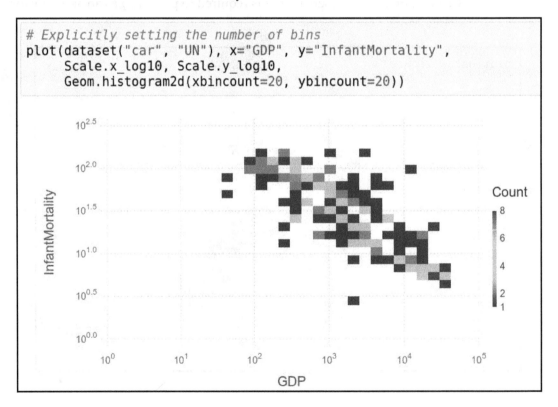

Smooth line plot

We worked on an example of line plot earlier. We can also create a smooth line plot, which estimates the function from the data.

Aesthetics are:

- x: Predictor data
- y: Response (function) data
- color: This can be used as an optional argument to categorize the dataset

Arguments are:

- smoothing: This specifies to what extent smoothing should be done

    Smaller values use more data (more fit) and larger values use less data (less fit).

- Method: The :lm and :loess methods are supported as arguments to generate the smooth curve

```
x_data = 0.0:0.1:3.0
y_data = x_data.^2 + rand(length(x_data))
plot(x=x_data, y=y_data,
    Geom.point,
    Geom.smooth(method=:loess,smoothing=0.9))
```

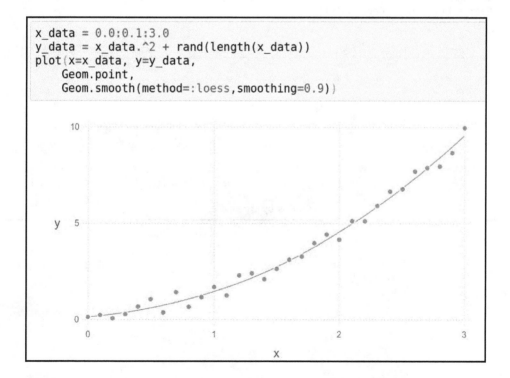

Subplot grid

Multiple plots can be made together as a grid, and they are organized by a few categorical vectors:

```
Julia> Geom.subplot_grid(elements::Gadfly.ElementOrFunction...)
```

Aesthetics are:

- xgroup and ygroup (optional): Use these to arrange the subplots on the *x* axis or *y* axis on the basis of the categorical data
- free_y_axis and free_x_axis (optional): By default, the values are false, which means the *y* axis or *x* axis scales can differ across different subplots

    If the value is true, then scales are set for individual plots

- If both xgroup and ygroup are bound, then a grid is formed

```
set_default_plot_size(20cm, 7.5cm)
plot(dataset("datasets", "OrchardSprays"),
    xgroup="Treatment", x="ColPos", y="RowPos", color="Decrease",
    Geom.subplot_grid(Geom.point))
```

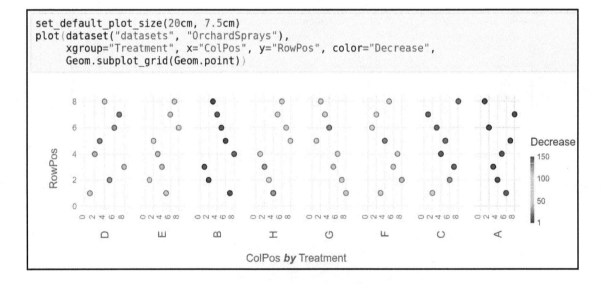

Using fixed scales:

```
using DataFrames
set_default_plot_size(8cm, 12cm)
widedf = DataFrame(x = [1:10], var1 = [1:10], var2 = [1:10].^2)
longdf = stack(widedf, [:var1, :var2])
plot(longdf, ygroup="variable", x="x", y="value",
    Geom.subplot_grid(Geom.point, free_y_axis=true))
```

Horizontal and vertical lines

Using `hline` and `vline`, we can draw horizontal and vertical lines across the canvas.

Aesthetics are:

- `xintercept`: The *x* axis intercept
- `yintercept`: The *y* axis intercept

Arguments are:

- `color`: The color of the generated lines
- `size`: We can also specify the width of the lines

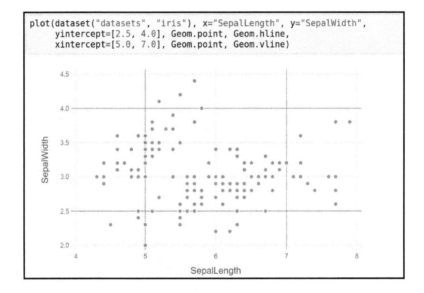

Plotting a ribbon

We can also plot a ribbon over the line plots.

Aesthetics are:

- `x`: The *x* axis
- `ymin` and `ymax`: The *y* axis, lower and upper bound
- `color` (optional): Categorically groups the data using different colors

Example:

```
xs = 0:0.1:20
df_cos = DataFrame(
    x=xs,
    y=cos(xs),
    ymin=cos(xs) .- 0.5,
    ymax=cos(xs) .+ 0.5,
    f="cos"
    )
df_sin = DataFrame(
    x=xs,
    y=sin(xs),
    ymin=sin(xs) .- 0.5,
    ymax=sin(xs) .+ 0.5,
    f="sin"
    )
df = vcat(df_cos, df_sin)
p = plot(df, x=:x, y=:y, ymin=:ymin, ymax=:ymax, color=:f, Geom.line,
Geom.ribbon)
```

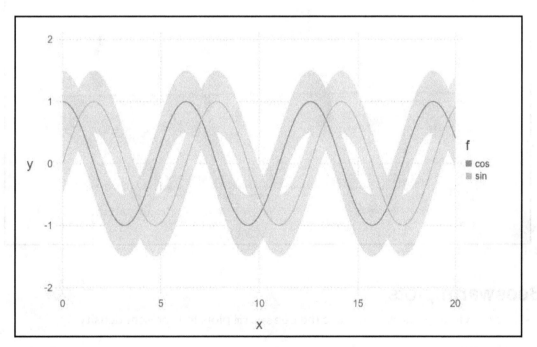

Violin plots

Violin plots are very specific to the use case. They are used to show the density.

Aesthetics are:

- x and y: The position on the *x* axis and *y* axis
- `width`: This represents the density according to the y value

```
plot(dataset("lattice", "singer"),
    x="VoicePart", y="Height", Geom.violin)
```

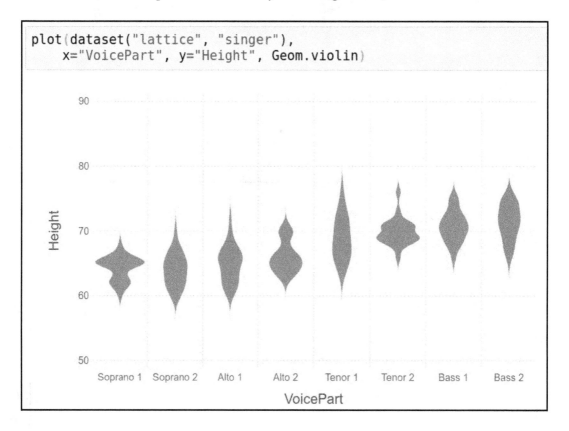

Beeswarm plots

Just like the violin plots, we can have the `beeswarm` plots to represent density.

Aesthetics are:

- x and y: The dataset for *x* axis and *y* axis
- `color` (optional)

Arguments are:

- `orientation`: This can be `:vertical` or `:horizontal`
- `padding`: The minimum distance between two points

```
# Binding categorial data to x
plot(dataset("lattice", "singer"),
    x="VoicePart", y="Height", Geom.beeswarm)
```

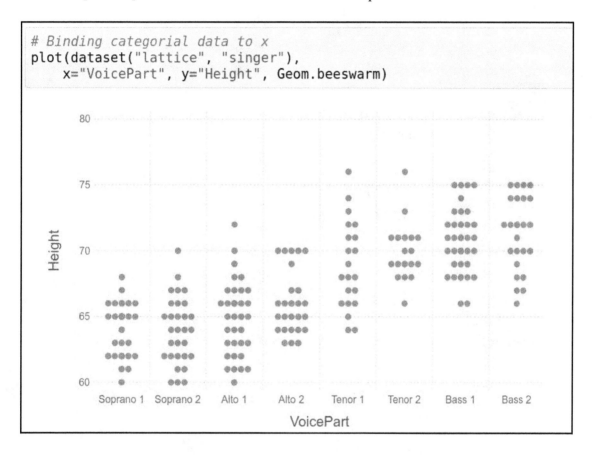

Elements – scale

This is used to transform the original data while retaining the original values. It maps one aesthetic to the same aesthetic.

x_continuous and y_continuous

These are used to map values to *x* and *y* coordinates.

Aesthetics are:

- x, xmin/xmax, and xintercept
- y, ymin/ymax, and yintercept

Arguments are:

- minvalue: Minimum x or y value
- maxvalue: Maximum x or y value
- labels: This can be either a function or nothing

    When a function is passed, a string is mapped to the value in x or y

- format: Formatting of the numbers

Variations are:

- Scale.x_continuous and Scale.y_continuous
- Scale.x_log10 and Scale.ylog10
- Scale.x_log2 and Scale.ylog2
- Scale.x_log and Scale.y_log
- Scale.x_asinh and Scale.y_asinh
- Scale.x_sqrt and Scale.y_sqrt

```
# Transform both dimensions
plot(x=rand(100), y=rand(100),
    Scale.x_log, Scale.y_log)
```

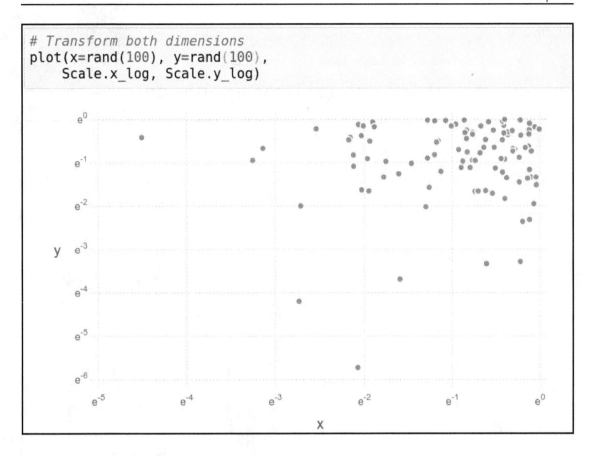

x_discrete and y_discrete

These are used to map the categorical data to the Cartesian coordinates. Regardless of the value, each value is mapped to a point.

Aesthetics are:

- x, xmin/xmax, and xintercept
- y, ymin/ymax, and yintercept

Arguments are:

- `labels`: This can be either a function or nothing

    When a function is passed, a string is mapped to the value in x or y:

```
# Treat numerical y data as categories
plot(x=rand(20), y=rand(20),
    Scale.x_discrete)
```

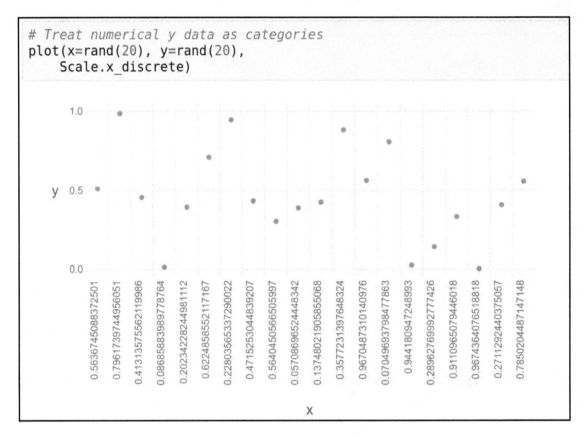

Continuous color scale

This creates a plot that uses a continuous color scale. This is used to represent the density.

Aesthetics are:

- color

Arguments are:

- `f`: The function defined that returns a color
- `minvalues` and `maxvalue`: The range of the value of the color scale

```
using Colors
x = repeat([1:10], inner=[10])
y = repeat([1:10], outer=[10])
plot(x=x,y=y,color=x+y, Geom.rectbin,
    Scale.ContinuousColorScale(Scale.lab_gradient(colorant"green",
                                                  colorant"white",
                                                  colorant"red")))
```

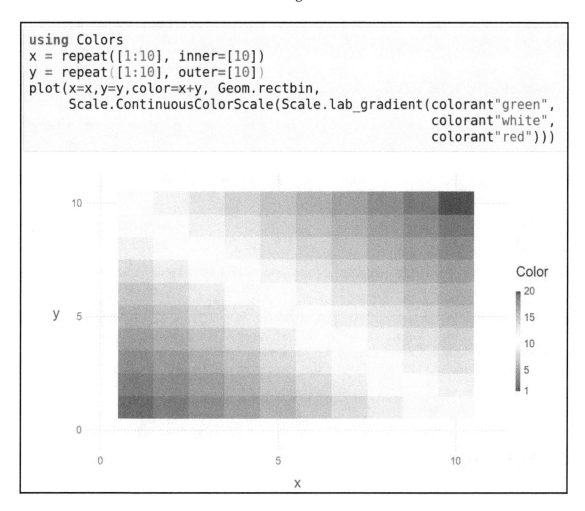

Elements – guide

These provide the special layout considerations to help us to better understand the data. They contain `xticks`, `yticks`, `xlabes`, `ylabels`, titles, and annotations, and many more.

Understanding how Gadfly works

We have gone through various plots in this chapter. Now, a brief introduction how Gadfly actually works.

First of all, subsets of the data source are mapped to the data objects for each layer in the plot:

- We have passed various scales to the plotting function. They are used to get the plottable aesthetics.
- A transformation of aesthetics is done, both layer wise and plot wise.
- A Compose context is created to fit the data into the screen coordinates by using aesthetics from all layers.
- Geometry is rendered individually for every layer.
- At last, the Guide is computed and rendered on top of the plot.

Summary

In this chapter, we learned to visualize in Julia using different graphics options.

We studied the PyPlot and how we can exploit the vast matplotlib library. We worked on various examples. We also went through Unicode plots, which are very lightweight and can be used in the terminal. Vega and Gadfly, the two most popular graphics libraries, were also explained in this chapter. Using different plots such as scatter, line, box, histogram, bar, and violin, we understood how and why it is important and helpful to visualize our data.

In the next chapter, we will study machine learning with Julia.

References

- http://dcjones.github.io/Gadfly.jl/
- https://github.com/stevengj/PyPlot.jl
- http://johnmyleswhite.github.io/Vega.jl/
- https://github.com/Evizero/UnicodePlots.jl

6
Supervised Machine Learning

It is often believed that data science is machine learning, which means in data science, we only train models of machine learning. But data science is much more than that. Data science involves understanding data, gathering data, munging data, taking the meaning out of that data, and then machine learning if needed.

In my opinion, machine learning is the most exciting field that exists today. With huge amounts of data that is readily available, we can gather invaluable knowledge. Lots of companies have made their machine learning libraries accessible and there are lots of open source alternatives that exist.

In this chapter, you will study the following topics:

- What is machine learning?
- Types of machine learning
- What is overfitting and underfitting?
- Bias-variance trade-off
- Feature extraction and selection
- Decision trees
- Naïve Bayes classifier

What is machine learning?

Generally, when we talk about machine learning, we get into the idea of us fighting wars with intelligent machines that we created but went out of control. These machines are able to outsmart the human race and become a threat to human existence. These theories are just created for our entertainment. We are still very far away from such machines.

So, the question is: what is machine learning? Tom M. Mitchell gave a formal definition:

> *"A computer program is said to learn from experience E with respect to some class of tasks T and performance measure P if its performance at tasks in T, as measured by P, improves with experience E."*

This implies that machine learning is teaching computers to generate algorithms using data without programming them explicitly. It transforms data into actionable knowledge. Machine learning has close association with statistics, probability, and mathematical optimization.

As technology grows, there is one thing that grows with it exponentially—data. We have huge amounts of unstructured and structured data growing at a very great pace. Lots of data is generated by space observatories, meteorologists, biologists, fitness sensors, surveys, and so on. It is not possible to manually go through this much amount of data and find patterns or gain insights. This data is very important for scientists, domain experts, governments, health officials, and even businesses. To gain knowledge out of this data, we need self-learning algorithms that can help us in decision making.

Machine learning evolved as a subfield of artificial intelligence, which eliminates the need to manually analyze large amounts of data. Instead of using machine learning, we make data-driven decisions by gaining knowledge using self-learning predictive models. Machine learning has become important in our daily lives. Some common use cases include search engines, games, spam filters, and image recognition. Self-driving cars also uses machine learning.

Some basic terminologies used in machine learning include:

- **Features**: Distinctive characteristics of the data point or record
- **Training set**: This is the dataset that we feed to train the algorithm that helps us to find relationships or build a model
- **Testing set**: The algorithm generated using the training dataset is tested on the testing dataset to find the accuracy
- **Feature vector**: An n-dimensional vector that contains the features defining an object
- **Sample**: An item from the dataset or the record

Uses of machine learning

Machine learning in one way or another is used everywhere. Its applications are endless. Let's discuss some very common use cases:

- **E-mail spam filtering**: Every major e-mail service provider uses machine learning to filter out spam messages from the Inbox to the Spam folder.
- **Predicting storms and natural disasters**: Machine learning is used by meteorologists and geologists to predict the natural disasters using weather data, which can help us to take preventive measures.
- **Targeted promotions/campaigns and advertising**: On social sites, search engines, and maybe in mailboxes, we see advertisements that somehow suit our tastes. This is made feasible using machine learning on the data from our past searches, our social profile, or e-mail contents.
- **Self-driving cars**: Technology giants are currently working on self-driving cars. This is made possible using machine learning on the feed of the actual data from human drivers, image and sound processing, and various other factors.
- Machine learning is also used by businesses to predict the market.
- It can also be used to predict the outcomes of elections and the sentiment of voters towards a particular candidate.
- Machine learning is also being used to prevent crime. By understanding the pattern of different criminals, we can predict a crime that can happen in the future and can prevent it.

One case that got a huge amount of attention was of a big retail chain in the United States using machine learning to identify pregnant women. The retailer thought of a strategy to give discounts on multiple maternity products, so that the women would become loyal customers and would baby purchase items with a high profit margin.

The retailer worked on the algorithm to predict the pregnancy using useful patterns in purchases of different products which are useful for pregnant women.

Once a man approached the retailer and asked for the reason that his teenage daughter is receiving discount coupons for maternity items. The retail chain offered an apology but later the father himself apologized when he got to know that his daughter was indeed pregnant.

This story may or may not be completely true, but retailers do analyze their customers' data routinely to find out patterns for targeted promotions, campaigns, and inventory management.

Machine learning and ethics

Let's see where machine learning is used very frequently:

- **Retailers**: In the previous example, we mentioned how retail chains use data for machine learning to increase their revenue as well as to retain their customers
- **Spam filtering**: E-mails are processed using various machine learning algorithms for spam filtering
- **Targeted advertisements**: In our mailbox, social sites, or search engines, we see advertisements of our liking

These are only some of the actual use cases that are implemented in the world today. One thing that is common between them is the user data.

In the first example, retailers are using the history of transactions done by the user for targeted promotions and campaigns and for inventory management, among other things. Retail giants do this by providing users a loyalty or sign-up card.

In the second example, the e-mail service provider uses trained machine learning algorithms to detect and flag spam. It does so by going through the contents of e-mail/attachments and classifying the sender of the e-mail.

In the third example, again the e-mail provider, social network, or search engine will go through our cookies, our profiles, or our mails to do the targeted advertising.

In all of these examples, it is mentioned in the terms and conditions of the agreement when we sign up with the retailer, e-mail provider, or social network that the user's data will be used but privacy will not be violated.

It is really important that before using data that is not publicly available, we take the required permissions. Also, our machine learning models shouldn't discriminate on the basis of region, race, and sex, or of any other kind. The data provided should not be used for purposes not mentioned in the agreement or if it is illegal in the region or country of existence.

Machine learning – the process

Machine learning algorithms are trained in keeping with the idea of how the human brain works. They are somewhat similar. Let's discuss the whole process.

The machine learning process can be described in three steps:

1. Input
2. Abstraction
3. Generalization

These three steps are the core of how the machine learning algorithm works. Although the algorithm may or may not be divided or represented in such a way, this explains the overall approach:

1. The first step concentrates on what data should be there and what shouldn't. On the basis of that, it gathers, stores, and cleans the data as per the requirements.
2. The second step entails the data being translated to represent the bigger class of data. This is required as we cannot capture everything and our algorithm should not be applicable for only the data that we have.
3. The third step focuses on the creation of the model or an action that will use this abstracted data, which will be applicable for the broader mass.

So, what should be the flow of approaching a machine learning problem?

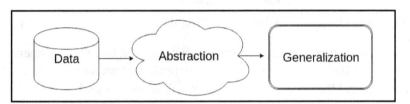

In this particular figure, we see that the data goes through the abstraction process before it can be used to create the machine learning algorithm. This process itself is cumbersome. We studied this process in the chapter related to data munging.

The process follows the training of the model, which is fitting the model into the dataset that we have. The computer does not pick up the model on its own, but it is dependent on the learning task. The learning task also includes generalizing the knowledge gained on the data that we don't have yet.

Therefore, training the model is based on the data that we currently have and the learning task includes generalization of the model for future data.

It depends on how our model deduces knowledge from the dataset that we currently have. We need to make such a model that can gather insights into something that wasn't known to us before can be useful and can be linked to future data.

Different types of machine learning

Machine learning is divided mainly into three categories:

- Supervised learning
- Unsupervised learning
- Reinforcement learning

In supervised learning, the model/machine is presented with inputs and the outputs corresponding to those inputs. The machine learns from these inputs and applies this learning in further unseen data to generate outputs.

Unsupervised learning doesn't have the required outputs; therefore it is up to the machine to learn and find patterns that were previously unseen.

In reinforcement learning, the machine continuously interacts with the environment and learns through this process. This includes a feedback loop.

What is bias-variance trade-off?

Let's understand what bias and variance are. First we will go through bias in our model:

- Bias is the difference between the predictions that have been generated by the model and the correct value that was expected or we should have received.
- When we get the new data, the model will work out and give predictions. Therefore, it means our model has a range of predictions it can generate.
- Bias is the correctness of this range of predictions.

Now, let's understand variance and how it affects the model:

- Variance is the variability of the model when the data points are changed or new data is introduced
- It shouldn't be required to tweak the model every time new data is introduced

As per our understanding of bias and variance, we can conclude that these affect each other. Therefore, while creating the model, we keep this trade-off in consideration.

Effects of overfitting and underfitting on a model

Overfitting happens when the model that we have created also starts considering the outliers or noise in our dataset. Therefore, it means our model is fitting the dataset rather too well.

The drawback of such a model is that it will not be able to generalize well. Such models have low bias and high variance.

Underfitting happens when the model that we have created is not able to find out the patterns or trend of the data as is desired. Therefore, it means the model is not fitting to the dataset well.

The drawback of such a model is that it is not able to give good predictions. Such models have high bias and low variance.

We should try to reduce both underfitting and overfitting. This is done through various techniques. Ensemble models are very good in avoiding underfitting and overfitting. We will study ensemble models in upcoming chapters.

Understanding decision trees

A decision tree is a very good example of "divide and conquer". It is one of the most practical and widely used methods for inductive inference. It is a supervised learning method that can be used for both classification and regression. It is non-parametric and its aim is to learn by inferring simple decision rules from the data and create such a model that can predict the value of the target variable.

Before taking a decision, we analyze the probability of the pros and cons by weighing the different options that we have. Let's say we want to purchase a phone and we have multiple choices in the price segment. Each of the phones has something really good, and maybe better than the other. To make a choice, we start by considering the most important feature that we want. And as such, we create a series of features that it has to pass to become the ultimate choice.

In this section, we will learn about:

- Decision trees
- Entropy measures
- Random forests

We will also learn about famous decision tree learning algorithms such as ID3 and C5.0.

Building decision trees – divide and conquer

A heuristic called recursive partitioning is used to build decision trees. In this approach, our data is split into similar classes of smaller and smaller subsets as we move along.

A decision tree is actually an inverted tree. It starts from the root and ends up at the leaf nodes, which are the terminal nodes. The splitting of the node into branches is based on logical decisions. The whole dataset is represented at the root node. A feature is chosen by the algorithm that is most predictive of the target class. Then it partitions the examples into distinct value groups of this particular feature. This represents the first set of the branches of our tree.

The divide-and-conquer approach is followed until the end point is reached. At each step, the algorithm continues to choose the best candidate feature.

The end point is defined when:

- At a particular node, nearly all the examples belong to the same class
- The feature list is exhausted
- A predefined size limit of the tree is reached

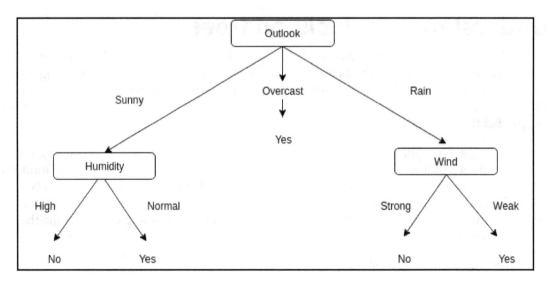

The preceding image is a very famous example of decision tree. Here, a decision tree is made to find out whether to go out or not:

- Outlook is the root node. This refers to all the possible classes of the environment

- Sunny, overcast, and Rain are the branches.
- Humidity and Wind are the leaf nodes, which are again split into branches, and a decision is taken depending on the favorable environment.

These trees can also be re-represented as if-then rules, which would be easily understandable. Decision trees are one of the very successful and popular algorithms, with a broad range of applications.

The following are some of the applications of decision trees:

- **Decision of credit card / loan approval**: Credit scoring models are based on decision trees, where every applicant's information is fed to decide whether a credit card / loan should be approved or not.
- **Medical diagnosis**: Various diseases are diagnosed using well-defined and tested decision trees based on symptoms, measurements, and tests.

Where should we use decision tree learning?

Although there are various decision tree learning methods that can be used for a variety of problems, decision trees are best suited for the following scenarios:

- Attribute-value pairs are scenarios where instances are described by attributes from a fixed set and values. In the previous example, we had the attribute as "Wind" and the values as "Strong" and "Weak". These disjoint possible values make it easy to create decision tree learning, although attributes with real values can also be used.
- The final output of the target function has a discreet value, like the previous example, where we had "Yes" or "No". The decision tree algorithm can be extended to have more than two possible target values. Decision trees can also be extended to have real values as outputs, but this is rarely used.
- The decision tree algorithm is robust to errors in the training dataset. These errors can be in the attribute values of the examples or the classification of the examples or both.
- Decision tree learning is also suited for missing values in a dataset. If the values are missing in some examples where they are available for attributes in other examples, then decision trees can be used.

Advantages of decision trees

- It is easy to understand and interpret decision trees. Visualizing decision trees is easy too.
- In other algorithms, data normalization needs to be done before they can be applied. Normalization refers to the creation of dummy variables and removing blank values. Decision trees, on the other hand, require very less data preparation.
- The cost involved in prediction using a decision tree is logarithmic with respect to the number of examples used in training the tree.
- Decision trees, unlike other algorithms, can be applied to both numerical and categorical data. Other algorithms are generally specialized to be used for only one type of variable.
- Decision trees can easily take care of the problems where multiple outputs is a possibility.
- Decision trees follow the white box model, which means a condition is easily explained using Boolean logic if the situation is observable in the model. On the other hand, results are comparatively difficult to interpret in a black box model, such as artificial neural networks.
- Statistical tests can be used to validate the model. Therefore, we can test the reliability of the model.
- It is able to perform well even if there is a violation in the assumptions from the true model that was the source of the data.

Disadvantages of decision trees

We've covered where decision trees are suited and their advantages. Now we will go through the disadvantages of decision trees:

- There is always a possibility of overfitting the data in decision trees. This generally happens when we create trees that are over-complex and are not possible to generalize well.
- To avoid this, various steps can be taken. One method is pruning. As the name suggests, it is a method where we set the maximum depth to which the tree can grow.
- Instability is always a concern with decision trees as a small variation in the data can result in generation of a different tree altogether.

- The solution to such a scenario is ensemble learning, which we will study in the next chapter.
- Decision tree learning may sometimes lead to the creation of biased trees, where some classes are dominant over others. The solution to such a scenario is balancing the dataset prior to fitting it to the decision tree algorithm.
- Decision tree learning is known to be NP-complete, considering several aspects of optimality. This holds even for the basic concepts.
- Usually, heuristic algorithms like greedy algorithms are used where a locally optimal decision is made at each node. This doesn't guarantee that we will have a decision tree that is globally optimal.
- Learning can be hard for the concepts such as Parity, XOR, and multiplexer problems, where decision trees cannot represent them easily.

Decision tree learning algorithms

There are various decision tree learning algorithms that are actually variations of the core algorithm. The core algorithm is actually a top-down, greedy search through all possible trees.

We are going to discuss two algorithms:

- ID3
- C4.5 and C5.0

The first algorithm, **ID3 (Iterative Dichotomiser 3)**, was developed by Ross Quinlan in 1986. The algorithm proceeds by creating a multiway tree, where it uses a greedy search to find each node and the features that can yield maximum information gain for the categorical targets. As trees can grow to the maximum size, which can result in over-fitting of data, pruning is used to make the generalized model.

C4.5 came after ID3 and eliminated the restriction that all features must be categorical. It does this by defining dynamically a discrete attribute based on the numerical variables. This partitions into a discrete set of intervals from the continuous attribute value. C4.5 creates sets of if-then rules from the trained trees of the ID3 algorithm. C5.0 is the latest version; it builds smaller rule sets and uses comparatively lesser memory.

How a decision tree algorithm works

The decision tree algorithm constructs the top-down tree. It follows these steps:

1. To know which element should come at the root of the tree, a statistical test is done on each instance of the attribute to determine how well the training examples can be classified using this attribute alone.
2. This leads to the selection of the best attribute at the root node of the tree.
3. Now at this root node, for each possible value of the attribute, the descendants are created.
4. The examples in our training dataset are sorted to each of these descendant nodes.
5. Now for these individual descendant nodes, all the previous steps are repeated for the remaining examples in our training dataset.
6. This leads to the creation of an acceptable tree for our training dataset using a greedy search. The algorithm never backtracks, which means it never reconsiders the previous choices and follows the tree downwards.

Understanding and measuring purity of node

The decision tree is built top-down. It can be tough to decide on which attribute to split on each node. Therefore, we find the feature that best splits the target class. Purity is the measure of a node containing only one class.

Purity in C5.0 is measured using entropy. The entropy of the sample of the examples is the indication of how class values are mixed across the examples:

- 0: The minimum value is an indication of the homogeneity in the class values in the sample
- 1: The maximum value is an indication that there is maximum amount of disorder in the class values in the sample

Entropy is given by:

$$\text{Entropy}(S) = \sum_{i=1}^{c} -p_i \, log_2(p_i)$$

In the preceding formula, *S* refers to the dataset that we have and *c* refers to the class levels. For a given class *i*, *p* is the proportion of the values.

When the purity measure is determined, the algorithm has to decide on which feature the data should be split. To decide this, the entropy measure is used by the algorithm to calculate how the homogeneity differs on splitting on each possible feature. This particular calculation done by the algorithm is the information gain:

$$\text{InfoGain}\left(F\right) = \text{Entropy}\left(S_1\right) - \text{Entropy}\left(S_2\right)$$

The difference between the entropy before splitting the dataset (*S1*) and the resulting partitions from splitting (*S2*) is called information gain (*F*).

An example

Let's apply what we've learned to create a decision tree using Julia. We will be using the example available for Python on `http://scikit-learn.org/` and Scikitlearn.jl by Cedric St-Jean.

We will first have to add the required packages:

```
julia> Pkg.update()
julia> Pkg.add("DecisionTree")
julia> Pkg.add("ScikitLearn")
julia> Pkg.add("PyPlot")
```

ScikitLearn provides the interface to the much-famous library of machine learning for Python to Julia:

```
julia> using ScikitLearn
julia> using DecisionTree
julia> using PyPlot
```

After adding the required packages, we will create the dataset that we will be using in our example:

```
julia> # Create a random dataset
julia> srand(100)
julia> X = sort(5 * rand(80))
julia> XX = reshape(X, 80, 1)
julia> y = sin(X)
julia> y[1:5:end] += 3 * (0.5 - rand(16))
```

This will generate a 16-element `Array{Float64,1}`.

Now we will create instances of two different models. One model is where we will not limit the depth of the tree, and in other model, we will prune the decision tree on the basis of purity:

```
# Fit regression model
regr_1 = DecisionTreeRegressor()
regr_2 = DecisionTreeRegressor(pruning_purity_threshold=0.05)
```

```
DecisionTree.DecisionTreeRegressor(Nullable(0.05),5,0,#undef)
```

We will now fit the models to the dataset that we have. We will fit both the models.

```
fit!(regr_1, XX, y)

DecisionTree.DecisionTreeRegressor(Nullable{Float64}(),5,0,Decision Tree
Leaves: 25
Depth:  8)
```

This is the first model. Here our decision tree has 25 leaf nodes and a depth of 8.

```
fit!(regr_2, XX, y)

DecisionTree.DecisionTreeRegressor(Nullable(0.05),5,0,Decision Tree
Leaves: 6
Depth:  4)
```

This is the second model. Here we prune our decision tree. This has 6 leaf nodes and a depth of 4.

Now we will use the models to predict on the test dataset:

```
julia> # Predict
julia> X_test = 0:0.01:5.0
julia> y_1 = predict(regr_1, hcat(X_test))
julia> y_2 = predict(regr_2, hcat(X_test))
```

This creates a 501-element `Array{Float64,1}`.

To better understand the results, let's plot both the models on the dataset that we have:

```julia
julia> # Plot the results
julia> scatter(X, y, c="k", label="data")
julia> plot(X_test, y_1, c="g", label="no pruning", linewidth=2)
julia> plot(X_test, y_2, c="r", label="pruning_purity_threshold=0.05",
linewidth=2)

julia> xlabel("data")
julia> ylabel("target")
julia> title("Decision Tree Regression")
julia> legend(prop=Dict("size"=>10))
```

Decision trees can tend to overfit data. It is required to prune the decision tree to make it more generalized. But if we do more pruning than required, then it may lead to an incorrect model. So, it is required that we find the most optimized pruning level.

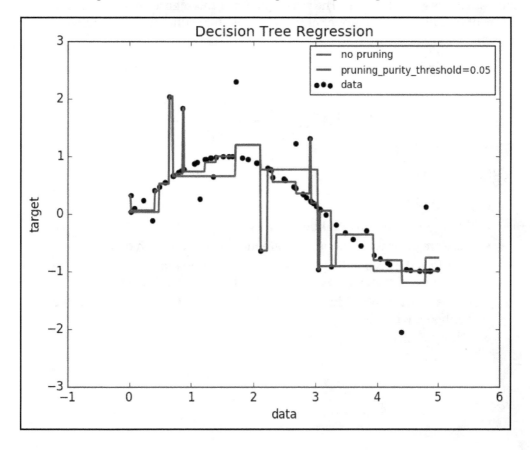

It is quite evident that the first decision tree overfits to our dataset, whereas the second decision tree model is comparatively more generalized.

Supervised learning using Naïve Bayes

Naïve Bayes is one of most famous machine learning algorithms to date. It is widely used in text classification techniques.

Naïve Bayes methods come under the set of supervised learning algorithms. It is a probabilistic classifier and is based on Bayes' theorem. It takes the "naïve" assumption that every pair of features is independent of one another.

And in spite of these assumptions, Naïve Bayes classifiers work really well. Their most famous use case is spam filtering. The effectiveness of this algorithm is justified by the requirement of quite a small amount of training data for estimating the required parameters.

These classifiers and learners are quite fast when compared to other methods.

$$P(A|B) = \frac{P(B|A)\ P(A)}{P(B)}$$

In this given formula:

- *A* and *B* are events.
- $P(A)$ and $P(B)$ are probabilities of *A* and *B*.
- These are prior probabilities and are independent of each other.
- $P(A \mid B)$ is the probability of *A* with the condition that *B* is true. It is the posterior probability of class (*A*, target) given predictor (*B*, attributes).
- $P(B \mid A)$ is the probability of *B* with the condition that *A* is true. It is the likelihood, which is the probability of the predictor given class.

Advantages of Naïve Bayes

Following are some of the advantages of Naïve Bayes:

- It is relatively simple to build and understand
- It can be trained easily and doesn't require a huge dataset
- It is comparatively fast
- Is not affected by irrelevant features

Disadvantages of Naïve Bayes

The disadvantage of Naïve Bayes is the "naïve" assumption that every feature is independent. This is not always true.

Uses of Naïve Bayes classification

Here are a few uses of Naïve Bayes classification:

- **Naïve Bayes text classification**: This is used as a probabilistic learning method and is actually one of the most successful algorithms to classify documents.
- **Spam filtering**: This is the best known use case of Naïve Bayes. Naïve Bayes is used to identify spam e-mail from legitimate e-mail. Many server-side e-mail filtering mechanisms use this with other algorithms.
- **Recommender systems**: Naïve Bayes can also be used to build recommender systems. Recommender systems are used to predict and suggest products the user may like in the future. It is based on unseen data and is used with collaborative filtering to do so. This method is more scalable and generally performs better than other algorithms.

To understand how Naïve Bayes classifiers actually work, we should understand the Bayesian rule. It was formed by Thomas Bayes in the 18th century. He developed various mathematical principles, which are known to us as Bayesian methods. These very effectively describe probabilities of events and how the probabilities should be revised when we have additional information.

Classifiers, based on Bayesian methods, use the training dataset to find out the observed probability of every class based on the values of all the features. So, when this classifier is used on unlabeled or unseen data, it makes use of the observed probabilities to predict to which class the new features belong. Although it is a very simple algorithm, its performance is comparable or better than most other algorithms.

Bayesian classifiers are best used for these cases:

- A dataset containing numerous attributes, where all of them should be considered simultaneously to calculate the probability of an outcome.
- Features with weak effects are generally ignored, but Bayesian classifiers use them too to generate predictions. Many such weak features can lead to a big change in the decision.

How Bayesian methods work

Bayesian methods are dependent on the concept that the estimation of likelihood of an event is based on the evidence at hand. The possible outcome of the situation is the event; for example, in a coin toss, we get heads or tails. Similarly, a mail can be "ham" or "spam". The trial refers to a single opportunity in which an event occurs. In our previous example, the coin toss is the trial.

Posterior probabilities

*posterior probability = conditional probability * prior probability/evidence*

In terms of classification, posterior probability refers to the probability that a particular object belongs to a class x when the observed feature values are given. For example, "what is the probability that it will rain given the temperature and percentage of humidity?"

P(rain | xi), xi = [45degrees, 95%humidity]

- Let xi be the feature vector of the sample i, where i" belongs to $\{1,2,3,.....n\}$
- Let wj be the notation of the class j, where j belongs to $\{1,2,3,.......n\}$
- $P(xi \mid wi)$ is the probability of the observing sample xi when it is given that it belongs to class wj

The general notation of posterior probabilities is:

$$P(wj \mid xi) = P(xi \mid wj) * P(wj)/P(xi)$$

The main objective of Naïve Bayes is to maximize the probability of the posterior probability on the given training data so that a decision rule can be formed.

Class-conditional probabilities

Bayesian classifiers assume that all the samples in the dataset are independent and identically distributed. Here, independence means that the probability of one observation is not affected by the probability of the other observation.

One very famous example that we discussed is the coin toss. Here the outcome of the first coin toss doesn't affect the subsequent coin tosses. The probability of getting the head or tail always remains 0.5 for an unbiased coin.

An added assumption is that the features have conditional independence. This is another "naïve" assumption, which means that the estimation of the likelihood or the class-conditional probabilities can be done directly from the training data without needing to evaluate all the probabilities of x.

Let's understand with an example. Suppose we have to create a server-side e-mail filtering application to decide if the mails are spam or not. Let's say we have around 1,000 e-mails and 100 e-mails are spam.

Now, we received a new mail with the text "Hello Friend". So, how should we calculate the class-conditional probability of the new message?

The pattern of the text consists of two features: "hello" and "friend". Now, we will calculate the class-conditional probability of the new mail.

Class-conditional probability is the probability of encountering "hello" when the mail is spam * the probability of encountering "friend" when the mail is spam:

$$P(X=[hello,world] \mid w=spam) = P(hello \mid spam) * P(friend \mid spam)$$

We can easily find out how many mails contained the word "hello" and how many mails contained the word "spam". However, we took the "naïve" assumption that one word doesn't influence the occurrence of the other. We know that "hello" and "friend" often occur together. Therefore, our assumption is violated.

Prior probabilities

Prior probability is the prior knowledge of the occurrence of an event. It is the general probability of the occurrence of the particular class. If the priors follow a uniform distribution, the posterior probabilities are determined using the class-conditional probabilities and also using the evidence term.

Prior knowledge is obtained using the estimation on the training data, when the training data is the sample of the entire population.

Evidence

There is one more required value to calculate posterior probability, and that is "evidence". The evidence P(x) is the probability of occurrence of the particular pattern x, which is independent of the class label.

The bag of words

In the previous example, we were doing classification of e-mails. For that, we classify a pattern. To classify a pattern, the most important tasks are:

- Feature extraction
- Feature selection

But how are good features recognized? There are some characteristics of good features:

- The features must be important to the use case that we are building the classifier for
- The selected features should have enough information to distinguish well between the different patterns and can be used to train the classifier
- The features should not be susceptible to distortion or scaling

We need to first represent the e-mail text document as a feature vector before we can fit it to our model and apply machine learning algorithms. The classification of the text document uses the bag-of-words model. In this model, we create the vocabulary, which is a collection of different words that occur in all the e-mails (training set) and then count how many times each word occurred.

Advantages of using Naïve Bayes as a spam filter

Here are the advantages of using Naïve Bayes as a spam filter:

- It can be personalized. It means that it can be trained on a per user basis. We sometime subscribe to newsletters or mailing lists or update about products, which may be spam to other users. Also, the e-mails that I receive have some words related to my work, which may be categorized as spam for other users. So, being a legitimate user, I would not like my mails going into spam. We may try to use the rules or filters, but Bayesian spam filtering is far more superior than these mechanisms.
- Bayesian spam filters are effective in avoiding false positives, by which it is very less probable that legitimate e-mail will be classified as spam. For example, we all get mails with the word "Nigeria" or claiming to be from Nigeria, which are actually phishing scams. But there is the possibility that I have a relative or a friend there, or I have some business there; therefore that mail may not be illegitimate to me.

Disadvantages of Naïve Bayes filters

Bayesian filters are vulnerable to Bayesian poisoning, which is a technique in which a large amount of legitimate text is sent with the spam mail. Therefore, the Bayesian filter fails there and marks it as "ham" or legitimate mail.

Examples of Naïve Bayes

Let us create some Naïve Bayes models using Julia:

```
julia> Pkg.update
julia> Pkg.add("NaiveBayes")
```

We added the required NaiveBayes package.

Now, let's create some dummy datasets:

```
julia> X = [1 1 0 2 1;
        0 0 3 1 0;
        1 0 1 0 2]
julia> y = [:a, :b, :b, :a, :a]
```

We created two arrays of X and y, where an element in y represents the column in X:

```
julia> m = MultinomialNB(unique(y), 3)
julia> fit(m, X, y)
```

We loaded an instance of MultinomialNB and fit our dataset to it:

```
julia> Xtest = [0 4 1;
        2 2 0;
        1 1 1]
```

Now we will use it to predict it on our test dataset:

```
julia> predict(m, Xtest)
```

The output that I got was:

```
julia> 3-element Array{Symbol,1}:
    :b
    :a
    :a
```

Which means the first column is b, second is a, and third is also a.

This example was on a dummy dataset. Let's apply Naïve Bayes on an actual dataset. We will be using the famous iris dataset in this example:

```
julia> #import necessary libraries

julia> using NaiveBayes
julia> using RDatasets

julia> iris = dataset("datasets", "iris")

julia> #observations in columns and variables in rows

julia> x = array(iris[:, 1:4])

julia> p,n = size(x)
julia> # By default species is a PooledDataArray

julia> y = [species for species in iris[:,5]]
```

We loaded RDatasets, which contains the iris dataset. We created arrays for the feature vectors (sepal length, sepal width, petal length, and petal width).

```
# how much data use for training
train_frac = 0.9
k = int(floor(train_frac * n))
idxs = randperm(n)
train = idxs[1:k]
test = idxs[k+1:end]
```

Now we will split the dataset for training and testing.

```
model = GaussianNB(unique(y), p)
fit(model, X[:, train], y[train])

accuracy = countnz(predict(model, X[:,test]).==
                y[test]) / countnz(test)

println("Accuracy: $accuracy")

Accuracy: 1.0
```

This is quite straightforward, fitting the dataset to a Naïve Bayes classifier. We are also calculating the accuracy to which our model worked. We can see that the accuracy was 1.0, which is 100%.

Summary

In this chapter, we learned about machine learning and its uses. Providing computers the ability to learn and improve has far-reaching uses in this world. It is used in predicting disease outbreaks, predicting weather, games, robots, self-driving cars, personal assistants, and much more.

There are three different types of machine learning: supervised learning, unsupervised learning, and reinforcement learning.

In this chapter, we learned about supervised learning, especially about Naïve Bayes and decision trees. In further chapters, we will learn more about ensemble learning and unsupervised learning.

References

- https://github.com/JuliaStats/MLBase.jl
- http://julialang.org/
- https://github.com/johnmyleswhite/NaiveBayes.jl
- https://github.com/bensadeghi/DecisionTree.jl
- https://github.com/bicycle1885/RandomForests.jl
- http://scikit-learn.org/stable/

7

Unsupervised Machine Learning

In the previous chapter, we learned about supervised machine learning algorithms and how we can use them in real-world scenarios.

Unsupervised learning is a little bit different and harder. The aim is to have the system learn something, but we ourselves don't know what to learn. There are two approaches to the unsupervised learning.

One approach is to find the similarities/patterns in the datasets. Then we can create clusters of these similar points. We make the assumption that the clusters that we found can be classified and can be provided with a label.

The algorithm itself cannot assign names because it doesn't have any. It can only find the clusters based on the similarities, but nothing more than that. To actually be able to find meaningful clusters, a good size of dataset is required.

It is used extensively in finding similar users, recommender systems, text classification, and so on.

We will discuss various clustering algorithms in detail. In this chapter, we will learn:

- Working with unlabeled data.
- What is unsupervised learning?
- What is clustering?
- Different types of clustering.

- The K-Means algorithm and Bisecting K-means. Its strengths and weaknesses.
- Hierarchical clustering.
- Agglomerative clustering. Its strengths and weaknesses.
- The DBSCAN algorithm.

We should also discuss the second approach before we can start delving deep into clustering. It will tell us how different clustering is from this approach and the use cases. The second approach is a kind of reinforcement learning. This involves rewards to indicate success to the algorithm. There are no explicit categorizations done. This type of algorithm is best suited for real-world algorithms. In this algorithm, the system behaves on the previous rewards or the punishments it got. This kind of learning can be powerful because there is no prejudice and there are no pre-classified observations.

This calculates the possibility of every action and knows beforehand what action will lead to what kind of result.

This trial and error method is computationally intensive and consumes a lot of time. Let's discuss the clustering approach that is not based on trial and error.

Understanding clustering

Clustering is a technique to divide data into groups (clusters) that are useful and meaningful. The clusters are formed capturing the natural structure of the data, which have meaningful relations with each other. It is also possible that this is only used at the preparation or the summarization stage for the other algorithms or further analysis. Cluster analysis has roles in many fields, such as biology, pattern recognition, information retrieval, and so on.

Clustering has applications in different fields:

- **Information retrieval**: To segregate the information into particular clusters is an important step in searching and retrieving information from the numerous sources or a big pool of data. Let's use the example of news aggregating websites. They create clusters of similar types of news making it easier for the user to go through the interesting sections.

  These news types can also have sub-classes creating a hierarchical view. For example, in the sports news section, we can have Football, Cricket, and Tennis, and other sports.

- **Biology**: Clustering finds a great use in biology. After years of research, biologists have classified most of the living things in hierarchies. Using the features of these classes, unknowns can be classified. Also, the existing data can be used to find similarities and interesting patterns.
- **Marketing**: Companies use customer and sales data to create clusters of similar users or segments where targeted promotions/campaigns can be run to get the maximum return on investment.
- **Weather**: Cluster analysis is used extensively in climate and weather analysis. Weather stations generate huge amount of data. Clustering is used to generate insights on this data and find out the patterns and important information.

How are clusters formed?

There are many methods to form clusters. Let's discuss some basic approaches of cluster creation:

- Start with grouping the data objects. This grouping should only happen based on the data that is describing the objects.
- Similar objects are grouped together. They may show a relationship with each other.
- Dissimilar objects are kept in other clusters.

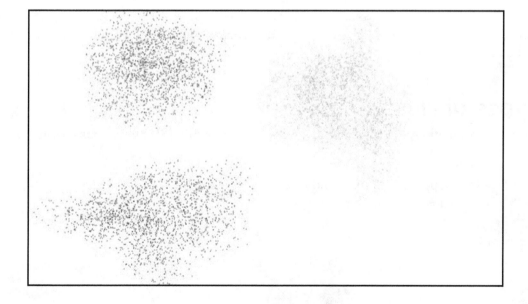

- The preceding plot clearly shows us some distinct clusters that are formed when there are more similarities between different data objects in a cluster and dissimilarities with data objects from other clusters.

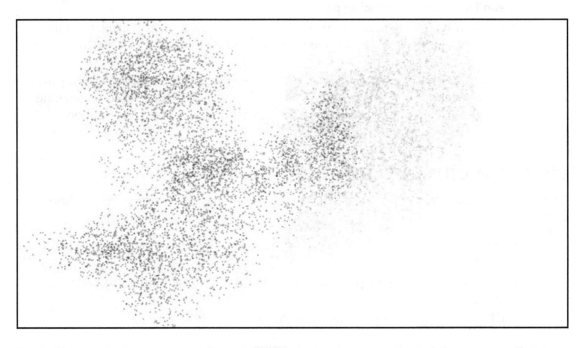

But in this particular representation of the data points, we can see that there are no definite clusters that can be formed. This is when there is some similarity between the data objects of the different clusters.

Types of clustering

There are different types of clustering mechanisms depending on the various factors:

- Nested or un-nested—hierarchical or partitional
- Overlapping, exclusive, and fuzzy
- Partial versus complete

Hierarchical clustering

If the clusters do not form subsets, then the cluster is said to be un-nested. Therefore, partitional clustering is defined as the creation of well-defined clusters, which do not overlap with each other. In such a cluster, the data points are located in one and only one cluster alone.

If the clusters have subclusters within them, then it is called hierarchical clustering.

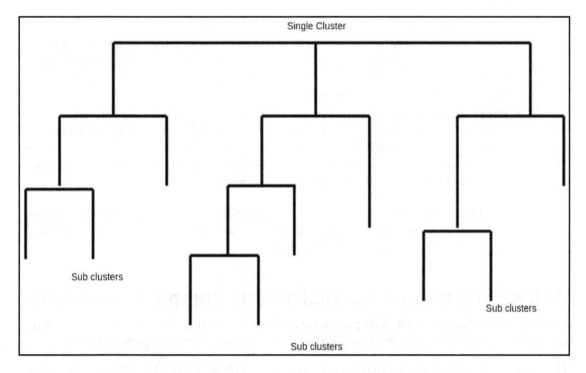

The preceding diagram represents a hierarchical cluster. Hierarchical clusters are the clusters organized as a tree.

Here, each cluster has its own child cluster. Each node can also be thought of as an individual system, having its own clusters obtained through partitioning.

Overlapping, exclusive, and fuzzy clustering

The techniques which leads to creation of different types of clusters can be categorized into three approaches:

- **Exclusive clusters**: In the section, How are clusters formed? We saw two images representing two different types of clusters. In the first image, we saw that the clusters are well defined and have a good separation between them. These are called exclusive clusters. In these clusters, the data points have a definite dissimilarity from the data points of the other clusters.
- **Overlapping clusters**: In the second image, we saw that there is no such definite boundary to separate two clusters. Here some of the data points can exist in any of the clusters. This situation comes when there is no such feature to distinguish the data point into any of the clusters.
- **Fuzzy clustering**: Fuzzy clustering is a unique concept. Here the data point belongs to each and every cluster and its relationship is defined by the weight which is between 1 (belongs exclusively) to 0 (doesn't belong). Therefore, clusters are considered as fuzzy sets. By the probabilistic rule, a constraint is added that the sum of weights of all the data points should be equal to 1.

    Fuzzy clustering is also known as probabilistic clustering. Generally, to have a definite relation, the data point is associated with the cluster for whom it has the highest membership weight.

Differences between partial versus complete clustering

In complete clustering, all the data points are assigned to a cluster because they accurately represent features of the cluster. These types of clusters are called complete clusters.

There can be some data points that may not belong to any of the clusters. This is when these data points represent noise or are outliers to the cluster. Such data points are not taken in any of the clusters, and this is called partial clustering.

K-means clustering

K-means is the most popular of the clustering techniques because of its ease of use and implementation. It also has a partner by the name of K-medoid. These partitioning methods create level-one partitioning of the dataset. Let's discuss K-means in detail.

K-means algorithm

K-means start with a prototype. It takes centroids of data points from the dataset. This technique is used for the objects lying in the n-dimensional space.

The technique involves choosing the K number of centroids. This K is specified by the user and is chosen considering various factors. It defines how many clusters we want. So, choosing a higher or lower than the required K can lead to undesired results.

Now going forward, each point is assigned to its nearest centroid. As many points get associated with a specific centroid, a cluster is formed. The centroid can get updated depending on the points that are part of the current cluster.

This process is done repeatedly until the centroid gets constant.

Algorithm of K-means

Understanding K-means algorithm will give us a better view of how to approach the problem. Let's understand step by step the K-means algorithm:

1. As per the defined K, select the number of centroids.
2. Assign data points to the nearest centroid. This step will form the clusters.
3. Compute the centroid of the cluster again.
4. Repeat steps 2 and 3 until the centroid gets constant.

In the first step, we use the mean as the centroid.

Step 4 says to repeat the earlier steps of the algorithm. This can sometimes lead to a large number of iterations with very little change. So, we generally use repeat steps 2 and 3 only if the newer computed centroid has more than 1% change.

Associating the data points with the closest centroid

How do we measure the distance between the computed centroid and the data point?

We use the Euclidean (L2) distance as the measure, and we assume that the data points are in the Euclidean space. We can also use different proximity measures if required, for example, Manhattan (L1) can also be used for the Euclidean space.

As the algorithm processes similarities with the different data points, it is good to have only the required set of features of the data points. With higher dimensional data, the computation increases drastically as it has to compute for each and every dimension iteratively.

There are some choices of the distance measure that can be used:

- **Manhattan (L1)**: This takes a median as the centroid. It works on the function to minimize the sum of the L1 distance of an object from the centroid of its cluster.
- **Squared Euclidean (L2^2)**: This takes a mean as the centroid. It works on the function to minimize the sum of the squared of the L2 distance of an object from the centroid of the cluster.
- **Cosine**: This takes a mean as the centroid. It works on the function to maximize the sum of the cosine similarity of an object from the centroid of the cluster.
- **Bregman divergence**: This takes a mean as the centroid. It minimizes the sum of the Bregman divergence of an object from the centroid of the cluster.

How to choose the initial centroids?

This is a very important step in the K-means algorithm. We start off by choosing the initial centroids randomly. This generally results in very poor clusters. Even if these centroids are well distributed, we do not get even close to the desired clusters.

There is a technique to address this problem—multiple runs with different initial centroids. After this, the set of the clusters is chosen, which has the minimum **Sum of Squares error (SSE)**. This may not always work well and may not always be feasible because of the size of the dataset and the computation power required.

In repeating the random initializing, the centroid may not be able to overcome the problem, but we have other techniques that we can use:

- Using hierarchical clustering, we can start with taking some sample points and use hierarchical clustering to make a cluster. Now we can take out the K number of clusters from this clustering and use the centroids of these clusters as the initial centroids. There are some constraints to this approach:
  - The sample data should not be large (expensive computation).
  - With the number of the desired clusters, K should be small.

- Another technique is to get the centroid of all the points. From this centroid, we find the point that is separated at maximum. We follow this process to get the maximum distant centroids, which are also randomly chosen. But there are some issues with this approach:
    - It is computationally intensive to find out the farthest point.
    - This approach sometimes produces undesirable results when there are outliers in the dataset. Therefore, we may not get the dense regions as required.

Time-space complexity of K-means algorithms

K-means doesn't require that much space as we only need to store the data points and the centroids.

The storage requirement of a K-means algorithm $O((m+K)n)$, where:

- m is number of points
- n is number of attributes

The time requirements of the K-means algorithm may vary, but generally they too are modest. The time increases linearly with the number of data points.

Time requirements of a K-means algorithm: $O(I*K*m*n)$, where:

- I is number of iterations required to converge to a centroid

K-means works best if the number of clusters required is significantly smaller than the number of data points on which the K-means is directly proportional to.

Issues with K-means

There are some issues associated with the basic K-means clustering algorithm. Let's discuss these issues in detail.

Empty clusters in K-means

There can be a situation where we get empty clusters. This is when there are no points allocated to a particular given cluster during the phase where points are assigned. This can be resolved as follows:

1. We choose a different centroid to the current choice. If it is not done, the squared error will be much larger than the threshold.
2. To choose a different centroid, we follow the same approach of finding the farthest such point from the current centroid. This generally eliminates the point that was contributing to the squared error.
3. If we are getting multiple empty clusters, then we have to repeat this process again several times.

Outliers in the dataset

When we are working with the squared error, then the outliers can be the decisive factor and can influence the clusters that are formed. This means that when there are outliers in the dataset, then we may not achieve the desired cluster or the cluster that truly represents the grouped data points may not similar features.

This also leads to a higher sum of squared errors. Therefore, a common practice is to remove the outliers before applying the clustering algorithm.

There can also be some situations where we may not want to remove the outliers. Some of the points, such as unusual activity on the Web, excessive credit, and so on, are interesting and important to the business.

Different types of cluster

There are limitations with K-means. The most common limitation of K-means is that it faces difficulty in identifying the natural clusters. By natural clusters we mean:

- Non-spherical/circular in shape
- Clusters of different sizes
- Clusters of different densities

K-means can fail if there are few denser clusters and a not so dense cluster.

Here is a diagram of clusters of different sizes:

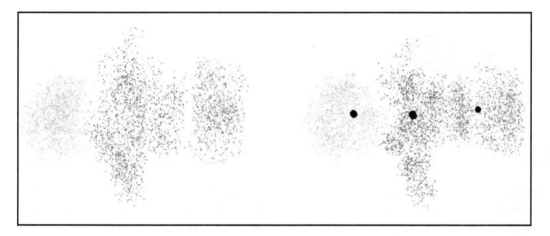

The preceding figure has two images. In the first image, we have original points and in the second image, we have three K-means clusters. We can see that these are not accurate. This happens when clusters are of different sizes.

Here is a diagram of clusters of different densities:

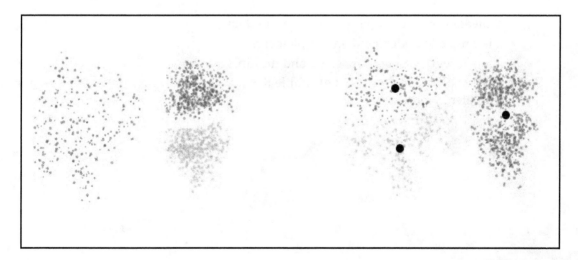

The preceding figure has two images. In the first image, we have original points and in the second image, we have three K-means clusters. The clusters are of different densities.

Here is a diagram of non-globular clusters:

The preceding figure has two images. In the first image, we have original points and in the second image, we have two K-means clusters. The clusters are non-circular or non-globular in nature and the K-means algorithm was not able to detect them properly.

K-means – strengths and weaknesses

There are many strengths and a few weaknesses of K-means. Let's discuss the strengths first:

- K-means can be used for various types of data.
- It is simple to understand and implement.
- It is efficient, even with repeated and multiple iterations.
- Bisecting K-means, a variant of simple K-means is more efficient. We will discuss that later in more detail.

Some weaknesses or drawbacks of K-means clustering include:

- It is not suitable for every type of data.
- As seen in the previous examples, it doesn't work well for clusters of different densities, sizes, or non-globular clusters.
- There are issues when there are outliers in the dataset.
- K-means has a big constraint in that it makes the cluster by computing the center. Therefore, our data should be such that can have a "center".

Bisecting K-means algorithm

Bisecting K-means is an extension of the simple K-means algorithm. Here we find out the K clusters by splitting the set of all points into two clusters. Then we take one of these clusters and split it again. The process continues until the K clusters are formed.

The algorithm of bisecting K-means is:

1. First we need to initialize the list of clusters that will have the cluster consisting of all the data points.
2. Repeat the following:
    1. Now we remove one cluster from the list of the clusters
    2. We now do trials of bisecting the cluster multiple times
    3. For n=1 to the number of trials in the previous step
3. The cluster is bisected using K-means:
    - Two clusters are selected from the result that has the lowest total sum of squared errors
    - These two clusters are added to the list of the clusters
4. The previous steps are performed until we have the K clusters in the list.

There are several ways we can split a cluster:

- Largest cluster
- Cluster which has the largest sum of squared errors
- Both

We will use the iris dataset from the RDatasets for this example:

```
using Clustering
using Gadfly
iris = dataset("datasets", "iris")
features = array(iris[:, 1:4])'
# group the data onto 3 clusters
result = kmeans( features, 3 )
plot(iris, x = "PetalLength", y = "PetalWidth",
        color = result.assignments, Geom.point)
```

This is a simple example of the famous iris dataset. We are clustering the data points using `PetalLength` and `PetalWidth`.

The result is as follows:

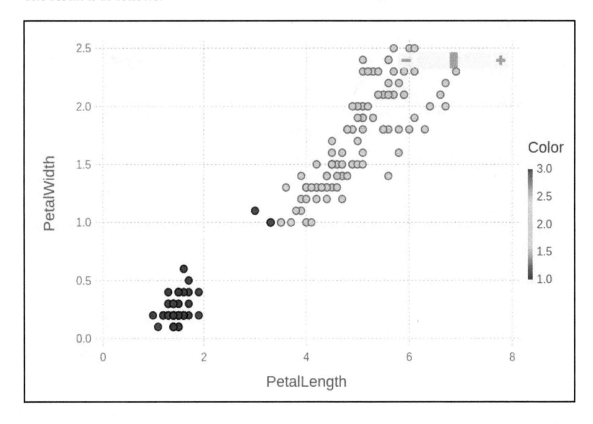

Getting deep into hierarchical clustering

This is the second most used clustering technique after K-means. Let's take the same example again:

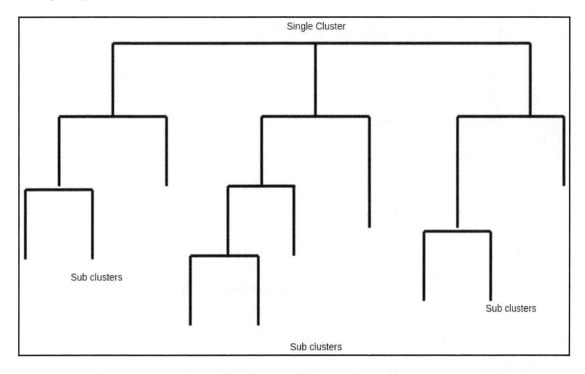

Here, the top most root represents all the data points or one cluster. Now we have three sub-clusters represented by nodes. All these three clusters have two sub-clusters. And these sub-clusters have further sub-clusters in them. These sub-clusters help in finding the clusters that are pure – that means, those which share most of the features.

There are two ways with which we can approach hierarchical clustering:

- **Agglomerative**: This is based on the concept of cluster proximity. We initially start with treating each point as the individual cluster and then step by step we merge the closest pairs.
- **Divisive**: Here we start with one cluster containing all the data points and then we start splitting it until clusters having individual points are left. In this case, we decide how the splitting should be done.

Hierarchical clusters are represented as a tree-like diagram, also known as a dendogram. This is used to represent a cluster-subcluster relationship and how the clusters are merged or split (agglomerative or divisive).

Agglomerative hierarchical clustering

This is the bottom-up approach of hierarchical clustering. Here, each observation is treated as an individual cluster. Pairs of these clusters are merged together on the basis of similarity and we move up.

These clusters are merged together based on the smallest distance. When these two clusters are merged, they are treated as a new cluster. These steps are repeated when there is one single cluster left in the pool of data points.

The algorithm of agglomerative hierarchical clustering is:

1. Firstly, the proximity matrix is computed.
2. The two closest clusters are merged.
3. The proximity matrix created in the first step is updated after the merging of the two clusters.
4. Step 2 and step 3 are repeated until there is only one cluster remaining.

How proximity is computed

Step 3 in the previous algorithm is a very important step. It is the proximity measure between the two clusters.

There are various ways to define this:

- **MIN**: The two closest points of different clusters define the proximity of these clusters. This is the shortest distance.
- **MAX**: Opposite to MIN, MAX takes the farthest point in the clusters and computes the proximity between these two which is taken as the proximity of these clusters.
- **Average**: One other approach is to take the average of all the data points of the different clusters and compute the proximity according to these points.

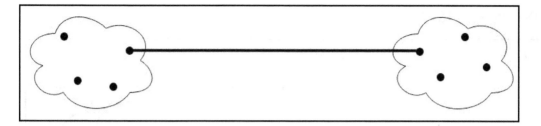

The preceding diagram depicts the proximity measure using MIN.

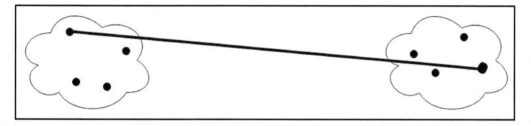

The preceding diagram depicts the proximity measure using MAX.

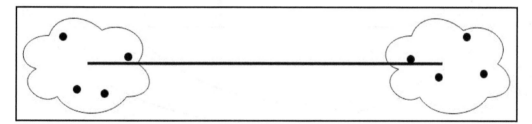

The preceding diagram depicts the proximity measure using Average.

These methods are also known as:

- **Single Linkage**: MIN
- **Complete Linkage**: MAX
- **Average Linkage**: Average

There is also another method known as the centroid method.

In the centroid method, the proximity distance is computed using two mean vectors of the clusters. At every stage, the two clusters are combined depending on which has the smallest centroid distance.

Let's take the following example:

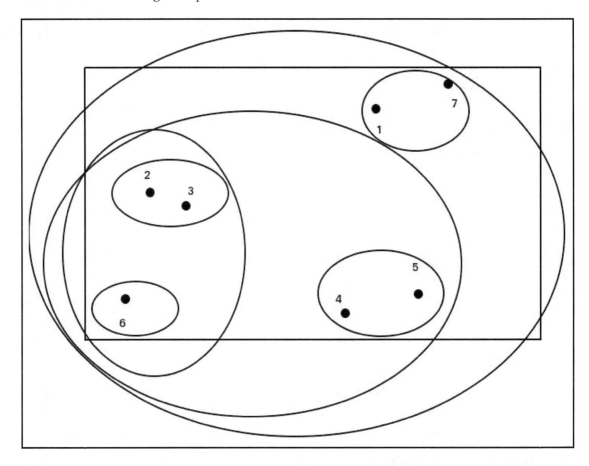

The preceding diagram shows seven points in an x-y plane. If we start to do agglomerative hierarchical clustering, the process would be as follows:

1. {1},{2},{3},{4},{5},{6},{7}.
2. {1},{2,3},{4},{5},{6},{7}.
3. {1,7},{2,3},{4},{5},{6},{7}.
4. {1,7},{2,3},{4,5},{6}.
5. {1,7},{2,3,6},{4,5}.
6. {1,7},{2,3,4,5,6}.
7. {1,2,3,4,5,6,7}.

This was broken down into seven steps to make the complete whole cluster.

This can also be shown by the following dendogram:

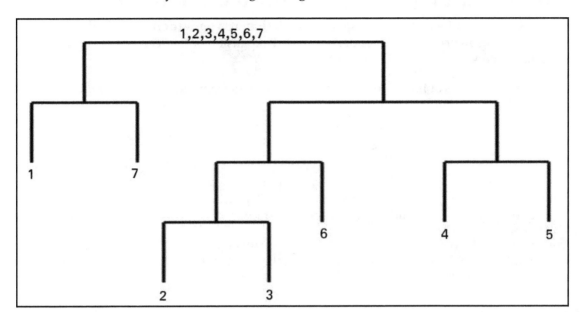

This represents the previous seven steps of the agglomerative hierarchical clustering.

Strengths and weaknesses of hierarchical clustering

The hierarchical clustering discussed earlier is sometimes more or less suited to a given problem. We will be able to comprehend this by understanding strengths and weaknesses of the hierarchical clustering:

- Agglomerative clustering lacks a global objective function. Such algorithms get the benefit of not having the local minima and no issues in choosing the initial points.
- Agglomerative clustering handles clusters of different sizes well.
- It is considered that agglomerative clustering produces better quality clusters.
- Agglomerative clustering is generally computationally expensive and doesn't work well with high-dimensional data.

Understanding the DBSCAN technique

DBSCAN refers to **Density-based Spatial Clustering of Applications with Noise**. It is a data clustering algorithm that uses density-based expansion of the seed (starting) points to find the clusters.

It locates the regions of high density and separates them from the others using the low densities between them.

So, what is density?

In the center-based approach, the density is computed at a particular point in the dataset by using the number of points in the specified radius. This is easy to implement and the density of the point is dependent on the specified radius.

For example, a large radius corresponds to the density at point m, where m is the number of data points inside the radius. If the radius is small, then the density can be 1 because only one point exists.

How are points classified using center-based density

- **Core point**: The points that lie inside the density-based cluster are the core points. These lie in the interior of the dense region.
- **Border point**: These points lie within the cluster, but are not the core points. They lie in the neighborhood of the core points. These lie on the boundary or edge of the dense region.
- **Noise points**: The points that are not the core points or the border points are the noise points.

DBSCAN algorithm

Points very close to each other are put together in the same cluster. Points lying close to these points are also put together. Points that are very far (noise points) are discarded.

The algorithm of the DBSCAN is given by:

1. Points are labeled as core, border, or noise points.
2. Noise points are eliminated.
3. An edge is formed between the core points using the special radius.

4. These core points are made into a cluster.
5. Border points associated to these core points are assigned to these clusters.

Strengths and weaknesses of the DBSCAN algorithm

The hierarchical clustering discussed earlier is sometimes more or less suited to a given problem. We will be able to comprehend this by understanding strengths and weaknesses of the hierarchical clustering.

- DBSCAN can handle clusters of different shapes and sizes. It is able to do this because it creates the definition of the cluster using the density.
- It is resistant to noise. It is able to perform better than K-means in terms of finding more clusters.
- DBSCAN faces issues with datasets that have varied densities.
- Also, it has issues dealing with high-dimensional data because it becomes difficult to find densities in such data.
- It's computationally intensive when computing nearest neighbors.

Cluster validation

Cluster validation is important as it tells us that the generated clusters are relevant or not. Important points to consider when dealing with the cluster validation include:

- It has the ability to distinguish whether non-random structure in the data actually exists or not
- It has the ability to determine the actual number of clusters
- It has the ability to evaluate how the data is fit to the cluster
- It should be able to compare two sets of clusters to find out which cluster is better

Example

We will be using `ScikitLearn.jl` in our example of agglomerative hierarchical clustering and DBSCAN.

As discussed previously, `ScikitLearn.jl` aims to provide a similar library such as the actual scikit-learn for Python.

We will first add the required packages to our environment:

```julia
julia> Pkg.update()
julia> Pkg.add("ScikitLearn")
julia> Pkg.add("PyPlot")
```

This also requires us to have the scikit-learn in our Python environment. If it is not already installed, we can install it using:

```
$ conda install scikit-learn
```

After this, we can start with our example. We will try out the different clustering algorithms available in ScikitLearn.jl. This is provided in the examples of ScikitLearn.jl:

```julia
julia> @sk_import datasets: (make_circles, make_moons, make_blobs)
julia> @sk_import cluster: (estimate_bandwidth, MeanShift, MiniBatchKMeans,
AgglomerativeClustering, SpectralClustering)

julia> @sk_import cluster: (DBSCAN, AffinityPropagation, Birch)
julia> @sk_import preprocessing: StandardScaler
julia> @sk_import neighbors: kneighbors_graph
```

We imported the datasets from the official scikit-learn library and the clustering algorithms. As some of these are dependent on the distance measure of neighbors, we also imported kNN:

```julia
julia> srand(33)

julia> # Generate datasets.

julia> n_samples = 1500
julia> noisy_circles = make_circles(n_samples=n_samples, factor=.5,
noise=.05)
julia> noisy_moons = make_moons(n_samples=n_samples, noise=.05)
julia> blobs = make_blobs(n_samples=n_samples, random_state=8)
julia> no_structure = rand(n_samples, 2), nothing
```

This particular snippet will generate the required datasets. The dataset generated will be of good enough size to test these different algorithms:

```julia
julia> colors0 = collect("bgrcmykbgrcmykbgrcmykbgrcmyk")
julia> colors = vcat(fill(colors0, 20)...)

julia> clustering_names = [
    "MiniBatchKMeans", "AffinityPropagation", "MeanShift",
    "SpectralClustering", "Ward", "AgglomerativeClustering",
    "DBSCAN", "Birch"];
```

We assigned names to these algorithms and colors to fill the image:

```julia
julia> figure(figsize=(length(clustering_names) * 2 + 3, 9.5))
julia> subplots_adjust(left=.02, right=.98, bottom=.001, top=.96,
wspace=.05, hspace=.01)

julia> plot_num = 1

julia> datasets = [noisy_circles, noisy_moons, blobs, no_structure]
```

Now, we assign how the images will be formed for different algorithms and datasets:

```julia
for (i_dataset, dataset) in enumerate(datasets)

    X, y = dataset
    # normalize dataset for easier parameter selection
    X = fit_transform!(StandardScaler(), X)

    # estimate bandwidth for mean shift
    bandwidth = estimate_bandwidth(X, quantile=0.3)

    # connectivity matrix for structured Ward
    connectivity = kneighbors_graph(X, n_neighbors=10,
            include_self=false)[:todense]()
```

Here, we are normalizing the dataset to easily select the parameters, and initializing the `kneighbors_graph` for the algorithms requiring the distance measure:

```julia
# PyCall does not support numpy sparse matrices
# make connectivity symmetric
connectivity = 0.5 * (connectivity + connectivity')

# create clustering estimators
ms = MeanShift(bandwidth=bandwidth, bin_seeding=true)
two_means = MiniBatchKMeans(n_clusters=2)
ward = AgglomerativeClustering(n_clusters=2, linkage="ward",
            connectivity=connectivity)
spectral = SpectralClustering(n_clusters=2,
                eigen_solver="arpack",
                affinity="nearest_neighbors")
```

Here, we are creating the clustering estimators, which are required by the algorithms to behave accordingly to the use case:

```
dbscan = DBSCAN(eps=.2)
affinity_propagation = AffinityPropagation(damping=.9, preference=-200)

average_linkage = AgglomerativeClustering(
    linkage="average", affinity="cityblock", n_clusters=2,
    connectivity=connectivity)

birch = Birch(n_clusters=2)
clustering_algorithms = [
    two_means, affinity_propagation, ms, spectral, ward, average_linkage,
    dbscan, birch]
```

The similar estimators for different algorithms.

After this, we use these algorithms on our datasets:

```
for (name, algorithm) in zip(clustering_names, clustering_algorithms)
    fit!(algorithm, X)
    y_pred = nothing
    try
        y_pred = predict(algorithm, X)
    catch e
        if isa(e, KeyError)
            y_pred = map(Int, algorithm[:labels_])
            clamp!(y_pred, 0, 27) # not sure why some algorithms return -1
        else rethrow() end
    end
    subplot(4, length(clustering_algorithms), plot_num)
    if i_dataset == 1
        title(name, size=18)
    end

    for y_val in unique(y_pred)
        selected = y_pred.==y_val
        scatter(X[selected, 1], X[selected, 2],
color=string(colors0[y_val+1]), s=10)
    end

    xlim(-2, 2)
    ylim(-2, 2)
    xticks(())
    yticks(())
    plot_num += 1
end
```

The result obtained is as follows:

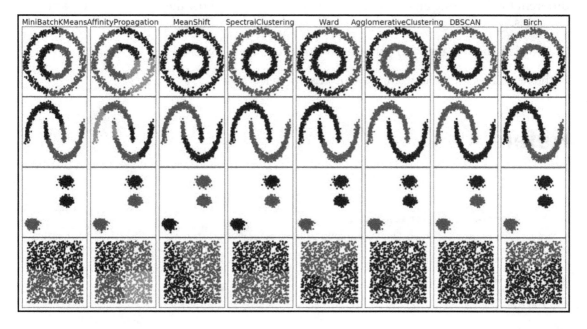

- We can see that agglomerative clustering and DBSCAN performed really well in the first two datasets
- Agglomerative clustering didn't perform well in the third dataset, whereas DBSCAN did
- Agglomerative clustering and DBSCAN both performed poorly on the fourth dataset

Summary

In this chapter, we learned about unsupervised learning and how it is different from Supervised learning. We discussed various use cases where Unsupervised learning is used.

We went through the different Unsupervised learning algorithms and discussed their algorithms, and strengths and weaknesses over each other.

We discussed various clustering techniques and how clusters are formed. We learned how different the clustering algorithms are from each other and how they are suited to particular use cases.

We learned about K-means, Hierarchical clustering, and DBSCAN.

In the next chapter, we will learn about Ensemble learning.

References

- https://github.com/JuliaLang/julia
- https://github.com/JuliaStats/Clustering.jl
- http://juliastats.github.io/
- https://github.com/stevengj/PyCall.jl
- https://github.com/cstjean/ScikitLearn.jl

8
Creating Ensemble Models

A group of people have the ability to take better decisions than a single individual, especially when each group member comes in with their own biases. The ideology is also true for machine learning.

When single algorithms are not capable to generate the true prediction function, then ensemble machine-learning methods are used. When there is more focus on the performance of the model rather than the training time and the complexity of the model, then ensemble methods are preferred.

In this chapter, we will discuss:

- What is ensemble learning?
- Constructing ensembles.
- Combination strategies.
- Boosting, bagging, and injecting randomness.
- Random forests.

What is ensemble learning?

Ensemble learning is a machine learning method where various models are prepared to work on the same problem. It is a process where multiple models are generated and the results obtained from them are combined to produce the final result. Moreover, ensemble models are inherently parallel; therefore, they are much more efficient at training and testing if we have access to multiple processors:

- **Ordinary methods of machine learning**: These use training data for learning a specific hypothesis.
- **Ensemble learning**: This uses training data to build a set of hypothesis. These hypotheses are combined to build the final model.

Therefore, it can be said that ensemble learning is the way toward preparing different individual learners for an objective function that utilizes different strategies, and in the long run, combines these learnings.

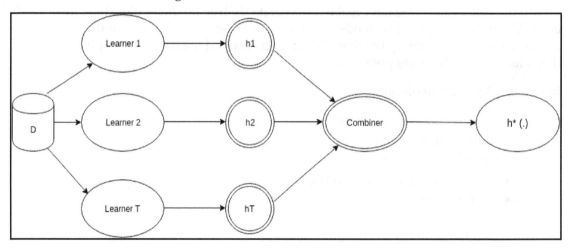

Understanding ensemble learning

Ensemble learning, as we discussed, combines the learning of the various individual learners. It is the aggregation of multiple learned models that aim to improve accuracy:

- Base learners: Each individual learner is called a base learner. Base learners may be suited for a specific situation, but are not good in generalization.
- Due to the weak generalization capability of the base learner, they are not suited for every scenario.
- Ensemble learning uses these base (weak) learners to construct a strong learner which results in a comparatively much more accurate model.
- Generally, decision tree algorithms are used as the base learning algorithm. Using the same kind of learning algorithm results in homogeneous learners. However, different algorithms can also be used, which will result in heterogeneous learners.

How to construct an ensemble

It is recommended that the base learners should be as diverse as possible. This enables the ensemble to handle and predict most of the situation with better accuracy. This diversity can be produced using different subsets of the dataset, manipulating or transforming the inputs, and using different techniques simultaneously for learning.

Also, when the individual base learners have a high accuracy then there is a good chance of having good accuracy with the ensemble.

Typically, construction of an ensemble is a two-step process:

1. The first step is to create the base learners. They are generally constructed in parallel, but if base learners are influenced by the previously formed base learners then they are constructed in a sequential manner.
2. The second step is to combine these base learners and create an ensemble which is best suited to the use case.

By using different types of base learners and combination techniques, we can altogether produce different ensemble learning models.

There are different ways to implement the ensemble model:

- Sub-sample the training dataset
- Manipulate the input features
- Manipulate the output features
- Inject randomness
- Learning parameters of the classifier can be modified

Combination strategies

Combination strategies can be classified into two categories:

- Static combiners
- Adaptive combiners

Static combiners: The combiner choice standard is autonomous of the component vector. Static methodologies can be comprehensively partitioned into trainable and non-trainable.

Trainable: The combiner goes through a different training stage to enhance the performance of the ensemble. Here are two approaches that are widely used:

- **Weighted averaging**: The yield of every classifier is weighted by its very own performance measure:
    - Measuring the accuracy of prediction on a different validation set
- **Stacked generalization**: The yield of the ensemble is treated as the feature vector to a meta-classifier

Non-trainable: Performance of the individual classifier does not have an affect on the voting. Different combiners might be utilized. This depends upon the sort of yield delivered by the classifier:

- **Voting**: This is used when a single class label is generated by every classifier. Every classifier votes for a specific class. The class that receives the larger part vote on the ensemble wins.
- **Averaging**: When a confidence estimate is created by every classifier then averaging is utilized. The class that has the highest number of posterior in the ensemble wins.
- **Borda counts**: This is used when a rank is produced by every classifier.

Adaptive combiners: This is a type of combiner function that is dependent on the feature vector given as input:

- A function that is local to every region
- Divide and conquer methodology creates modular ensembles and simple classifiers specializing in different regions of I/O space
- The individual specialists are required to perform well in their region of ability and not for all inputs

Subsampling training dataset

The learner is considered to be unstable if the output classifier has to undergo radical changes when there are some small variations in the training data:

- **Unstable learners**: Decision trees, neural networks, and so on
- **Stable learners**: Nearest neighbor, linear regression, and so on

This particular technique is more suited for the unstable learners.

Two very common techniques used in subsampling are:

- Bagging
- Boosting

Bagging

Bagging is also known as Bootstrap Aggregation. It generates the additional data that is used for training by using sub-sampling on the same dataset with replacement. It creates multiple combinations with repetitions to generate the training dataset of the same size.

As sampling with replacement is done, on an average, each classifier is trained on 63.2% of the training example.

After training on these multiple datasets, bagging combines the result by majority voting. The class that received the most number of votes wins. By using these multiple datasets, bagging aims to reduce the variance. Accuracy is improved if the induced classifiers are uncorrelated.

Random forest, a type of ensemble learning, uses bagging and is one of the most powerful methods.

Let's go through the bagging algorithm.

Training:

- For iteration, *t=1 to T*:
    - Sample randomly from the training dataset with replacement *N* samples
    - Base learner is trained (for example, decision tree or neural network) on this sample

Test:

- For test sample, *t=1 to T*:
    - Start all the models that were trained
    - Prediction is done on the basis of the following:
        - **Regression**: Averaging
        - **Classification**: Majority vote

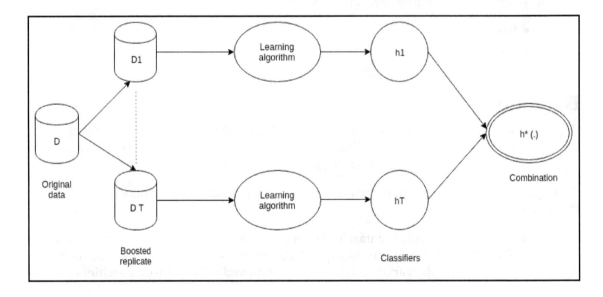

When does bagging work?

Bagging works in scenarios where there would have been over-fitting if it wasn't used. Let's go through these scenarios:

- **Under-fitting**:
    - **High bias**: Models are not good enough and don't fit the training data well
    - **Small variance**: Whenever there is a change in the dataset, there is a very small change that needs to be done in the classifier
- **Over-fitting**:
    - **Small bias**: Models fit too well to the training data
    - **Large variance**: Whenever there is a small change in the dataset, there is a large or drastic change that needs to be done in the classifier

Bagging aims to reduce the variance without affecting the bias. Therefore, the dependency of the model on the training dataset is reduced.

Boosting

Boosting is different to the bagging approach. It is based on the PAC framework, which is the Probably Approximately Correct framework.

PAC learning: The probability of having larger confidence and smaller accuracy than the misclassification error:

- **Accuracy**: This is the percentage of correctly classifying the samples in the test dataset
- **Confidence**: This is the probability of achieving the accuracy in the given experiment

Boosting approach

The boosting approach is based on the concept of the "weak learner". When an algorithm performs somewhat better than 50% in binary classification tasks, then it is called a weak learner. The approach is to combine multiple weak learners together, and the aim is to:

- Improve confidence
- Improve accuracy

This is done by training these different weak learners on different datasets.

Boosting algorithm

- Training:
    - Samples are taken randomly from the dataset.
    - First, learner *h1* is trained on the sample.
    - Accuracy of this learner, *h1*, is evaluated on the dataset.
    - A similar process is followed using different samples for multiple learners. They are divided such that they classify differently.

- Test:
    - On the test dataset, the learning is applied using the majority vote of all the learners

Confidence can also be boosted in a similar way, as boosting the accuracy with some trade-off.

Boosting is less of an algorithm and rather it is a "framework". The main aim of this framework is to take a weak learning algorithm W and turn it into a strong learning algorithm. We will now discuss AdaBoost, which is short for "adaptive boosting algorithm". AdaBoost became famous because it was one of the first successful and practical boosting algorithms.

It does not require a large number of hyper-parameters to be defined and executes in a polynomial time. The benefit of this algorithm is that it has the ability to automatically adapt to the data given to it.

AdaBoost – boosting by sampling

- After *n* iterations, a weak learner having distribution *D* over the training set is provided by the boosting:
    - All examples have the equal probability of being selected as the first component
- Sub-sampling of the training set is done in accordance with distribution *Dn* and a model is trained by the weak learner
- The weights of misclassified instances are adjusted in a way that subsequent classifiers work on comparatively difficult cases
- A distribution *D(n+1)* is generated with the probability of misclassified samples

increasing and correctly classified samples decreasing
- After *t* iterations, according to the performance of the models, the votes of individual hypotheses are weighted

The strength of AdaBoost derives from the adaptive resampling of examples, not from the final weighted combination.

What is boosting doing?

- Every classifier has a specialization on the specific subset of dataset
- An algorithm concentrates on examples with increasing levels of difficulty
- Boosting is able to reduce variance (similar to bagging)
- It is also able to eliminate the consequences of high bias of the weak learner (not present in bagging)
- Train versus test errors performance:
  - We can reduce the train errors to nearly 0
  - Overfitting is not present and is evident by the test errors

The bias and variance decomposition

Let's discuss how bagging and boosting affect the bias-variance decomposition of the classification error:

- Features of errors that can be expected from a learning algorithm:
  - A bias term is a measure of performance of the classifier with respect to the target function
  - Variance terms measure the robustness of the classifier; if there is a change in the training dataset, then how is the model affected by it?
- Bagging and boosting are capable to reduce the variance term, and therefore reducing the errors in the model
- It is also proved that boosting attempts to reduce the bias term since it focuses on misclassified samples

Manipulating the input features

One other technique with which we can generate multiple classifiers is by manipulating the set of input features which we feed to the learning algorithm.

We can select different subsets of features and networks of different sizes. The input features subsets may be manually selected rather than in an automated fashion. This technique is widely used in image processing: one of the very famous examples is Principle Component Analysis.

The ensemble classifier generated in many experiments was able to perform like an actual human.

It was also found that when we delete even a few of the features that we gave as the input, it affects the performance of the classifier. This affects the overall voting, and the ensemble thus generated is not able to perform up to the expectations.

Injecting randomness

This is another universally useful technique for producing an ensemble of classifiers. In this method, we inject randomness into the learner algorithm. Neural networks with back-propagation are also created using the same technique for hidden weights. On the off chance that the calculation is connected to the same preparing illustrations, but with various starting weights, the subsequent classifier can be very diverse.

One of the most computationally costly parts of outfits of decision trees involves preparing the decision tree. This is quick for decision stumps; however, for more profound trees, it can be restrictively costly.

The costly part is picking the tree structure. Once the tree structure is picked, it is extremely cheap to fill in the leaves (which is the predictions of the trees) utilizing the training data. A shockingly productive and successful option is to utilize trees with altered structures and random features. Accumulations of trees are called forests, thus classifiers fabricated like this are called random forests.

It takes three arguments:

- The training data
- The depth of the decision trees
- The number form

The calculation produces each of the K trees freely which makes it simple to parallelize. For every tree, it develops a full binary tree of a given depth. The elements utilized at the branches of this tree are chosen randomly, regularly with substitution, implying that the same element can seem numerous at times, even in one branch. Based on the training data, the leaves that will perform the actual predictions are filled. This last step is the main time when the training data is utilized. The subsequent classifier then only involves the voting of the K-numerous random trees.

The most astonishing thing about this methodology is that it works strikingly well. It tends to work best when the greater part of the components are not significant, since the quantity of features chosen for any given tree is minimal. A portion of the trees will query the useless features.

These trees will basically make random forecasts. Be that as it may, a portion of the trees will query good features and will make good forecasts (on the grounds that the leaves are assessed in light of the training data). In the event that you have enough trees, the arbitrary ones will wash out as noise, and just the good trees will affect the final classification.

Random forests

Random forests were developed by Leo Breiman and Adele Cutler. Their strength in the field of machine learning has been shown nicely in a blog entry at Strata 2012: "Ensembles of decision trees (often known as random forests) have been the most successful general-purpose algorithm in modern times", as they "automatically identify the structure, interactions, and relationships in the data".

Moreover, it has been noticed that "most Kaggle solutions have no less than one top entry that vigorously utilizes this methodology". Random forests additionally have been the preferred algorithm for recognizing the body part in Microsoft's Kinect, which is a movement detecting information gadgets for Xbox consoles and Windows PCs.

Random forests comprises of a group of decision trees. We will consequently begin to analyze decision trees.

A decision tree, as discussed previously, is a tree-like chart where on each node there is a choice, in view of one single feature. Given an arrangement of features, the tree is navigated from node to node, as indicated by these decisions, until you come to a leaf. The name of this leaf is the expectation for the given list of features. A straightforward decision tree could be utilized to choose what you have to bring with you when going out.

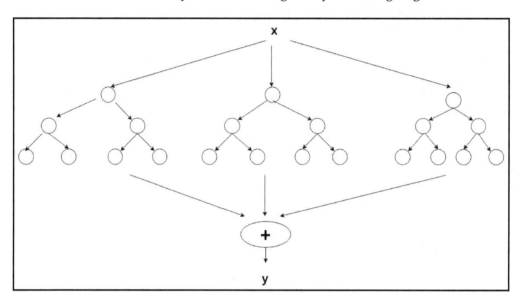

Each tree is constructed in the following way:

- Randomly take an *n* sample case where n is the number of cases in the training set.
    - Replacement is used to select these n cases. This particular set of data is used to construct the tree.
- The node is split by $x<X$, where X is the number of input variables. The X doesn't change with the growth of the forest.
- Pruning is not done as trees are allowed to go the maximum depth.

The error rate in a random forest is dependent on the following (as given in the original paper):

- When correlation among the trees increases, the error rate in the random forest increases
- When individual trees are weak, the error rate increases and it decreases when the individual trees are strengthened

It is found that x, which was mentioned previously, has an effect on correlation and strength. Increasing x increases both strength and correlation, and decreasing x decreases both. We try to find the particular value or the range where the x should lie to have the minimal error.

We use the **oob** (**out of bag**) error to find the best value or the range of the value of x.

This tree does not classify every one of the points effectively. We could transform this by expanding the tree depth. Thus, the tree can foresee the specimen data 100% effectively, just by taking in the noise in the examples. In the most extreme case, the calculation is proportional to a word reference containing each specimen. This is known as over-fitting and prompts awful results when utilizing it for out of test forecasts. Keeping in mind the end goal to overcome over-fitting, we can prepare numerous decision trees by presenting weights for the examples and just considering an irregular subset of the features for every split. A definite conclusion of the random forest will be controlled by a lion's share vote on the trees' forecasts. This method is otherwise called bagging. It diminishes the variance (errors from noise in the training set) without expanding the bias (errors because of the insufficient adaptability of the model).

Features of random forests

- A random forest is highly accurate as compared to the existing algorithms.
- It can be used effectively and efficiently on big data. They are fast and don't require expensive hardware to run.
- One of the key features of a random forest is its ability to deal several numbers of input variables.
- A random forest can show the generalization error estimate during the process of construction of the forest. It can also give the important variables for the classification.
- When the data is sparse, a random forest is an effective algorithm with good accuracy. It can also work on prediction of missing data.
- The models generated can be utilized later on data that we might receive in the future.
- In unbalanced datasets, it provides the feature to balance the error present in the class population.
- Some of these features can be used for unsupervised clustering too and also as an effective method for outlier detection.
- One other key feature of a random forest is that it doesn't overfit.

How do random forests work?

To comprehend and utilize the different choices, additional data about how they are figured is valuable. The vast majority of the alternatives rely upon two information objects produced by random forests.

At the point when the training set for the present tree is drawn by sampling with replacement, around 33% of the cases are left well enough alone for the example.

As more and more trees are added to the random forest, the information from the oob helps to generate the estimate of the classification error. After the construction of every tree, the greater part of the information keeps running down the tree, and vicinities are computed for every pair of cases.

On the other hand, if the same terminal node is shared by two cases then we increase their proximity by 1. After the complete analysis, these proximities are normalized. Proximities are utilized as a part of supplanting missing information, finding outliers, and delivering in-depth perspectives of the information.

The out-of-bag (oob) error estimate

Random forests eliminate the requirement to cross-validate to achieve the unbiased estimate of the test set error. During the construction, it is estimated as follows:

- Every tree is constructed utilizing an alternate bootstrap sample from the original information. Around 33% of the cases are left alone for the bootstrap test and not utilized as a part of the development of the kth tree.
- There may be some cases that were not considered during the construction of the trees. We put these cases down the kth to achieve a classification. It produces a classification test set in around 33% of the trees. Towards the end of the run, take j to be the class that received the vast majority of the votes each time the case n was oob. The number of times that j is not equivalent to the true class of n at the midpoint of all the cases is the oob error estimate. This follows being unbiased in the various tests.

Gini importance

The impurity measure is frequently used for decision trees. Misclassification is measured and is called gini impurity which applies in the context where there are multiple classifiers present.

There is also a gini coefficient. This is applicable to binary classification. It needs a classifier that is able to rank the sample according to the probability of being in the right class.

Proximities

As mentioned before, we don't prune the trees while constructing the random forest. Therefore, the terminal nodes don't have many numbers of instances.

To find the proximity measure, we run all the cases from the training set down the tree. Let's say case x and case y arrive at the same terminal node, we then increase the proximity by 1.

After the run, we take twice the number of trees and divide the proximity of the case which was increased by 1 by this number.

Implementation in Julia

Random forests are available in the Julia-registered packages from Kenta Sato:

```
Pkg.update() Pkg.add("RandomForests")
```

This is a CART-based random forest implementation in Julia. This package supports:

- Classification models
- Regression models
- Out-of-bag (OOB) errors
- Feature importances
- Various configurable parameters

There are two separate models available in this package:

- Classification
- Regression

Each model has its own constructor that is trained by applying the fit method. We can configure these constructors with some keyword arguments listed as follows:

```
RandomForestClassifier(;n_estimators::Int=10,
                        max_features::Union(Integer, FloatingPoint,
Symbol)=:sqrt,
                        max_depth=nothing,
                        min_samples_split::Int=2,
                        criterion::Symbol=:gini)
```

This one is for the classification:

```
RandomForestRegressor(;n_estimators::Int=10,
                       max_features::Union(Integer, FloatingPoint,
Symbol)=:third,
                       max_depth=nothing,
                       min_samples_split::Int=2)
```

This one is for the regression:

- `n_estimators`: This is the number of weak estimators
- `max_features`: This is the number of candidate features at each split
    - If Integer is given, the fixed number of features are used
    - If FloatingPoint is given, the proportions of the given value (0.0, 1.0] are used
    - If Symbol is given, the number of candidate features is decided by a strategy
        - `:sqrt`: `ifloor(sqrt(n_features))`
        - `:third`: `div(n_features, 3)`
- `max_depth`: The maximum depth of each tree
    - The default argument nothing means there is no limitation of the maximum depth

- `min_samples_split`: The minimum number of sub-samples to try to split a node
- `criterion`: The criterion of the impurity measure (classification only)
    - `:gini`: Gini index
    - `:entropy`: Cross entropy

`RandomForestRegressor` always uses the mean squared error for its impurity measure. Currently, there are no configurable criteria for the regression model.

Learning and prediction

For our example, we will be using the amazing "DecisionTree" package provided by Ben Sadeghi.

The package supports the following available models:

- `DecisionTreeClassifier`
- `DecisionTreeRegressor`
- `RandomForestClassifier`
- `RandomForestRegressor`
- `AdaBoostStumpClassifier`

Installation is straightforward:

```
Pkg.add("DecisionTree")
```

Let us start with the classification example:

```
using RDatasets: dataset
using DecisionTree
```

We now take the famous iris dataset:

```
iris = dataset("datasets", "iris")
features = convert(Array, iris[:, 1:4]);
labels = convert(Array, iris[:, 5]);
```

This generates a pruned tree classifier:

```
# train full-tree classifier
model = build_tree(labels, features)
# prune tree: merge leaves having >= 90% combined purity (default: 100%)
model = prune_tree(model, 0.9)
# pretty print of the tree, to a depth of 5 nodes (optional)
print_tree(model, 5)
```

```
Feature 3, Threshold 3.0
L-> setosa : 50/50
R-> Feature 4, Threshold 1.8
    L-> Feature 3, Threshold 5.0
        L-> versicolor : 47/48
        R-> Feature 4, Threshold 1.6
            L-> virginica : 3/3
            R-> Feature 1, Threshold 7.2
                L-> versicolor : 2/2
                R-> virginica : 1/1
    R-> Feature 3, Threshold 4.9
        L-> Feature 1, Threshold 6.0
            L-> versicolor : 1/1
            R-> virginica : 2/2
        R-> virginica : 43/43
```

It generates such a tree given in the previous image. We now apply this learned model:

```
# apply learned model
apply_tree(model, [5.9,3.0,5.1,1.9])
# get the probability of each label
apply_tree_proba(model, [5.9,3.0,5.1,1.9], ["setosa", "versicolor",
"virginica"])
# run n-fold cross validation for pruned tree,
# using 90% purity threshold pruning, and 3 CV folds
accuracy = nfoldCV_tree(labels, features, 0.9, 3)
```

It generates the following result:

```
Fold 1
Classes:
3x3 Array{Int64,2}:
  15   0   0
   1  13   0
   0   1  20
Any["setosa","versicolor","virginica"]
Matrix:
Accuracy:
3x3 Array{Int64,2}:
  18   0   0
   0  18   5
   0   1   8
3x3 Array{Int64,2}:
  17   0   0
   0  11   2
   0   3  17
0.96
Kappa:    0.9391727493917275

Fold 2
Classes:  Any["setosa","versicolor","virginica"]
Matrix:
Accuracy: 0.88
Kappa:    0.8150431565967939

Fold 3
Classes:  Any["setosa","versicolor","virginica"]
Matrix:
Accuracy: 0.9
Kappa:    0.8483929654335963

Mean Accuracy: 0.9133333333333332
```

Now let's train the random forest classifier:

```
# train random forest classifier
# using 2 random features, 10 trees, 0.5 portion of samples per tree
(optional), and a maximum tree depth of 6 (optional)
model = build_forest(labels, features, 2, 10, 0.5, 6)
```

It generates the random forest classifier:

```
3x3 Array{Int64,2}:
 14   0   0
  2  15   0
  0   5  14
3x3 Array{Int64,2}:
 19   0   0
  0  15   3
  0   0  13
3x3 Array{Int64,2}:
 17   0   0
  0  14   1
  0   0  18
```

Now we will apply this learned model and check the accuracy:

```
# apply learned model
apply_forest(model, [5.9,3.0,5.1,1.9])
# get the probability of each label
apply_forest_proba(model, [5.9,3.0,5.1,1.9], ["setosa", "versicolor",
"virginica"])
# run n-fold cross validation for forests
# using 2 random features, 10 trees, 3 folds and 0.5 of samples per tree
(optional)
accuracy = nfoldCV_forest(labels, features, 2, 10, 3, 0.5)
```

The result is as follows:

```
Fold 1
Classes:  Any["setosa","versicolor","virginica"]
Matrix:
Accuracy: 0.86
Kappa:    0.7904191616766468

Fold 2
Classes:  Any["setosa","versicolor","virginica"]
Matrix:
Accuracy: 0.94
Kappa:    0.9096929560505719

Fold 3
Classes:  Any["setosa","versicolor","virginica"]
Matrix:
Accuracy: 0.98
Kappa:    0.9698613622664255

Mean Accuracy: 0.9266666666666666
```

```
3-element Array{Float64,1}:
 0.86
 0.94
 0.98
```

Now let's train a regression tree:

```
n, m = 10^3, 5 ;
features = randn(n, m);
weights = rand(-2:2, m);
labels = features * weights;
# train regression tree, using an averaging of 5 samples per leaf
(optional)
model = build_tree(labels, features, 5)
apply_tree(model, [-0.9,3.0,5.1,1.9,0.0])
# run n-fold cross validation, using 3 folds, averaging of 5 samples per
leaf (optional)
# returns array of coefficients of determination (R^2)
r2 = nfoldCV_tree(labels, features, 3, 5)
```

It generates the following tree:

```
Fold 1
Mean Squared Error:     3.300846200596437
Correlation Coeff:      0.8888432175516764
Coeff of Determination: 0.7880527098784421

Fold 2
Mean Squared Error:     3.453954624611847
Correlation Coeff:      0.8829598153801952
Coeff of Determination: 0.7713110081750566

Fold 3
Mean Squared Error:     3.694792045651598
Correlation Coeff:      0.8613929927227013
Coeff of Determination: 0.726445409019041

Mean Coeff of Determination: 0.7619363756908465

3-element Array{Float64,1}:
 0.788053
 0.771311
 0.726445
```

Now training a regression forest is made straightforward by the package:

```
# train regression forest, using 2 random features, 10 trees,
# averaging of 5 samples per leaf (optional), 0.7 of samples per tree
(optional)
model = build_forest(labels,features, 2, 10, 5, 0.7)
# apply learned model
apply_forest(model, [-0.9,3.0,5.1,1.9,0.0])
# run n-fold cross validation on regression forest
# using 2 random features, 10 trees, 3 folds, averaging of 5 samples/leaf
(optional),
# and 0.7 porition of samples per tree (optional)
# returns array of coefficients of determination (R^2)
r2 = nfoldCV_forest(labels, features, 2, 10, 3, 5, 0.7)
```

It generates the following output:

```
Fold 1
Mean Squared Error:     1.9810655619597397
Correlation Coeff:      0.9401674806129654
Coeff of Determination: 0.8615574830022655

Fold 2
Mean Squared Error:     1.9359831066335886
Correlation Coeff:      0.950439305213504
Coeff of Determination: 0.8712750380735376

Fold 3
Mean Squared Error:     2.120355686915558
Correlation Coeff:      0.9419270107183548
Coeff of Determination: 0.8594402239360724

Mean Coeff of Determination: 0.8640909150039585

3-element Array{Float64,1}:
 0.861557
 0.871275
 0.85944
```

Why is ensemble learning superior?

To comprehend the generalization power of ensemble learning being superior to an individual learner, Dietterich provided three reasons.

These three reasons help us understand the reason for the superiority of ensemble learning leading to a better hypothesis:

- The training information won't give adequate data to picking a single best learner. For instance, there might be numerous learners performing similarly well on the training information set. In this way, joining these learners might be a superior decision.
- The second reason is that, the search procedures of the learning algorithms may be defective. For instance, regardless of the possibility that there exists a best hypothesis, the learning algorithms may not be able to achieve that due to various reasons including generation of an above average hypothesis. Ensemble learning can improve on that part by increasing the possibility to achieve the best hypothesis.
- The third reason is that one target function may not be present in the hypothesis space that we are searching in. This target function may lie in a combination of various hypothesis spaces, which is similar to combining various decision trees to generate the random forest.

There are numerous hypothetical studies on acclaimed ensemble techniques. For example, boosting and bagging are the methods to achieve these three points discussed.

It is also observed that boosting does not experience the ill effects of over-fitting even after countless, and now and then it is even ready to diminish the generalization error after the training error has achieved zero. Although numerous scientists have considered this marvel, hypothetical clarifications are still in belligerence.

The bias-variance decomposition is frequently utilized as a part of studying the execution of ensemble techniques. It is observed that bagging is able to nearly eliminate the variance, and by doing so becomes ideal to attach to learners that experience huge variance, such as unstable learners, decision trees, or neural networks.

Boosting is able to minimize the bias, notwithstanding diminishing the variance, and by doing so becomes more viable to weak learners such as decision trees.

Applications of ensemble learning

Ensemble learning is used widely in applications, such as:

- Optical character recognition
- Text categorization
- Face recognition
- Computer-aided medical diagnosis

Ensemble learning can be used in nearly all scenarios where machine learning techniques are used.

Summary

Ensemble learning is a method for generating highly accurate classifiers by combining weak or less accurate ones. In this chapter, we discussed some of the methods for constructing ensembles and went through the three fundamental reasons why ensemble methods are able to outperform any single classifier within the ensemble.

We discussed bagging and boosting in detail. Bagging, also known as Bootstrap Aggregation, generates the additional data that is used for training by using sub-sampling on the same dataset with replacement. We also learned why AdaBoost performs so well and understood in detail about random forests. Random forests are highly accurate and efficient algorithms that don't overfit. We also studied how and why they are considered as one of the best ensemble models. We implemented a random forest model in Julia using the "DecisionTree" package.

References

- http://cs.nju.edu.cn/zhouzh/zhouzh.files/publication/springerEBR09.pdf
- http://web.engr.oregonstate.edu/~tgd/publications/mcs-ensembles.pdf
- http://www.machine-learning.martinsewell.com/ensembles/ensemble-learning.pdf
- http://web.cs.wpi.edu/~xkong/publications/papers/ecml11.pdf

9
Time Series

The capacity to demonstrate and perform decision modeling and examination is a crucial component of some real-world applications ranging from emergency medical treatment in intensive care units to military commands and control frameworks. Existing methodologies and techniques for deduction have not been progressively viable with applications where exchange offs between decision quality and computational tractability are essential.
A successful way to deal with time-critical element decision modeling should give express backing to the demonstration of transient procedures and for managing time-critical circumstances.

In this chapter, we will cover:

- What is Forecasting?
- Decision-making processes
- What is Time Series?
- Types of models
- Trend analysis
- Analysis of seasonality
- ARIMA
- Smoothing

What is forecasting?

Let's take the example of an organization that needs to find out the demand for its inventory in the near future, to maximize the return on investment.

For instance, numerous stock frameworks apply for indeterminate demand. The stock parameters in these frameworks require evaluations of the demand and forecast error distributions.

The two phases of these frameworks, forecasting and stock control, are frequently analyzed autonomously. It is essential to comprehend the cooperation between demand estimating and stock control since this impacts the execution of the stock framework.

Forecasting requirements include:

- Each decision gets to be operational sooner or later, so it ought to be based on figures of future conditions.
- Figures are required all through an organization and they should absolutely not be created by a disconnected gathering of forecasters.
- Forecasting is never "wrapped up". Forecasts are required constantly, and as time proceeds onward, the effect of the forecasts on real execution is measured, original forecasts are overhauled, and decisions are adjusted, and this goes on in a loop.

The decision maker makes use of forecasting models to carry out the decisions. They are regularly utilized to demonstrate the procedure to research the effect of various strategies reflectively.

It is helpful to break the components of decision making into three groups:

- Uncontrollable
- Controllable
- Resources (that define the problem situation)

Decision-making process

What is a system? Frameworks are shaped with parts set up together in a specific way, keeping in mind the end goal to meet a specific a target. The relationship between the parts figures out what the framework does and its overall capacities. Along these lines, the connections in a framework are regularly more critical than the individual parts. When all is said and done, the frameworks that are building blocks for different frameworks are called subsystems.

The dynamics of a system

A framework that does not change is a static framework. A hefty portion of business frameworks are rapid frameworks, which mean that their states change after some time. We allude to the way a framework changes after some time as the framework's conduct. What's more, when the framework's improvement takes a typical pattern, we say the framework has a behavior pattern. Whether a framework is static or dynamic relies upon how it changes over time.

The decision-making process has the following components:

- **Performance measure (or indicator)**: The development of powerful measures is seen as important in every organization. Performance measures give the desirable levels of results, that is, the target of your choice. The goal is essential in recognizing the anticipating action:
    - **Strategic**: Return on Investment, growth, and innovations
    - **Tactical**: Cost, quantity, and customer satisfaction
    - **Operational**: Target setting and conformance with standard
- **Resources**: Resources are the consistent components that don't change amid the time range of the forecast. Resources are the variables that characterize the decision issue. Strategic decisions ordinarily have longer time horizons than both the tactical and the operational choices.
- **Forecasts**: Forecast information originates from the environment of the decision maker. Uncontrollable inputs must be determined or predicted.
- **Decisions**: Decision inputs are the collection of all conceivable approaches that are possible.
- **Interaction**: Associations among the preceding decision parts are the logical, scientific functions representing the circumstances and end result connections among inputs, resources, forecasts, and the result. At the point when the result of a decision relies upon the strategy, we transform one or more parts of the risky circumstance with the aim of realizing an attractive change in some other part of it. We succeed in the event that we know about the connection among the parts of the issue.
- **Actions**: Decision making includes the choice of a strategy that is chosen by the decision maker. The way that our strategy influences the result of a choice relies upon how the forecasts and different inputs are interrelated and how they identify with the result.

What is TimeSeries?

A time series is an arrangement of insights, typically gathered at standard intervals. Time series information normally happens in numerous applications:

- **Economics**: For example, monthly data for unemployment, hospital admissions, and so on
- **Finance**: For example, daily exchange rate, a share price, and so on
- **Environmental**: For example, daily rainfall, air quality readings, and so on
- **Medicine**: For example, ECG brain wave activity every 2 to 8 seconds

The techniques for time series investigation predate those for general stochastic procedures and Markov chains. The goals of time series analysis are to portray and outline time series data, fit low-dimensional models, and to make desirable forecasts.

Trends, seasonality, cycles, and residuals

One straightforward strategy for depicting a series is that of classical disintegration. The idea is that the arrangement can be segmented into four components:

- **Trend (Tt)**: Long-term movements in the mean
- **Seasonal effects (It)**: Cyclical fluctuations related to the calendar
- **Cycles (Ct)**: Other cyclical fluctuations (such as a business cycle)
- **Residuals (Et)**: Other random or systematic fluctuations

The idea is to create separate models for these four elements and then combine them:

- **Additively**: $Xt = Tt + It + Ct + Et$
- **Multiplicatively**: $Xt = Tt\ It\ Ct\ Et$

Difference from standard linear regression

The information is not inexorably independent and is not, as a matter of course, indistinguishably distributed. One characteristic for time series is that it is a rundown of observations where the ordering matters. Sequence is essential on the grounds that there is reliance and changing the sequence could change the importance of the information.

Basic objectives of the analysis

The basic objective usually is to determine a model that describes the pattern of the time series. Uses for such a model are:

- Describing the important features of the time series pattern
- Explaining how the past affects the future or how two time series can "interact"
- Forecasting future values of the series
- Serving as a control standard for a variable that measures the quality of products in some manufacturing situations

Types of models

There are two basic types of "time domain" model:

- Ordinary regression models that use time indices as x-variables:
    - Helpful for an initial description of the data and form the basis of several simple forecasting methods
- ARIMA models (for Autoregressive Integrated Moving Average):
    - Models that relate the present value of a series to past values and past prediction errors

Important characteristics to consider first

Some important questions to first consider when looking at a time series are:

- Is there a trend?
    - The pattern in which the measurements tend to increase or decrease over time.
- The effect of seasonality?
    - Is there a regularly repeating pattern of highs and lows related to calendar time such as seasons, quarters, months, days of the week, and so on?

- Are there any outliers?
  - In regression, outliers are at a distance from the trend line. With time series data, the outliers are at a distance from other data.
- Is there a period unrelated to seasonality factors?
- Is there a constant variance over a definite period of time?
- Are there any abrupt changes to either side?

The following plot is an example of random numbers over time. By a time series plot, we simply mean that the variable is plotted against time. Similar plots can be made for heartbeats over time, market fluctuations, seismic graphs, and so on.

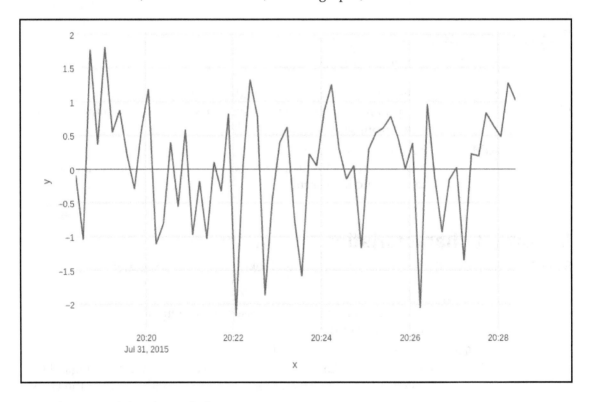

Some features of the plot include:

- There is no consistent trend (upward or downward) over the entire time span. The series appears to slowly wander up and down.
- There are some obvious outliers.
- It's difficult to judge whether the variance is constant or not.

Systematic pattern and random noise

As in most different analyses, in time series analysis it is accepted that the information comprises of a systematic pattern (as a set arrangement of identifiable segments) and random noise (error), which typically makes the pattern hard to recognize. Most of the time, series analysis systems include some type of filtering through noise, keeping in mind the end goal to make the pattern more identifiable.

Two general aspects of time series patterns

Most of the time, series patterns can be portrayed regarding two fundamental classes of segments:

- Pattern
- Regularity

A pattern is a generally straight or (regularly) nonlinear part that progresses after some time and does not rehash (probably) inside the time range caught by our data.

Regularity may have a formally similar nature; in any case, it rehashes itself in systematic intervals after some time. These two general classes of time series components may coexist in actual real-life data.

For instance, offers of an organization can quickly grow over the years, yet they still follow predictable seasonal patterns (for example, as much as 30% of yearly deals every year are made in October, while just 10% are made in March).

Trend analysis

There are no demonstrated "programmed" systems to distinguish pattern segments in the time series data. In any case, the length of the pattern is repetitive (increasing or decreasing in a consistent manner) and some portion of data analysis is ordinarily not extremely difficult. In the event that the time series information contains considerable errors, then the initial phase during the time spent pattern distinguishing proof is smoothing.

Smoothing

Smoothing dependably includes some type of neighborhood averaging of data such that the non-systematic parts of individual perceptions offset each other. The most widely recognized method is moving normal smoothing. This replaces every component of the series by either the simple or weighted normal of n encompassing components, where n is the width of the smoothing "window".

Medians can be utilized rather than means. Here are some advantages of medians:

- Within the smoothing window, its results are less biased by outliers
- If there are outliers in the data, middle smoothing regularly delivers smoother or more "reliable" curves than moving normal, taking into account the same window width

The fundamental weakness of middle smoothing is that without clear outliers it might deliver more jagged curves than moving normal and it doesn't take into account weighting.

Fitting a function

Numerous monotonous time series information can be satisfactorily approximated by a linear function. If there is a reasonable monotonous nonlinear part, the data initially should be changed to evacuate the nonlinearity. Normally a logarithmic, exponential, or (less frequently) polynomial function can be utilized.

Analysis of seasonality

Seasonal dependency (seasonality) is another general part of the time series design. For example, if we see a time series graph of buying trends, we can see that there is a huge spike during the end of October and December every year. This pattern repeats every year.

Autocorrelation correlogram

Seasonal patterns of time series can be analyzed by means of correlograms. The correlogram graphically and numerically shows the **autocorrelation function (ACF),** which are serial relationship coefficients (and their standard errors) for sequential lags in a predetermined range of lags.

Ranges of two standard errors for every lag are generally set apart in correlograms, yet commonly the size of autocorrelation is of more interest than its dependability.

The following is the correlogram for the `mtcars` dataset:

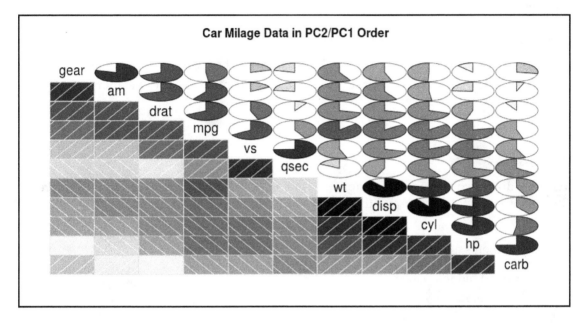

Examining correlograms

We must remember while examining correlograms that autocorrelations for successive lags are formally dependent. For example, if the primary component is firmly related to the second, and the second to the third, then the main component should likewise be to some degree related to the third one, and so on.

Partial autocorrelations

Another helpful strategy to inspect serial dependencies is to look at the **partial autocorrelation capacity** (**PACF**), an expansion of autocorrelation, where the dependence on the intermediate components (those inside the lag) is eliminated.

Removing serial dependency

Serial dependency for a specific lag of k can be evacuated by differencing the series, that is, changing over every *i*th component of the series into its difference from the *(i-k)*th component.

There are two explanations behind such changes:

- Seasonal dependencies of a hidden nature can be recognized in the series
- ARIMA and other procedures require that we make the series stationary, which itself requires removing the seasonal dependencies

ARIMA

We have discussed the numerical modeling of the procedure of time series analysis. In real life, patterns are not so clear and the observations generally have a considerable amount of errors.

The requirements are to:

- Find hidden patterns
- Generate forecasts

Let's now understand ARIMA and how it can help us with getting these.

Common processes

- Autoregressive procedure:
  - Most time series comprise of components that are serially dependent as in you can evaluate a coefficient or an arrangement of coefficients that depict back-to-back components of the series from particular, time-lagged (past) components.
  - Stationary prerequisite. The autoregressive procedure is stable only within a certain range of parameters that the parameters fall into. Previous effects can pile up and affect the consecutive points and the series may not be stationary.

- Moving normal procedure. Autonomous from the autoregressive procedure, every component in the series can likewise be influenced by the past error (or arbitrary shock) that can't be represented by the autoregressive component.
- Invertibility necessity. There is a "duality" between the moving normal procedure and the autoregressive procedure:
    - The moving normal equation can be transformed into an autoregressive structure. In any case, undifferentiated from the stationary condition depicted over, this must be done if the moving normal parameters take after specific conditions, that is, if the model is invertible. Also, the series won't be stationary.

ARIMA methodology

Autoregressive moving average model.

The general model presented by Box and Jenkins (1976) incorporates autoregressive, and in addition, moving normal parameters and unequivocally incorporates differencing in the detailing of the model.

In particular, the three sorts of parameters in the model are:

- The autoregressive parameters (p)
- The quantity of differencing passes (d)
- Moving normal parameters (q)

In the documentation presented by Box and Jenkins, models are abridged as ARIMA (p, d, q).

Identification

The input series for ARIMA should be stationary. It must have a steady mean, difference, and autocorrelation through time. Subsequently, for the most part, the series first should be differenced until it is stationary (this, likewise, regularly requires log changing the data to make the variance stable).

The quantity of times the series should be differenced to accomplish stationarity is reflected in the "d" parameter. So as to decide the fundamental level of differencing, we need to look at the plot of the data and auto-correlogram.

Noteworthy changes in level (solid upward or descending changes) ordinarily require first order nonseasonal (lag=1) differencing:

- Solid changes of incline generally require second order nonseasonal differencing

Estimation and forecasting

The next step is estimation. Here the parameters are assessed (utilizing function minimization systems) so that the sum of squared residuals is minimized. The assessments of the parameters are utilized as a part of the last stage (forecasting) to compute new estimations of the series (past those incorporated into the input dataset) and confidence intervals for those predicted values.

The estimation procedure is performed on changed (differenced) information before the forecasted figures are produced. It is required that the series should be integrated so that the forecasts are communicated in values compatible with the input data.

The constant in ARIMA models

With the standard autoregressive and moving normal parameters, ARIMA models may likewise incorporate a constant. The representation of this constant is dependent on the model that is fit:

- If in the model there are no autoregressive parameters present, then the mean of the series is the expected value of the constant
- If in the model there are autoregressive parameters present, then the intercept is represented by the constant

Identification phase

Before the estimation can start, we have to settle on (distinguish) the particular number and kind of ARIMA parameters to be evaluated. The significant instruments utilized as a part of the ID stage are:

- Plots of the arrangement
- Correlograms of autocorrelation (ACF)
- Partial autocorrelation (PACF)

The choice is not direct and in less typical cases requires experience as well as a decent arrangement of experimentation with option models (and also the specialized parameters of ARIMA).

In any case, a good amount of experimental time series patterns can be adequately approximated utilizing one of the five fundamental models. These models are based on the shape of the **autocorrelogram (ACF)** and **partial auto correlogram (PACF)**:

- One autoregressive parameter (p):
  - ACF: Exponential decay
  - PACF: Spike at lag 1
  - No correlation for other lags
- Two autoregressive parameters (p):
  - ACF: A sine-wave shape pattern or a set of exponential decays
  - PACF: Spikes at lags 1 and 2
  - No correlation for other lags
- One moving average parameter (q):
  - ACF: Spike at lag 1
  - No correlation for other lags
  - PACF: Damps out exponentially
- Two moving average parameters (q):
  - ACF: Spikes at lags 1 and 2
  - No correlation for other lags
  - PACF: A sine-wave shape pattern or a set of exponential decays
- One autoregressive (p) and one moving average (q) parameter:
  - ACF: Exponential decay starting at lag 1
  - PACF: Exponential decay starting at lag 1

Seasonal models

A series in which a pattern repeats seasonally over time requires special models.

This is similar to the simple ARIMA parameters in seasonal models:

- Seasonal autoregressive (ps)
- Seasonal differencing (ds)
- Seasonal moving normal parameters (qs)

For instance, let's take the model (0,1,2)(0,1,1).

This depicts a model that incorporates:

- No autoregressive parameters
- Two general moving normal parameters
- One regular moving normal parameter

The seasonal lag utilized for the seasonal parameters is normally decided amid the identification proof stage and should be expressly indicated.

The general suggestions concerning the choice of parameters to be assessed (taking into account ACF and PACF) likewise apply to seasonal models. The principle distinction is that in seasonal series, ACF and PACF will indicate sizable coefficients at products of the seasonal lag.

Parameter estimation

There are a few distinct techniques for assessing the parameters. Every one of them should fundamentally deliver the same estimates, yet might be pretty much proficient for any given model. Generally, amid the parameter estimation stage, a function minimization calculation is utilized to maximize the probability (likelihood) of the watched series given the parameter values.

This requires the computing of the (conditional) aggregates of squares (SS) of the residuals, given the separate parameters.

In practice, this requires the calculation of the (conditional) sums of squares (SS) of the residuals, given the respective parameters.

Different methods have been proposed to compute the SS for the residuals:

- The approximate maximum likelihood method according to McLeod and Sales (1983)
- The approximate maximum likelihood method with backcasting
- The exact maximum likelihood method according to Melard (1984)

Evaluation of the model

- **Parameter estimates**:
    - Report surmised *t* values, figured from the parameter standard errors
    - If there is no significance, then the separate parameter can most of the time be dropped from the model without considerably influencing the overall fit of the model
- **Other quality criteria**: Another clear and normal measure of the quality of the model is the exactness of its forecasts created taking into account partial data so that the forecasts can be contrasted and known (unique) observations

Interrupted time series ARIMA

We might want to assess the effect of one or more discrete occasions on the qualities in the time series. These kinds of interruptions on time series analysis are portrayed in subtle elements in McDowall, McCleary, Meidinger, and Hay (1980). McDowall, et al., recognize three noteworthy sorts of effects that are conceivable:

- Permanent abrupt
- Permanent gradual
- Abrupt temporary

Exponential smoothing

Exponential smoothing has turned out to be exceptionally well known as a forecasting strategy for various types of time series data. The strategy was freely created by Brown and Holt. Brown worked for the US Navy during World War II, where his task was to design a tracking system for fire-control information to compute the location of submarines. Later, he connected this strategy to the forecasting of interest for spare parts (an inventory control issue).

Simple exponential smoothing

A simple model for a time series t would be to consider every observation as comprising of a constant (*b*) and an error component (epsilon), that is: $Xt = b + t$.

The constant b is generally steady in every fragment of the series; however, it may change gradually after some time. On the off chance of fitting, then one approach to seclude the genuine estimation of b, and therefore the orderly or unsurprising part of the series, is to figure a sort of moving normal, where the current and quickly new observations are doled out more prominent weight than the particular older observations.

Exponential smoothing fulfills precisely such weighting where exponentially smaller weights are doled out to older observations. The specific formula for simple exponential smoothing is as follows:

$$St = a*Xt + (1-a)*St\text{-}1$$

At the point when connected recursively to each progressive observation in the series, each new smoothed value (forecast) is figured as the weighted normal of the present observation and the past smoothed observation.

The past smoothed observation was processed from the past observed value and the smoothed quality before the past perception, and so on. Subsequently, each smoothed value is the weighted normal of the past perceptions where the weights decrease exponentially relying upon the estimation of the parameter (alpha).

On the off chance that it is equivalent to 1 (one), then the past perceptions are overlooked altogether; if it is equivalent to 0 (zero), then the present perception is disregarded totally, and the smoothed worth comprises completely of the past smoothed quality (which is processed from the smoothed perception before it, and so on; along these lines every single smoothed quality will be equivalent to the underlying smoothed worth S0). Estimations in the middle will deliver transitional results:

- If it is equal to 1, then the past observations are ignored completely
- If it is equal to 0, then the current observation is ignored completely:
  - The smoothed value consists completely of the past smoothed value (which, in turn, is computed from the smoothed observation before it, and so on; thus all smoothed values will be equal to the initial smoothed value, S0). Estimations in the middle will deliver transitional results.

The hypothetical model for the process hidden in the observed time series, simple exponential smoothing, will frequently create precise forecasts.

Indices of lack of fit (error)

The most direct method for assessing the exactness of the forecasts in light of a specific value is to just plot the observed values and the one-stage ahead of forecasts. This plot can likewise incorporate the residuals (scaled against the right Y axis), so that locales of better or most noticeably bad fit can likewise effectively be distinguished.

This visual check of the precision of forecasts is frequently the most intense technique for figuring out if or not the present exponential smoothing model fits the data:

- **Mean error**: The **mean error** (ME) quality is essentially processed as the normal error value (normal of observed minus one-stage ahead forecast):
    - Clearly, a downside of this measure is that positive and negative error values can counterbalance each other, so this measure is not a decent marker of general fit.

- **Mean absolute error**: The **mean absolute error** (MAE) value is processed as the normal absolute error value:
    - If the value is 0 (zero) then the fit (forecast) is considered perfect.
    - Compared with the mean squared error value, this measure of fit will neglect anomalies, therefore, one of a kind or uncommon large error values will influence the MAE less than the MSE value.

- Sum **of squared error (SSE) and mean squared error**: These values are calculated as the aggregate (or normal) of the squared error values. This is the most normally utilized absence of-fit indicator as a part of statistical fitting strategies.

- **Percentage error (PE)**: All the preceding measures depend on the actual error value. It might appear to be sensible to rather express the absence of fit as far as the relative deviation of the one-stage ahead forecasts from the observed values, which is with respect to the magnitude of the observed values.
    - For instance, when attempting to foresee month-to-month deals that may fluctuate generally from month to month, we might be fulfilled if our expectation "hits the objective" with about ±10% precision. At the end of the day, the outright errors might be of less interest, but rather more are the relative errors in the forecasts:

$$PEt = 100*(Xt - Ft)/Xt$$

Here Xt is the observed value at time t, and Ft is the forecasts (smoothed values).

- **Mean percentage error (MPE)**: This value is computed as the average of the PE values.
- **Mean absolute percentage error (MAPE)**: As is the situation with the mean error value, a mean percentage error close to 0 (zero) can be created by substantial positive and negative rate percentage errors that offset each other. Consequently, a superior measure of relative general fit is the mean absolute percentage error. Additionally, this measure is generally more significant than the mean squared mistake:
    - For instance, realizing that the normal forecast is "off" by ±5% is a helpful result all by itself, though a mean squared error of 30.8 is not quickly interpretable.
- **Automatic search for best parameter**: A quasi-Newton function minimization procedure (the same as in ARIMA) is utilized to minimize either the mean squared error, mean absolute error, or mean total rate error.
- **The initially smoothed value S0**: We require a S0 value keeping in mind the end goal to process the smoothed quality (forecast) for the main observation in the series. Depending upon the decision of the parameter (that is, when it is near zero), the underlying value for the smoothing procedure can influence the nature of the forecasts for some observations.

Implementation in Julia

TimeSeries is a registered package. So like other packages, we can add it to your Julia packages:

```
Pkg.update()
Pkg.add("TimeSeries")
```

The TimeArray time series type

```
immutable TimeArray{T, N, D<:TimeType, A<:AbstractArray} <:
AbstractTimeSeries

timestamp::Vector{D}
values::A
colnames::Vector{UTF8String}
meta::Any
```

```
function TimeArray(timestamp::Vector{D},
values::AbstractArray{T,N},
colnames::Vector{UTF8String},
meta::Any)
nrow, ncol = size(values, 1), size(values, 2)
nrow != size(timestamp, 1) ? error("values must match length of
timestamp") :
ncol != size(colnames,1) ? error("column names must match width of
array") :
timestamp != unique(timestamp) ? error("there are duplicate dates") :
~(flipdim(timestamp, 1) == sort(timestamp) || timestamp ==
sort(timestamp)) ? error("dates are mangled") :
flipdim(timestamp, 1) == sort(timestamp) ?
new(flipdim(timestamp, 1), flipdim(values, 1), colnames, meta) :
new(timestamp, values, colnames, meta)
end
end
```

There are four fields for the type:

- `timestamp`: The timestamp field consists of a vector of values of a child type of `TimeType`, in practice, either `Date` or `DateTime`. The `DateTime` type is similar to the Date type except it represents time frames smaller than a day. For the construction of a TimeArray to work, this vector needs to be sorted. If the vector includes dates that are not sequential, the construction of the object will error out. The vector also needs to be ordered from the oldest to latest date, but this can be handled by the constructor and will not prohibit an object from being created.

- `values`: The values field holds the data from the time series and its row count must match the length of the timestamp array. If these do not match, the constructor will fail. All the values inside the values array must be of the same type.

- `colnames`: The `colnames` field is a vector of type UTF8 String and contains the names of the columns for each column in the values field. The length of this vector must match the column count of the values array, or the constructor will fail.

- `meta`: The meta field defaults to holding nothing, which is represented by type Void. This default is designed to allow programmers to ignore this field. For those who wish to utilize this field, `meta` can hold common types such as String or more elaborate user-defined types. One might want to assign a name to an object that is immutable versus relying on variable bindings outside of the object's type fields.

We'll be using historical financial datasets available in the `MarketData` package:

```
Pkg.add("MarketData")
using TimeSeries
using MarketData
```

Now let's go through the data:

```
ohlc[1]
```

This produces the following output:

```
1x4 TimeSeries.TimeArray{Float64,2,Date,Array{Float64,2}} 2000-01-03 to
2000-01-03

              Open      High      Low       Close
2000-01-03 |  104.88    112.5     101.69    111.94
```

Let's go through some more records and statistics:

```
ohlc[[1:3;9]]
```

This produces the following output:

```
4x4 TimeSeries.TimeArray{Float64,2,Date,Array{Float64,2}} 2000-01-03 to
2000-01-13

              Open      High      Low       Close
2000-01-03 |  104.88    112.5     101.69    111.94
2000-01-04 |  108.25    110.62    101.19    102.5
2000-01-05 |  103.75    110.56    103.0     104.0
2000-01-13 |  94.48     98.75     92.5      96.75
```

We can also go through them using the column names:

```
500x2 TimeSeries.TimeArray{Float64,2,Date,Array{Float64,2}} 2000-01-03 to
2001-12-31

              Open      Close
2000-01-03 |  104.88    111.94
2000-01-04 |  108.25    102.5
2000-01-05 |  103.75    104.0
2000-01-06 |  106.12    95.0

2001-12-26 |  21.35     21.49
2001-12-27 |  21.58     22.07
2001-12-28 |  21.97     22.43
2001-12-31 |  22.51     21.9
```

To access the records using Date, it can be done as follows:

```
ohlc[[Date(2000,1,3),Date(2000,2,4)]]
```

It will give the following output:

```
2x4 TimeSeries.TimeArray{Float64,2,Date,Array{Float64,2}} 2000-01-03 to
2000-02-04

             Open      High      Low       Close
2000-01-03 | 104.88    112.5     101.69    111.94
2000-02-04 | 103.94    110.0     103.62    108.0
```

We can also list the records over the range of the dates:

```
ohlc[Date(2000,1,10):Date(2000,2,10)]
```

It produces the following output:

```
23x4 TimeSeries.TimeArray{Float64,2,Date,Array{Float64,2}} 2000-01-10 to
2000-02-10

             Open      High      Low       Close
2000-01-10 | 102.0     102.25    94.75     97.75
2000-01-11 | 95.94     99.38     90.5      92.75
2000-01-12 | 95.0      95.5      86.5      87.19
2000-01-13 | 94.48     98.75     92.5      96.75

2000-02-07 | 108.0     114.25    105.94    114.06
2000-02-08 | 114.0     116.12    111.25    114.88
2000-02-09 | 114.12    117.12    112.44    112.62
2000-02-10 | 112.88    113.88    110.0     113.5
```

We can also use two different columns:

```
ohlc["Open"][Date(2000,1,10)]
```

It produces the following output:

```
1x1 TimeSeries.TimeArray{Float64,1,Date,Array{Float64,1}} 2000-01-10 to
2000-01-10

             Open
2000-01-10 | 102
```

Using time constraints

There are some specific methods that can segment on time ranges if the condition is met.

when

The when method allows aggregating elements from a `TimeArray` into specific time periods.

For example: `dayofweek` or `month`. Here are some dates methods with examples:

```
day    Jan 3, 2000 = 3
dayname   Jan 3, 2000 = "Monday"
week   Jan 3, 2000 = 1
month Jan 3, 2000 = 1
monthname    Jan 3, 2000 = "January"
year   Jan 3, 2000 = 2000
dayofweek    Monday = 1
dayofweekofmonth   Fourth Monday in Jan = 4
dayofyear    Dec 31, 2000 = 366
quarterofyear   Dec 31, 2000 = 4
dayofquarter    Dec 31, 2000 = 93
```

from

```
from(cl, Date(2001, 10, 24))
```

This will give the following output:

```
47x1 TimeSeries.TimeArray{Float64,1,Date,Array{Float64,1}} 2001-10-24 to
2001-12-31

             Close
2001-10-24 | 18.95
2001-10-25 | 19.19
2001-10-26 | 18.67
2001-10-29 | 17.63

2001-12-26 | 21.49
2001-12-27 | 22.07
2001-12-28 | 22.43
2001-12-31 | 21.9
```

to

```
to(cl, Date(2000, 10, 24))
```

This code will generate the following output:

```
206x1 TimeSeries.TimeArray{Float64,1,Date,Array{Float64,1}} 2000-01-03 to
2000-10-24
```

	Close
2000-01-03	111.94
2000-01-04	102.5
2000-01-05	104.0
2000-01-06	95.0
2000-10-19	18.94
2000-10-20	19.5
2000-10-23	20.38
2000-10-24	18.88

findwhen

This is probably one of the most used and efficient methods. It tests a condition and returns the `Date` or `DateTime` vector:

```
red = findwhen(ohlc["Close"] .< ohlc["Open"]);
```

This will generate the following output:

```
252x4 TimeSeries.TimeArray{Float64,2,Date,Array{Float64,2}} 2000-01-04 to
2001-12-31
```

	Open	High	Low	Close
2000-01-04	108.25	110.62	101.19	102.5
2000-01-06	106.12	107.0	95.0	95.0
2000-01-10	102.0	102.25	94.75	97.75
2000-01-11	95.94	99.38	90.5	92.75
2001-12-14	20.73	20.83	20.09	20.39
2001-12-20	21.4	21.47	20.62	20.67
2001-12-21	21.01	21.54	20.8	21.0
2001-12-31	22.51	22.66	21.83	21.9

find

The `find` method is similar to `findwhen`. It tests a condition and returns a vector of Int, representing the row in the array where the condition is true:

```
green = find(ohlc["Close"] .> ohlc["Open"]);
```

This will generate the following output:

```
244x4 TimeSeries.TimeArray{Float64,2,Date,Array{Float64,2}} 2000-01-03 to
2001-12-28

                Open      High      Low       Close
2000-01-03 |  104.88    112.5     101.69    111.94
2000-01-05 |  103.75    110.56    103.0     104.0
2000-01-07 |  96.5      101.0     95.5      99.5
2000-01-13 |  94.48     98.75     92.5      96.75

2001-12-24 |  20.9      21.45     20.9      21.36
2001-12-26 |  21.35     22.3      21.14     21.49
2001-12-27 |  21.58     22.25     21.58     22.07
2001-12-28 |  21.97     23.0      21.96     22.43
```

Mathematical, comparison, and logical operators

These methods are also supported by the TimeSeries package.

To use mathematical operators:

- \+ or .+: Mathematical element-wise addition
- – or .-: Mathematical element-wise subtraction
- * or .*: Mathematical element-wise multiplication
- ./: Mathematical element-wise division
- .^: Mathematical element-wise exponentiation
- % or .%: Mathematical element-wise remainder

To use comparison operators:

- .> element-wise greater-than comparison
- .< element-wise less-than comparison
- .== element-wise equivalent comparison

- .>= element-wise greater-than or equal comparison
- .<= element-wise less-than or equal comparison
- .!= element-wise not-equivalent comparison

To use logical operators:

- & element-wise logical AND
- | element-wise logical OR
- !, ~ element-wise logical NOT
- $ element-wise logical XOR

Applying methods to TimeSeries

Common transformation of time series data involves:

- Lagging
- Leading
- Calculating change
- Windowing operations and aggregation operations

Lag

The `lag` method is putting yesterday's value in today's timestamp:

```
cl[1:4]

#Output
4x1 TimeSeries.TimeArray{Float64,1,Date,Array{Float64,1}} 2000-01-03 to
2000-01-06

              Close
2000-01-03 | 111.94
2000-01-04 | 102.5
2000-01-05 | 104.0
2000-01-06 | 95.0
```

It is applying lag on this:

```
lag(cl[1:4])
```

It generates the following output:

```
3x1 TimeSeries.TimeArray{Float64,1,Date,Array{Float64,1}} 2000-01-04 to
2000-01-06

             Close
2000-01-04 | 111.94
2000-01-05 | 102.5
2000-01-06 | 104.0
```

Lead

Lead is opposite to the lag:

```
lead(cl[1:4])
```

The output generated is as follows:

```
3x1 TimeSeries.TimeArray{Float64,1,Date,Array{Float64,1}} 2000-01-03 to
2000-01-05

             Close
2000-01-03 | 102.5
2000-01-04 | 104.0
2000-01-05 | 95.0
```

As the cl is 500 rows long we can lead till that. For now, we will lead by 400:

```
lead(cl, 400)
```

The output generated is as follows:

```
100x1 TimeSeries.TimeArray{Float64,1,Date,Array{Float64,1}} 2000-01-03 to
2000-05-24

             Close
2000-01-03 | 19.5
2000-01-04 | 19.13
2000-01-05 | 19.25
2000-01-06 | 18.9

2000-05-19 | 21.49
2000-05-22 | 22.07
2000-05-23 | 22.43
2000-05-24 | 21.9
```

Percentage

One of the most common time series operations is to calculate the change in percentage:

```
percentchange(cl)
```

The output generated is as follows:

```
499x1 TimeSeries.TimeArray{Float64,1,Date,Array{Float64,1}} 2000-01-04 to
2001-12-31

              Close
2000-01-04 | -0.0843
2000-01-05 | 0.0146
2000-01-06 | -0.0865
2000-01-07 | 0.0474

2001-12-26 | 0.0061
2001-12-27 | 0.027
2001-12-28 | 0.0163
2001-12-31 | -0.0236
```

This shows the percentage change from the previous record.

Combining methods in TimeSeries

Two `TimeArrays` can be merged to generate a meaningful array.

Merge

Merge joins two TimeArrays. By default, it joins using an inner join:

```
merge(op[1:4], cl[2:6], :left)
```

The output generated is as follows:

```
4x2 TimeSeries.TimeArray{Float64,2,Date,Array{Float64,2}} 2000-01-03 to
2000-01-06

              Open       Close
2000-01-03 | 104.88     NaN
2000-01-04 | 108.25     102.5
2000-01-05 | 103.75     104.0
2000-01-06 | 106.12     95.0
```

In the previous example, we provided the type of join we want to perform. We can also do right or outer joins.

Collapse

The `collapse` method is used to compress data into a larger time frame.

Map

This is used for transformations in the timeseries data. The first argument of this method is a binary function (the time stamp and the values). This method returns two values, respectively the new time stamp and the new vector of values:

```
a = TimeArray([Date(2015, 10, 24), Date(2015, 11, 04)], [15, 16],
["Number"])
```

The output generated is as follows:

```
 2x1 TimeSeries.TimeArray{Int64,1,Date,Array{Int64,1}} 2015-10-24 to
2015-11-04

               Number
2015-10-24 |  15
2015-11-04 |  16
```

You apply the map method as follows:

```
map((timestamp, values) -> (timestamp + Dates.Year(1), values), a)
```

This transforms the records for the particular time provided:

```
2x1 TimeSeries.TimeArray{Int64,1,Date,Array{Int64,1}} 2016-10-24 to
2016-11-04

               Number
2016-10-24 |  15
2016-11-04 |  16
```

Summary

In this chapter, we learned about what is forecasting and why it is needed in a business. Forecasting helps to identify the demand and take necessary steps, as well as in other domains it helps to predict weather, and so on. The decision-making process is highly affected by the results of forecasting. Time Series is the arrangement of insights, typically gathered at standard intervals. It has been used in various domains such as medical, weather, finance markets, and so on.

We also learned about the different types of models and how to analyze trends in Time Series. We also took into consideration seasonality effects on the Time series analysis. We discussed ARIMA in detail and also explored the Time Series library of Julia.

References

- http://timeseriesjl.readthedocs.io/en/latest/
- https://documents.software.dell.com/statistics/textbook/time-series-analysis
- http://home.ubalt.edu/ntsbarsh/stat-data/forecast.htm
- http://userwww.sfsu.edu/efc/classes/biol71/timeseries/timeseries1.htm
- https://onlinecourses.science.psu.edu/stat51/node/47
- http://www.itl.nist.gov/div898/handbook/pmc/section4/pmc4.htm

10

Collaborative Filtering and Recommendation System

Every day, we are immersed with decisions and choices. These can range from our clothes to the movies we can watch or what to eat when we order online. We take decisions in business, too. For instance, which stock we should invest in. The set of choices that we have can vary depending on what we are actually doing and what we want. For example, when buying clothes online from Flipkart or Amazon we see hundreds or thousands of choices. Amazon's Kindle store is so huge that no one can read all the books in their lifetime. To make these decisions, we require some background information and maybe a little help in knowing what can be best for us.

Generally, individuals depend on suggestions from their companions or the counsel of specialists to choose and make decisions. They may observe their friends or trusted people to make the same decisions as them. These include either paying a good amount on the ticket and go to watch a movie, or order a specific pizza that the individual has not tasted before, or start reading a book the individual knows nothing about.

The way these suggestions are made have limits. These are not dependent on the likings or the "taste" of the user. There might be many movies or pizzas or books that one may like and their friends or their company won't on whose his decisions are usually made. This specific taste of the user cannot be taken care of by the traditional way of suggestions or recommendations.

In this chapter, we will learn:

- What are recommendation systems?
- Association rule mining.
- Content-based filtering.

- What is collaborative filtering?
- What is user-based and item-based collaborative filtering?
- Building a recommendation engine.

What is a recommendation system?

Recommendation frameworks use learning methods for making customized suggestions for data, items, or services. These recommendation systems generally have some level of interaction with the target individual. The amount of data that has been collected in recent years and the data that is being generated today proved a great boon for these recommendation systems.

Today, many recommendation systems are in operation and produce millions of recommendations per day:

- Recommendations on e-commerce websites regarding the books, clothes, or items to buy
- Advertisements suited to our tastes
- Type of properties that we may be interested in
- Travel packages suited to our tastes and budget

The current generation of recommender systems are able to make worthy recommendations and are scaled to millions of products and target users. It is required that even if the number of products or users increase, the recommender system should continue to work. But this becomes another challenge, as to get better recommendations the algorithm would process more data which would increase the time taken for recommendations. If we limit the data that is processed, the recommendations generated may not be that effective or have the quality that the user would trust.

We need to create the balance and devise the mechanisms to process more data in a less amount of time.

This is done by utilizing user-based collaborative filtering or item-based collaborative filtering. Before we go further in collaborative filtering, we will also go through association rule mining.

A recommender framework is an essential part of the data and e-business system. It is an effective technique for empowering clients to channel through vast data and item spaces. It also helps the user to find the product right at the front which the user might not have been able to search for or might not have bought if the recommendation system hadn't been there in place. This also helps in increasing the sales as more and more users find the correct item that they would be interested in buying.

A lot of research has been made to improve the recommender systems and it has been accepted that there is no recommender system that can fit to every kind of problem.

Algorithms cannot work without the user interaction or the data. Interaction with the user is needed to:

- Understand the user
- Provide recommendations generated to the user

This is a big challenge to collect the "good" data from the user, that is, eliminating or removing the noisy data that can have an affect on the recommendations that will be generated.

Some users generally traverse through various information on the Internet, while some are focused only on the data they are interested in. Also, some users are very concerned about their privacy and don't allow the data collection process to happen.

Actually, the current recommender systems generally give good recommendations when fed with clean and useful data. A lot of effort is put into the data collection and cleaning phase where we understand which data is actually of use to the user.

The utility matrix

Generally, we encounter entities belonging to two classes in recommender systems:

- Users
- Items

Users may have a liking for specific items and we need to find this liking and show the items matching the criteria to them.

Let's take an example of the matrix of user ratings for movies. We will make a user-movie matrix where the the ratings would be values in this matrix:

	Star Wars IV	The Godfather	LOTR 1	LOTR 2	LOTR 3	The Notebook	Titanic
User 1		4			3	3	
User 2	5			3			2
User 3	5		5		4		
User 4		4				3	
User 5	2				3	4	5

In this particular example, we can see that user 1 has given a rating of 4 to "The Godfather", a rating of 3 to "LOTR 3" (The Lord of the Rings 3), and a rating of 3 to "The Notebook", but the user has not given ratings to other movies, which is generally due to the reason that the user has not watched the movie. It is also a possibility that the user preferred not to share views regarding the movie.

The values range from 1 to 5, 1 being the lowest and 5 being the highest rating for a movie. It is evident that the matrix is sparse, which means that most of the entries are unknown. In the real world, the data that we encounter is more sparse and we are required to fill these blank spaces with the probable ratings from the user and thus give the recommendations.

Association rule mining

Association rule mining is finding associations or patterns among a collection of items which occur frequently. It is also known as **Market basket analysis**.

Its main aim is to understand the buying habits of the customer, which is done by finding the correlations and patterns among the items that customers intended to buy or actually bought. For example, a customer who buys a computer keyboard is also likely to buy a computer mouse or a pen drive.

The rule is given by:

- Antecedent → Consequent [support, confidence]

Measures of association rules

Let A, B, C, D, and E .... represent different items.

Then we need to generate association rules, for example:

- $\{A, J\} \rightarrow \{C\}$
- $\{M, D, J\} \rightarrow \{X\}$

The first rule here means that when A and J are bought together then there is a high probability of the customer buying C too.

Similarly, the second rule means that when M, D, and J are bought together there is a high probability of the customer buying X too.

These rules are measured by:

- **Support**: Support refers to the total coverage. It is the probability of items bought together over the total transactions:
  - Support, $X \rightarrow Y$: $P(X,Y)$
  - (transactions containing both X and Y)/(total number of transactions)
- **Confidence**: Confidence refers to the accuracy. It is the probability of buying the second item if the first item is bought:
  - Confidence, $X \rightarrow Y$: $P(Y|X)$
  - (transactions that contain both X and Y) / (transactions that contain only X)

Some items are not bought that frequently and they may not be of that much importance to the algorithm. To generate these rules, these items need to to be dropped. These are defined by the two thresholds, which are called:

- Minimum support
- Minimum confidence

How to generate the item sets

- Item sets that have the required minimal support are chosen.
- If $\{X,Y\}$ fulfills the criteria for the minimal support, then X and Y also fulfill that criteria. The vice-versa is not true.

Apriori algorithm: Subsets belonging to the frequent item sets are themselves frequent:

1. First, all the item sets are found based on the n:
   - For example, when $n=2$, $\{\{X,Y\}, \{Y,Z\}, \{X,S\}, \{S,Y\}\}$

2. Now we merge these sets to a higher level:
   - $\{\{X,Y,Z\}, \{X,Y,S\}, \{Y,Z,S\}, \{X,Z,S\}\}$

3. Out of these merged sets, we check how many of these have the required minimum support:
   - We eliminate those sets whose minimum support couldn't be generated

4. We keep on increasing the level to the point where no more sets can be generated that have the required minimal support

How to generate the rules

When the number of item sets is small, the brute-force method is used:

- Subsets of all the item sets are generated. The empty set is not included.
- Confidence of these subsets is computed.
- Rules having higher confidence are selected.

Content-based filtering

Content-based filtering creates a profile of the user and uses this profile to give relevant recommendations to the user. The profile of the user is created by the history of the user.

For example, an e-commerce company can track the following details of the user to generate recommendations:

- Items ordered in the past
- Items viewed or added to the cart but not purchased
- User browsing history to identify what kinds of products the user may be interested in

The user may or may not have manually given ratings to these items, but various factors can be considered to evaluate their relevance to the user. Based on this, new items are recommended to the user that would be interesting to that user.

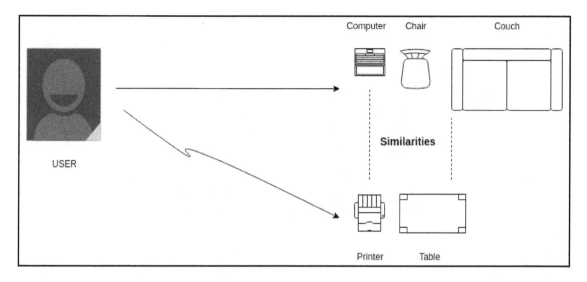

The process as shown, takes the attributes from the user profile and matches them with the attributes of the items available. When there are relevant items available, these are considered to be of interest to the user and are recommended.

Therefore, the recommendations are heavily dependent on the profile of the user. If the user profile correctly represents the user likings and interests then the recommendations produced would be accurate and if the profile is not the current representation of the user's preferences then the recommendations produced may not be accurate.

Steps involved in content-based filtering

There are multiple steps involved in generating recommendations using content-based filtering. These steps are as follows:

- Analyzing attributes of the items. There is a possibility that the items that are the candidates for the recommendation don't have the valid structure of the information. Therefore, the first step is to extract these attributes from the items in a structured way:
  - For instance, for an e-commerce company, these attributes are the properties or features of the products available in their catalog
- Generating the profile of the user. The user profile is created considering various factors. This is done using machine learning techniques. The various factors that can be considered are:
  - Order history

- Item view history
- User browsing history to identify what kind of products the user may be interested in

  In addition to these, the feedback from the user is also taken into account. For example, if the user was satisfied after ordering a product, how many times the user viewed a product and how much time was spent on it.

- The recommender using the preceding two generated components. The following generated user profile and the item attributes that are extracted are matched against each other using various techniques. Different weights are provided to the different attributes of both user and item. We then generate recommendations that can be ordered on the basis of relevance.

Generating a user profile is a typical task and it needs to be exhaustive to generate a more accurate profile.

Social networks help to build a user profile. That is a treasure trove of the information that is manually provided by the user. The user gives the details, such as:

- Type of products interested in, such as which type of books, music, and so on
- Products disliked such as some particular cuisine, cosmetic brands, and so on

After we start giving user recommendations, we also have the capability to receive feedback, which helps the recommender to produce better recommendations:

- **Explicit feedback**: When we buy an item on an e-commerce website, we generally receive a feedback form after 2-3 days of initial use. The primary aim of this form is to help the company to know if we actually liked the product and if not, what could have been done to make it better. This is called explicit feedback. This enables the recommender system to know that the product was not completely suited for the user or a better product could have been recommended.
- **Implicit feedback**: The user may not be required to manually fill out the feedback or may choose not to do so. In such a scenario, the user's activities are analyzed and monitored to know what the response was of the user towards the product.

Feedback may also be present as the comments on the product review section on these e-commerce sites. These comments can be mined, and sentiment of the user can be extracted.

Although having direct feedback from the user makes it easier for the system, most users choose to ignore this particular feedback.

Advantages of content-based filtering

There are many advantages of using content-based filtering:

- Content-based filtering is dependent only on the user that we are generating recommendations for. These are not dependent on the other users' ratings or profiles.
- The recommendations generated can be explained to the user as they are dependent on the user's profile and the attributes of the items present.
- As the recommendations are not based on the ratings of the items, but on the attributes of these items and the profile of the users, the newer items that have not yet been bought or rated can be recommended too.

Limitations of content-based filtering

There are some limitations of content-based filtering too:

- As content-based filtering requires the user profile, for a new user it can be difficult to generate recommendations. To give good quality recommendations, we need to analyze the user's activity and still the recommendations generated may not be as per to the user's liking.
- When the attributes or the features of the items are not readily available, the content-based filtering faces difficulty to give recommendations. Also, sufficient domain knowledge is also needed to understand these attributes.
- Content-based filtering is also dependent on the feedback provided by the user. So, we need to analyze and monitor for the user feedback continuously. In the scenario where the system can't understand if it is positive or negative feedback, then it may not give such relevant recommendations.
- CBF also has the tendency to limit the recommendations to a very specific set. It may not be able to recommend similar or related items that the user might be interested in.

Collaborative filtering

Collaborative filtering is a famous algorithm that is based on the likings or the behavior of other users or peers unlike the content-based filtering that we studied in the previous section.

Collaborative filtering:

- If the user likes some of the things that other users or peers have shown an inclination to, then the preferences of these users can be recommended to the desired user
- It is referred to as the "nearest neighbor recommendation"

To implement collaborative filtering, some assumptions are made:

- Likings or the behavior of peers or other users can be taken into consideration to understand and predict for the desired user. Therefore, an assumption is made that the desired user has similar tastes as the other users taken into consideration here.
- If the user got a recommendation in the past based on ratings of a group of users, then the user would have a similar taste with that group.

There are different types of collaborative filtering:

- **Memory-based collaborative filtering**: Memory-based collaborative filtering is based on the rating of the users to compute the similarity between the users or even the items. This is used to make the recommendations:
    - It makes use of the rating matrix
    - Recommendations are generated for the desired user using this rating matrix at any given time
- **Model-based collaborative filtering**: Model-based collaborative filtering depends on the training data and the learning algorithm to create the model. This model is used to generate the recommendations using the actual data:
    - This method fits the model to the provided matrix to generate the recommendations on the basis of this model

The basic procedure for collaborative filtering includes:

- As CF is highly based on the group whose preferences are considered, it is recommended to find the peer group with similar tastes
- The items that we will consider recommending should be there in the list of items from the group, but not of the user
- After creating the matrix, the items are given a particular score depending on the various factors
- The items that receive the highest scores are recommended
- To keep improving and adding the recommendations as new items are added to the list from the group, the preceding steps are performed again on a desired interval

There are some advantages and disadvantages with collaborative filtering. Let's go through the advantages:

- It is easier to understand where attributes of the user are properly formed
- Users and products are simple systems and don't need specific understanding to build the recommender
- The recommendations produced are generally good

There are some drawbacks to collaborative filtering, too:

- As discussed earlier, collaborative filtering requires a lot of user feedback. Also, these users need to be reliable.
- A standardization is also required for the attributes of the items.
- Assumption of past behavior will influence the present choices.

Baseline prediction methods

A baseline is the simplest and easiest prediction that can be formed. It is important to calculate a baseline to know about the accuracy of the models we generate and validity of the results of the algorithms that we produce:

- **Classification**: The baseline for classification problems can be formed by considering that most of the results of the predictions will be from the class with the most observations.

- **Regression**: The baseline for regression problems can be formed by considering that most of the results of the predictions will be a central tendency measure, such as mean or median.
- **Optimization**: Random samples in the domain are fixed when working on the optimization problem.

When we have chosen the baseline prediction methods and have the results we can compare them with the results of the models that we generated.

If the models that we generated are not able to out perform these baseline methods then most likely we need to work on the model to improve the accuracy.

User-based collaborative filtering

User-based collaborative filtering makes use of the main idea of collaborative filtering which is finding similar users that have past ratings or behavior somewhat similar to the target user.

This approach is also called k-Nearest Neighbour collaborative filtering.

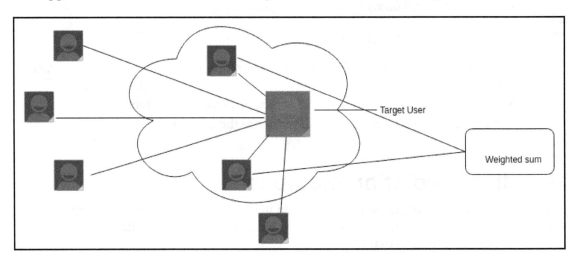

If we have n number of users and x number of items, then we will have a matrix $R \rightarrow n*x$. In the preceding diagram, we can see that there is one target user and multiple other users. Out of these other users, two of them are similar to the target user. Therefore, the previous ratings or behavior can be utilized for generating the recommendations.

Other than the matrix mentioned above, we also need a function to compute the similarity between the users to calculate which users' ratings can be used to generate the recommendations.

To find the similarity between the users (u,v), we find the nearest neighbors using the Pearson Correlation coefficient (Pearson's r):

$$s(u, v) = \frac{\sum_{i \in I_u \cap I_v} (r_{u,i} - \bar{r}_u)(r_{v,i} - \bar{r}_v)}{\sqrt{\sum_{i \in I_u \cap I_v} (r_{u,i} - \bar{r}_u)^2} \sqrt{\sum_{i \in I_u \cap I_v} (r_{v,i} - \bar{r}_v)^2}}$$

This computes the neighborhood $N \subseteq U$ of neighbors of u:

- Perfectly positive correlation = 1
- Perfectly negative correlation = -1

Pearson Correlation has a drawback in that it may show two users as similar even if they have very few ratings in common. To treat this, we can apply a threshold on the items that are rated by both the users.

Cosine similarity: This is another method to find similar users. This takes a different approach than Pearson Correlation.

Unlike Pearson correlation, which uses statistical approach, cosine similarity uses the vector-space approach. In this method, users are not part of the matrix but are represented by |I|-dimensional vectors.

To measure the similarity between two users (vectors), it computes the cosine distance. This is the dot product of the vectors and divides it by taking the product of their L2 (Euclidean) norms.

$$s(u,v) = \frac{\mathbf{r}_u \cdot \mathbf{r}_v}{\|\mathbf{r}_u\|_2 \|\mathbf{r}_v\|_2} = \frac{\sum_i r_{u,i} r_{v,i}}{\sqrt{\sum_i r_{u,i}^2} \sqrt{\sum_i r_{v,i}^2}}$$

When there is no rating for a particular item, the dot product becomes 0 and it drops out.

Now to generate the recommendation, we use:

$$p_{u,i} = \bar{r}_u + \frac{\sum_{u' \in N} s(u,u')(r_{u',i} - \bar{r}_{u'})}{\sum_{u' \in N} |s(u,u')|}$$

This computes the weighted average of the user's rating of the neighbors taking similarity as the weights. It is the most commonly used practice.

Here are some drawbacks of user-based collaborative filtering:

- Sparsity: the matrix formed is usually very sparse and sparsity increases with the increase in number of users and items
- It is not always easy to effectively find nearest neighbors and make recommendations
- It is not very scalable and becomes computationally heavy with the increase in the number of users and items
- Sparse matrices may not be able to predict actual sets of like-minded people

Item-item collaborative filtering

There are some drawbacks to the user-based collaborative filtering, one of them is scalability. To find the nearest neighbors, we find similarities between the neighbors, which involves a lot of computation. It may not be feasible to apply user-based collaborative filtering to systems having millions of users because of high computation power requirements.

So, item-based collaborative filtering is used instead of user-based collaborative filtering to achieve the desired scalability. It looks for patterns such as a few items liked and an other few items disliked by the same set of users, then these are considered to be like-minded and items are recommended.

It is still required that we find the similar items in the item set by using k-Nearest Neighbor or a similar algorithm.

Let's consider a scenario where a user has rated a few items. After a few days, that particular user revisits those items and changes their rating. By changing their rating, the user is essentially going to another neighbor.

Therefore, it is not always recommended to pre-compute the matrix or find the nearest neighbors. This is generally done when the recommendations are actually needed.

Algorithm of item-based collaborative filtering

- For (*i=1 to I*) where *I* refers to every item available:
    - For each customer, *x* who rated *I*
        - For each item *K* purchased by the same customer, *x*
- Save that customer, *x* purchased both *I* and *K*
    - For each item *K*
        - Find the similarity between *I* and *K*

This particular similarity is found using the same methods as used in user-based collaborative filtering:

- Cosine-based similarity
- Correlation-based similarity

A weighted average is used to generate the recommendations.

Let S be the set of items which is similar to i, then predictions can be made. The equation that defines the item-based collaborative filtering is as follows:

$$p_{u,i} = \frac{\sum_{j \in S} s(i,j)(r_{u,j} - b_{u,i})}{\sum_{j \in S} |s(i,j)|} + b_{u,i}$$

For the number of neighbors k, u would have rated some items which are taken into consideration.

Building a movie recommender system

The dataset is maintained by the "GroupLens research" and is available for free at http://g rouplens.org/datasets/movielens/.

We will be working on the dataset of 20 million ratings (ml-20m.zip). This contains:

- 20 million ratings
- 465,000 tag applications applied to 27,000 movies by 138,000 users

We will work on an ALS recommender, which is a matrix factorization algorithm that uses **Alternating Least Squares with Weighted-Lamda-Regularization (ALS-WR)**.

Let's consider that we have a matrix with users, u, and items, i:

Matrix, M (ui) = { r (if item i is rated by the user, u)

0 (if item i is not rated by user, u) }

Here, r represents the ratings submitted.

Consider that we have *m* number of users and *n* number of movies.

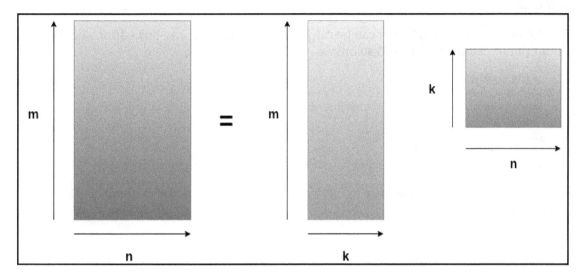

With *m* number of users and *n* number of movies, we create a matrix of users and movies (*m*n*).

The recommendations are generated for any user-movie pair as follows:

$$(i,j), r_{ij}=u_i \cdot m_j, \forall i,j$$

Here, *(i,j)* is the user-movie pair.

Julia has a package, `RecSys.jl`, created by Abhijith Chandraprabhu (https://github.com/abhijithch). The package can be installed as follows:

```
Pkg.update()
Pkg.clone("https://github.com/abhijithch/RecSys.jl.git")
```

We will initiate Julia in parallel mode:

```
julia -p <number of worker processes>
```

As we will be working on a huge dataset it is recommended to initiate the Julia process in parallel.

There is `movielens.jl` in the examples section. We will be using this to generate recommendations for us.

Keep it in the directory where it can be called and open it using any text editor, such as Atom (Juno), Sublime, Vim, and so on:

```
using RecSys

import RecSys: train, recommend, rmse

if isless(Base.VERSION, v"0.5.0-")
    using SparseVectors
end
```

This example will use the package `RecSys` and we are importing the methods `train`, `recommend`, and `rmse`:

```
type MovieRec
    movie_names::FileSpec
    als::ALSWR
    movie_mat::Nullable{SparseVector{AbstractString,Int64}}

    function MovieRec(trainingset::FileSpec, movie_names::FileSpec)
        new(movie_names, ALSWR(trainingset, ParShmem()), nothing)
    end

    function MovieRec(trainingset::FileSpec, movie_names::FileSpec,
    thread::Bool)
    new(movie_names, ALSWR(trainingset, ParThread()), nothing)
    end

    function MovieRec(user_item_ratings::FileSpec,
    item_user_ratings::FileSpec, movie_names::FileSpec)
        new(movie_names, ALSWR(user_item_ratings, item_user_ratings,
        ParBlob()), nothing)
    end
end
```

This creates a composite type, which is a collection of named fields whose instances can be treated as a single value. This is a user-defined data type.

This user-defined data type has three fields and three methods. The field `als` belongs to the type ALSWR, which is defined in RecSys.

The function uses multiple dispatches for the different types of inputs, which could be provided:

- `trainingset` and `movie_names`
- `trainingset`, `movie_names`, and `thread`
- `user_item_ratings`, `item_user_ratings`, and `movie_names`

```
function movie_names(rec::MovieRec)
    if isnull(rec.movie_mat)
        A = read_input(rec.movie_names)
        movie_ids = convert(Array{Int}, A[:,1])
        movie_names = convert(Array{AbstractString}, A[:,2])
        movie_genres = convert(Array{AbstractString}, A[:,3])
        movies = AbstractString[n*" - "*g for (n,g) in
        zip(movie_names, movie_genres)]
        M = SparseVector(maximum(movie_ids), movie_ids, movies)
        rec.movie_mat = Nullable(M)
    end

    get(rec.movie_mat)
end
```

This creates a function, `movie_names`, which is made to work with the `movielens` dataset to handle the data types and missing values in the CSV file, which we use as the input to the recommender system.

Now, to train the system, we will use the train function:

`train(als, num_iterations, num_factors, lambda)`

In this particular scenario, we will do as follows:

`train(movierec::MovieRec, args...) = train(movierec.als, args...)`

This trains the model for the `movielens` dataset using ALS:

```
rmse(movierec::MovieRec, args...; kwargs...) = rmse(movierec.als, args...;
kwargs...)
```

We can also initiate the test for the recommendations that will be produced:

```
rmse(als, testdataset)
```

To start the recommendations, do as follows:

```
recommend(movierec::MovieRec, args...; kwargs...) = recommend(movierec.als,
args...; kwargs...)

function print_recommendations(rec::MovieRec, recommended::Vector{Int},
watched::Vector{Int}, nexcl::Int)
    mnames = movie_names(rec)

    print_list(mnames, watched, "Already watched:")
    (nexcl == 0) || println("Excluded $(nexcl) movies already watched")
    print_list(mnames, recommended, "Recommended:")
    nothing
end
```

This will print the recommendations on screen.

The recommendations that I received were:

```
[96030] Weekend It Lives, The (Ax 'Em) (1992) - Horror
[96255] On Top of the Whale (Het dak van de Walvis) (1982) - Fantasy
[104576] Seasoning House, The (2012) - Horror|Thriller
[92948] Film About a Woman Who... (1974) - Drama
[6085] Neil Young: Human Highway (1982) - Comedy|Drama
[94146] Flower in Hell (Jiokhwa) (1958) - Crime|Drama
[92083] Zen (2009) - Drama
[110603] God's Not Dead (2014) - Drama
[105040] Dragon Day (2013) - Drama|Sci-Fi|Thriller
[80158] Cartoon All-Stars to the Rescue (1990) -
Animation|Children|Comedy|Drama|Fantasy
```

We will call the function test to generate the recommendations:

```
function test(dataset_path)
    ratings_file = DlmFile(joinpath(dataset_path, "ratings.csv");
    dlm=',', header=true)
    movies_file = DlmFile(joinpath(dataset_path, "movies.csv");
    dlm=',', header=true)
    rec = MovieRec(ratings_file, movies_file)
    @time train(rec, 10, 10)

    err = rmse(rec)
    println("rmse of the model: $err")

    println("recommending existing user:")
    print_recommendations(rec, recommend(rec, 100)...)

    println("recommending anonymous user:")
```

```
u_idmap = RecSys.user_idmap(rec.als.inp)
i_idmap = RecSys.item_idmap(rec.als.inp)
# take user 100
actual_user = isempty(u_idmap) ? 100 : findfirst(u_idmap, 100)
rated_anon, ratings_anon = RecSys.items_and_ratings(rec.als.inp,
actual_user)
actual_movie_ids = isempty(i_idmap) ? rated_anon : i_idmap[rated_anon]
nmovies = isempty(i_idmap) ? RecSys.nitems(rec.als.inp) :
maximum(i_idmap)
sp_ratings_anon = SparseVector(nmovies, actual_movie_ids,
ratings_anon)
print_recommendations(rec, recommend(rec, sp_ratings_anon)...)

println("saving model to model.sav")
clear(rec.als)
localize!(rec.als)
save(rec, "model.sav")
nothing
end
```

- This function takes the dataset path as an argument. Here we will provide the path of the directory where we extracted the ml-20m.zip, which we downloaded from grouplens.
- It takes the ratings file and the movies file and creates an object "rec" of type MovieRec, which we created earlier.
- We pass the object to rmse to find out the error.
- It calls print_recommendations, which calls the recommend function to generate the recommendations for the existing user.
- It saves the model for further use.

Summary

In this chapter, we learned what recommendation engines are and how they are important to businesses as well as what value they provide to the customer. We discussed association rule mining and market basket analysis and how this simple method is being used in the industry. Then we went through content-based filtering and its advantages and disadvantages. We then discussed collaborative filtering and different types of collaborative filtering, namely user-based and item-based collaborative filtering. The aim of user-based collaborative filtering is finding similar users that have past ratings or behavior somewhat similar to the target user, whereas item-based collaborative filtering looks for patterns in ratings of items to find like-minded users and to recommend items.

11
Introduction to Deep Learning

Innovators have always longed to make machines that can think. At the point when programmable PCs were first considered, individuals pondered whether they might get to be wise, over a hundred years before one was constructed (Lovelace in 1842).

Today, **artificial intelligence** (**AI**) is a flourishing field with numerous reasonable applications and dynamic exploration points. We look to intelligent programming to automate routine work, process image and audio and extract meaning out of it, automate diagnoses of several diseases, and much more.

In the beginning, when artificial intelligence (AI) was picking up, the field handled and tackled issues that are mentally difficult for individuals, yet moderately straightforward for computers. These issues can be depicted by a rundown of formal, scientific principles. The genuine test for artificial intelligence turned out to be unraveling the undertakings that are simple for individuals to perform yet hard for individuals to depict formally. These issues we explain naturally, for example the ability of humans to understand speech (and sarcasm) and our ability to identify images, especially faces.

This arrangement is to permit computers to learn by gaining experience and to comprehend the world as far as a chain or a tree of facts, with every fact defined as far as its connection to more straightforward facts. By understanding these facts, this methodology maintains a strategic distance from the requirement for human administrators to formally indicate the greater part of the information that the computer needs.

The progressive system of facts permits the computer to learn convoluted ideas by building them out of more straightforward ones. In the event that we draw a diagram indicating how these ideas are based on top of each other, the chart is profound, with numerous layers. Thus, we call this way to deal with AI deep learning.

A number of the early accomplishments of AI occurred in moderately sterile and formal situations and it was not necessary for computers to have much learning of the world. Let's take an example:

- IBM's Deep Blue chess-playing framework in 1997 defeated Mr. Gary Kasparov, the world champion at the time.

We should also consider these factors:

- Chess is obviously an extremely basic world.
- It contains just 64 blocks and 32 elements that can only move in predefined ways.
- Although conceiving a fruitful chess system is a huge achievement, the test is not due to the difficulty of describing the arrangement of chess elements and passable moves to the computer.
- Chess can be totally portrayed by an extremely short rundown of totally formal principles, effortlessly given earlier by the software engineer.

Computers perform better than human beings in some of the tasks and worse in others:

- Abstract tasks that are among the most difficult mental endeavors for a person are among the simplest for a computer. Computers are much better suited for such tasks.
    - An example of this is performing complex mathematical tasks.
- Subjective and natural tasks are performed much better by the average human being than a computer.
    - A man's ordinary life requires a tremendous measure of information about the world.
    - A lot of this learning is subjective and natural, and accordingly difficult to express formally.
    - Computers need to catch this same information so as to act in a wise way. One of the key difficulties in artificial intelligence is the means by which you get this casual learning onto a computer.

A few artificial intelligence ventures have looked to hard-code information about the world in formal dialects. A computer can reason about articulations in these formal dialects, consequently utilizing legitimate deduction rules. This is known as the information base way to deal with artificial intelligence. None of these activities have prompted a noteworthy success.

The difficulties confronted by frameworks depending on hard-coded information propose that AI frameworks require the capacity to obtain their own particular learning, by extracting patterns from crude information. This is known as machine learning, which we studied in previous chapters.

The execution of these straightforward machine-learning calculations depends vigorously on the representation of the information they are given.

For instance, when logistic regression is utilized to suggest the future weather, the AI framework does not look at the patient straightforwardly:

- The specialist tells the framework a few bits of important data, for example, the varying temperatures, wind direction and speed, humidity, and so on.
- Every bit of the data incorporated into the representation of the weather is known as a feature. Logistic regression figures out how each of these features of the weather relates to different weather in different seasons or in other locations.
- In any case, it can't influence the way that the features are defined in any capacity.

One answer for this issue is to utilize the machine, figuring out how to find the mapping from the representation to yield as well as the representation itself. This methodology is known as representation learning. Learned representations frequently bring about much-preferred execution over what can be acquired with hand-planned representations. They additionally permit AI frameworks to quickly adjust to new tasks, with negligible human intercession.

A representation learning calculation can find a decent arrangement of features for a straightforward undertaking in minutes, or for a complex assignment in hours to months. Physically outlining highlights for a complex work require a lot of human time and effort, much more than for computers.

In this chapter we will go through multiple topics, starting with the basic introduction:

- Basic foundations
- Differences between machine learning and deep learning
- What is deep learning?
- Deep feed-forward networks
- Single and multi-layer neural networks
- Convolution networks
- Practical methodology and applications

Revisiting linear algebra

Linear algebra is a widely used branch of mathematics. Linear algebra is a part of discrete mathematics and not of continuous mathematics. A good understanding is needed to understand the machine learning and deep learning models. We will only revise the mathematical objects.

A gist of scalars

A scalar is just a single number (as opposed to a large portion of alternate objects examined in linear algebra, which are generally arrays of various numbers).

A brief outline of vectors

A vector is an organized collection or an array of numbers. We can recognize every individual number by its index in that list. For example:

$$x = [x1, x2, x3, x4 ..... xn]$$

- Vectors can also be thought of as identifying points in space.
- Each element represents the value of coordinate along a different axis.
- We can also index the positions of these values in the vector. Therefore, it makes it easier to access the specific value of the array.

The importance of matrices

- A matrix is a two-dimensional array of numbers.
- Every component is identified by two indexes rather than only one.
- For example, a point in 2D space may be identified as (3,4). It means that the point is 3 points on the x axis and 4 points on the y axis.
- We can also have arrays of such numbers as[(3,4), (2,4), (1,0)]. Such an array is called a matrix.

What are tensors?

If more than two-dimensions are needed (matrix) then we use tensors.

This is an array of numbers without a defined number of axes.

Such objects have a structure as follows: *T (x, y, z)*

[(1,3,5), (11,12,23), (34,32,1)]

Probability and information theory

Probability theory is a scientific system for speaking to questionable explanations. It gives a method for evaluating instability and adages for inferring new indeterminate statements.

In applications of AI, we utilize probability theory as follows:

- The laws of probability define how AI frameworks ought to reason, so algorithms are designed to figure or approximate different expressions inferred on utilizing probability theory
- Probability and statistics can be utilized to hypothetically investigate the behavior of proposed AI frameworks

While probability theory permits us to put forth indeterminate expressions and reason within the sight of uncertainty, data permits us to measure the degree of uncertainty in a probability distribution.

Why probability?

Machine learning makes substantial utilization of probability theory unlike other branches of computer science that are mainly dependent on the deterministic nature of the computer system:

- This is on the grounds that machine learning must dependably manage uncertain quantities.
- Some of the time it may also be necessary to manage stochastic (non-deterministic) amounts. Uncertainty and stochasticity can emerge from numerous sources.

All exercises require some capacity to reason within the sight of uncertainty. Actually, with past numerical explanations that are valid by definition, it is difficult to think about any suggestion that is completely valid or any occasion that is totally ensured to happen.

Uncertainty has are three possible sources:

- Existing stochasticity in the framework that is being modeled.
    - For instance, while playing a card game we make the assumption that the cards are truly shuffled in a random fashion.
- Fragmented observability. When a greater part of the variables that drive the conduct of the framework cannot be observed then even deterministic frameworks can seem stochastic.
    - For instance, in a question with multiple-choice options as answers, one choice leads to the correct answer while others will result in nothing. The result given the challenger's decision is deterministic, yet from the candidate's perspective, the result is indeterminate.
- Fragmented modeling. When we utilize a model that must dispose of a portion of the data we have observed, the disposed-of data results in instability in the model's expectations.
    - For instance, assume we manufacture a robot that can precisely watch the area of each article around it. In the event that the robot discretizes space while anticipating the future area of these objects, then the discretization makes the robot quickly become dubious about the exact position of the articles: every item could be any place inside the discrete cell that it was seen to possess.

A probability can be seen as the augmentation of rationale to manage uncertainty. Rationale gives an arrangement of formal rules for figuring out what suggestions are inferred to be true or false given the suspicion that some other arrangement of recommendations is true or false.

Probability hypothesis gives an arrangement of formal principles for deciding the probability of a suggestion being genuine given the probability of the different recommendations.

Differences between machine learning and deep learning

Machine learning and deep learning intend to accomplish the same objective, but, they are distinctive and amount to various thoughts. Machine learning is the most major of the two and scientists and mathematicians have been doing research on it for a few decades now. Deep learning is a comparatively new idea. Deep learning is based on learning via neural networks (multiple layers) to achieve the goal. Understanding the difference between the two is important to know where we should apply deep learning and which problems can be solved using machine learning.

It was understood that a more intense approach to construct pattern recognition algorithms is achieved by utilizing the information that can be effortlessly mined relying only upon the area and the deciding objective.

For instance, in image recognition we accumulate various pictures and expand the algorithm on that. Utilizing the information as a part of these pictures, our model can be trained to recognize creatures, human appearances, or different examples.

Machine learning is connected to different areas and now it is not limited to image or character recognition. It is currently utilized intensely as a part of robotics, financial markets, self-driving cars, and genome analysis. We learned about machine learning in previous chapters and now we can go further to understand how different it is from deep learning.

What is deep learning?

Deep learning started becoming popular in 2006. It is also known as hierarchical learning. Its applications are wide and it has increased the scope of artificial intelligence and machine learning. There is a huge interest in deep learning from the community.

Deep learning refers to a class of machine learning techniques which:

- Perform unsupervised or supervised feature extraction.
- Perform pattern analysis or classification by exploiting multiple layers of non-linear information processing.

It consists of a hierarchy of features or factors. In this hierarchy, lower-level features help in defining higher-level features. Artificial neural networks are typically used in deep learning.

- Conventional machine learning models learn patterns or clusters. Deep neural networks learn computations with a very small number of steps.
- Generally speaking, the deeper the neural network, the more powerful it gets.
- Neural networks are updated according to the new data made available.
- Artificial neural networks are fault tolerant, which means that if some part of the network is destroyed, then that may affect the performance of the network, but the key functioning of the network may still be retained.
- Deep learning algorithms learn multiple levels of representation and do the computations in parallel, which may be of increasing complexity.

If we fast forward to today, there is a widespread enthusiasm for something that many refer to as deep learning. The most prominent sorts of deep learning models, as they are utilized as a part of extensive scale image recognition tasks, are known as Convolutional Neural Nets, or essentially ConvNets.

Deep learning emphasizes the sort of model that we need to utilize (such as a deep convolutional multi-layer neural system) and that we can utilize information to fill in the missing parameters.

With deep learning comes incredible obligation. Since we are beginning with a model of the world which has a high dimensionality, we truly require a great deal of information which we also call big data, and a considerable measure of computational force (General Purpose GPUs/ High performance computing). Convolutions are utilized widely as a part of deep learning (particularly computer vision applications).

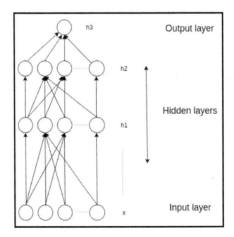

In the previous image we saw three layers:

- **Output layer**: Here this predicts a supervised target
- **Hidden layer**: Abstract representations of the intermediary functions
- **Input layer**: Raw inputs

Artificially simulated neurons stand for the building blocks of the multi-layer artificial neural systems. The essential idea is to simulate a human brain and how it solves a complex problem. The main idea to manufacture neural systems was based upon these theories and models.

Numerous more significant leaps were brought about in the last few decades with regards to deep-learning algorithms. These can be utilized to make feature indicators from unlabeled information and also to pre-train deep neural networks, which are the neural systems that are made out of numerous layers.

Neural networks are an interesting issue in scholastic exploration, as well as in huge innovation organizations, for example for companies such as Facebook, Microsoft, and Google, who are investing heavily in deep-learning research.

Complex neural networks fueled by deep-learning calculations are considered as best in class with regards to critical problem solving. For example:

- **Google's image search**: We can search images on the Internet using the Google image search tool. This can be done by uploading an image or giving the URL of the image to search for on the Internet.
- **Google Translate**: This tool can read text in images and understand speech to translate or tell meaning in several languages.

One other very famous application is used in the self-driving cars, created by Google or Tesla. They are powered by deep learning to find out the best path, drive through the traffic in real time, and perform necessary tasks as they would if they were being driven by a human driver.

Deep feedforward networks

Deep feedforward networks are the most famous deep learning models. These are also called the following:

- Feedforward neural networks.
- **Multi-layer perceptrons (MLPs)**

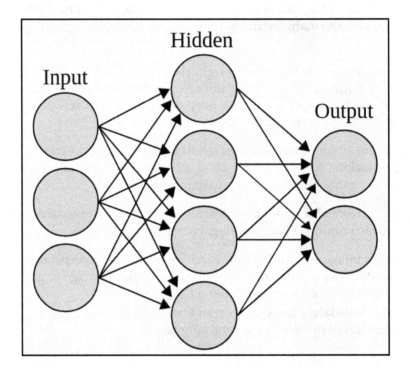

The aim of the feed-forward neural network is to learn by their parameters and define a function that maps to the output *y:*

$$y = f(x, theta)$$

As also depicted in the image, the feedforward neural networks are called such because of their data flows in one direction. It starts from the *x* and passes through the function for the intermediate calculations to generate *y*.

When such systems also include connections to the previous layer (feedback), then these are known as recurrent neural networks.

Feedforward systems are of great significance to machine learning experts. They frame the premise of numerous imperative business applications. For instance, the convolutional systems utilized for natural language processing from speech are a specific sort of feedforward system.

Feedforward systems are a reasonable stepping stone on the way to recurrent networks. These systems have numerous natural language applications. Feedforward neural networks are called networks since they are represented by forming together numerous different functions. The model is connected with a directed acyclic graph portraying how the functions are created together.

For example, we have three functions – *f(1)*, *f(2)*, and *f(3)*.

They are chained or associated together as follows:

$$f(x) = f(3)(f(2)(f(1)(x)))$$

These chain structures are the most normally utilized structures of neural systems. For this situation:

- *f(1)* is known as the first layer of the network.
- *f(2)* is known as the second layer, and so on.
- The general length of the chain gives the depth of the model. It is from this wording the name "deep learning" emerges.
- The final layer of a feedforward network is known as the output or yield layer.

Amid neural network training, we follow these steps:

1. Drive *f(x)* to coordinate *f*(x)*. The training information has data with noise and inexact data off **(x)* assessed at different training sets.
2. Every example of *x* is associated by a label $y \approx f*(x)$.
3. The training cases determine straightforwardly what the yield layer must do at every point *x*. That is, it must create a value that is near *y*.

Understanding the hidden layers in a neural network

The conduct of alternate layers is not straightforwardly specified by the training information. The learning algorithm must choose how to utilize those layers to create the desired yield, yet the training information does not say what every individual layer ought to do.

Rather, it is the learning algorithm which must choose how to utilize these layers to best execute an estimation off *. Since the training information does not demonstrate the desired yield for each of these layers, these layers are called hidden layers.

The motivation of neural networks

- These systems are called neural on the grounds that they are approximately motivated by neuroscience.
- Each concealed or hidden layer of the system is generally vector-valued.
- The dimension of y of these hidden layers decides the width of the model.
- Every component of the vector might be translated as assuming a part comparable to a neuron.
- As opposed to thinking about the layer as exhibiting a single vector-to-vector function, it should be thought that the layer comprises of numerous units that work in parallel, each exhibiting a vector-to-scalar function.
- Each unit looks like a neuron in respect that it gets a contribution from numerous different units and registers its own activation value.
- Using numerous layers of vector-valued representation is drawn from neuroscience.
- The decision of the function $f(i)(x)$ used to figure out these representations is somewhat guided by neuroscientific observations about the functions that organic neurons process.

We studied regularization in previous chapters. Let's study why this is important and required for deep learning models.

Understanding regularization

The main issue in machine learning is the means by which to make an algorithm that will perform well on the training information, as well as on new inputs. Numerous techniques utilized as a part of machine learning are expressly intended to diminish test errors, potentially to the detriment of increased training errors. These techniques are referred to aggregately as regularization.

There are many types of regularization accessible to the deep-learning specialist. More effective regularization systems have been one of the research efforts in the field.

There are numerous regularization systems.

- Additional constraints on a machine learning model
    - For example, including constraints on the parameter values.
- Additional terms in the target functions that can be taken as comparing to a delicate requirement on the parameter values
- If done strategically and carefully, these additional requirements and constraints can result in enhanced performance on the testing data
- These constraints and restrictions can also be used to encode specific sorts of prior learning
- These constraints and restrictions can also lead to generalization of the model
- Ensemble methods also use regularization to generate better results

With regards to deep learning, most regularization procedures depend on regularizing estimators. To regulate the estimator:

- We need to exchange increased bias for reduced variance
- An effective regularizer is one that makes a profitable exchange, which means it decreases the variance drastically whilst not excessively expanding the bias

In overfitting and generalization we concentrate on these situations for the model that we are training:

- Avoid the true information on the producing process to take into account the underfitting and inducing bias
- Include the true information on the producing process
- Include information on the producing process and additionally numerous other information on producing processes to take into account the overfitting where variance instead of bias rules the estimation error

The objective of regularization is to take a model to the second process that is mentioned.

An excessively complex model family does not, as a matter of course, incorporate the target function or the genuine information producing process. In any case, most utilizations of deep-learning algorithms are where the genuine information producing procedure is in all likelihood outside the model family. Deep learning algorithms are normally connected, to a great degree, to complicated use cases such as image recognition, speech recognition, self-driving cars, and so on.

This means that controlling the complexity of the nature of the model is not just a matter of finding a model of the appropriate size with the right set of parameters.

Optimizing deep learning models

Optimization methods are vital in designing algorithms to extract desired knowledge from huge volumes of data. Deep learning is a rapidly evolving field where new optimization techniques are generated.

Deep learning algorithms include enhancement in numerous connections. For instance, performing deduction in models, for example, PCA, includes taking care of an improvement issue.

We regularly utilize diagnostic optimization to compose verifications or configuration calculations. Of the majority of the numerous optimization issues required in deep learning, the most difficult is preparing the neural network.

It is very common to contribute days, or even months, of time to many machines with a specific end goal to solve even a single case of the neural system-training problem. Since this issue is so critical and thus expensive, a specific arrangement of optimization strategies has been produced for enhancing it.

The case of optimization

To find the parameters θ of a neural network that significantly lessen a cost function $J(\theta)$, commonly incorporates an execution measure assessed on the whole training set and additionally extra regularization terms.

An optimization used as a training algorithm for a machine learning task is different from immaculate optimization. More complex algorithms adjust their learning rates amid training or influence data contained in the second derivatives of the cost function. Finally, a few optimization methodologies are created by joining basic optimization algorithms into higher-level strategies.

Optimization algorithms utilized for the training of deep learning models are different from conventional optimization algorithms in a few ways:

- Machine learning typically acts in a roundabout way. In most machine-learning situations, we think about some execution measure P, that is defined as for the test set and may likewise be obstinate. We accordingly upgrade P just in a roundabout way. We decrease a different cost function $J(\theta)$ with the expectation that doing so will enhance P.

This is as opposed to pure optimization, where minimizing J is an objective all by itself. Optimization algorithms for preparing deep learning models likewise commonly incorporate some specialization on the specific structure of machine learning target functions.

Implementation in Julia

There are many good and tested libraries for deep learning in popular programming languages:

- Theano (Python) can utilize both CPU and GPU (from the MILA Lab at the University of Montreal)
- Torch (Lua) is a Matlab-like environment (from Ronan Collobert, Clement Farabet, and Koray Kavukcuoglu)
- Tensorflow (Python) makes use of data flow graphs
- MXNet (Python, R, Julia, C++)
- Caffe is the most popular and widely used
- Keras (Python) based on Theano
- Mocha (Julia) by Chiyuan Zhang

We will mainly go through Mocha for Julia, which is an amazing package written by Chiyuan Zhang, a PhD student at MIT.

To start, add the package as follows:

```
Pkg.update()
Pkg.add("Mocha")
```

Network architecture

Network architecture in Mocha refers to a set of layers:

```
data_layer = HDF5DataLayer(name="data", source="data-list.txt",
batch_size=64, tops=[:data])
ip_layer   = InnerProductLayer(name="ip", output_dim=500, tops=[:ip],
bottoms=[:data])
```

- The input of the `ip_layer` has the same name as the output of the `data_layer`
- The same name connects them

A topological sort is carried out by Mocha on a collection of layers.

Types of layers

- Data layers
    - These layers read information from the source and feed them to the top layers
- Computation layers
    - These take the input stream from the base layers, do the calculations, and feed the results generated to the top layers
- Loss layers
    - These layers take processed results (and ground truth names/labels) from the base layers and figure a scalar loss value
    - Loss values from all the layers and regularizers in a net are included to characterize the final loss function of the net
    - The net parameters in the back propagation are trained with the help of the loss function

- Statistics layers
    - These take information from the base layers and generate valuable insights like classification accuracy
    - Insights are gathered all through the various iterations
    - `reset_statistics` can be utilized to unequivocally reset the statistics aggregation
- Utility Layers

Neurons (activation functions)

Let's understand real neural nets (brains). Neuroscience is the study of the functioning of the brain and has given us good evidence about the way in which it works. Neurons are the real information storage of the brain. It is also very important to understand their connection strengths, namely how strongly one neuron can influence those neurons connected to it.

Learning or the repetition of a task and exposure to new stimulating procedures or environment often leads to activity in the brain which is actually the neurons acting according to the new data being received.

The neurons, and therefore the brain, behave very differently to different stimuli and environments. They may react or get excited more in some scenarios as compared to others.

Some understanding of this is important in getting to know about artificial neural networks:

- Neurons can be connected to any layer
- The neuron of every layer will influence the yield in the forward pass and the slope in the backward pass consequently, unless it is an identity neuron
- By default, layers have an identity neuron

Let's go through the various types of neurons that we can utilize to make the network:

- `class Neurons.Identity`
    - This is an activation function whose input is not changed.
- `class Neurons.ReLU`
    - Rectified Linear Unit. Amid the forward pass, this restrains all restraints underneath some limit ϵ, normally 0.
    - It processes point-wise $y=max(\epsilon,x)$.

- class Neurons.LreLU
  - Leaky Rectified Linear Unit. A Leaky ReLU can settle the "dying ReLU" issue.
  - ReLU's can "die" if a sufficiently substantial gradient changes the weights such that the neuron never activates on new information.
- class Neurons.Sigmoid
  - Sigmoid is a smoothed step function
  - It produces roughly 0 for negative information with vast absolute values and estimated 1 for huge positive inputs
  - The point-wise equation is $y=1/(1+e-x)y=1/(1+e-x)$
- class Neurons.Tanh
  - Tanh is a variation of Sigmoid
  - It takes values in $\pm1\pm1$ rather than the unit interim
  - The point-wise equation is $y=(1-e-2x)/(1+e-2x)$

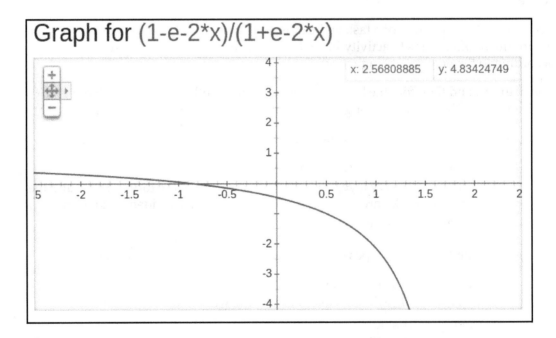

Graph for (1-e-2*x)/(1+e-2*x)

x: 2.56808885   y: 4.83424749

Understanding regularizers for ANN

We studied regularizers in our previous sections. Regularizers include additional penalties or restrictions for network parameters to confine the complexity of the model. In a popular deep-learning framework, caffe, it is known as decay.

Weight decay and regularization are comparable in back-propagation. The theoretical contrast in the forward pass is that when regarded as weight decay, they are not considered as being a piece of the objective function.

By default, Mocha similarly eliminates the forward calculation for regularizers with a specific end goal to decrease the quantity of calculations. We utilize the term regularization rather than weight decay since it is less demanding to comprehend.

- class `NoRegu`: No regularization
- class `L2Regu`: L2 regularizer
- class `L1Regu`: L1 regularizer

Norm constraints

Norm restrictions are a more immediate method for limiting the complexity of the model by unequivocally contracting the parameters in each of the n cycles if the standard or norm of the parameters surpasses a given threshold.

- class `NoCons`: No constraints
- class `L2Cons`: Restrict the Euclidean norm of parameters. Threshold and contracting are applied to every parameter. In particular, the threshold is applied to each filter for the filters parameter of a convolution layer.

Using solvers in deep neural networks

Mocha contains broadly useful stochastic (sub-) gradient-based solvers. These can be utilized to prepare deep neural networks.

A solver is developed by indicating a lexicon of solver parameters that give vital configuration:

- General settings like stop conditions
- Parameters particular to a specific calculation

Additionally, it is generally recommended to take some short breaks between training iterations to print progress or for saving a snapshot. These are called coffee breaks in Mocha.

Solver algorithms

- class SGD: Stochastic Gradient Descent with momentum.
    - lr_policy: Learning rate policy.
    - mom_policy: Momentum policy.
- class Nesterov: Stochastic Nesterov accelerated gradient method.
    - lr_policy: Learning rate policy.
    - mom_policy: Momentum policy.
- class Adam: A Method for Stochastic Optimization
    - lr_policy: Learning rate policy.
    - beta1: Exponential decay factor for first order moment estimates. *0<=beta1<1*, default *0.9*
    - beta2: Exponential decay factor for second order moment estimates, *0<=beta1<1*, default *0.999*.
    - epsilon: Affects the scaling of the parameter updates for numerical conditioning, default *1e-8*.

Coffee breaks

Training can become a very computationally intensive iteration of several loops. It is generally recommended to take some short breaks between training iterations to print progress or for saving a snapshot. These are called coffee breaks in Mocha. They are performed as follows:

```
# report training progress every 1000 iterations
add_coffee_break(solver, TrainingSummary(), every_n_iter=1000)

# save snapshots every 5000 iterations
add_coffee_break(solver, Snapshot(exp_dir), every_n_iter=5000)
```

This prints the training summary every 1,000 iterations and saves a snapshot every 5,000 iterations.

Image classification with pre-trained Imagenet CNN

MNIST is a handwritten digit recognition dataset. It contains the following:

- 60,000 training examples
- 10,000 test examples
- 28 x 28 single channel grayscale images

We can use `get-mnist.sh` script to download the dataset

It calls `mnist.convert.jl` to convert the binary dataset into a HDF5 file that Mocha can read.

`data/train.hdf5` and `data/test.hdf5` will be generated when the conversion finishes.

We are using Mocha's native extension here to get faster convolution:

```
ENV["MOCHA_USE_NATIVE_EXT"] = "true"

using Mocha

backend = CPUBackend()
init(backend)
```

This configures Mocha to use the native background and not the GPU (CUDA).

Now, we will proceed with defining the network structure. We will start by defining a data layer that will read the HDF5 file. This will be the input for the network.

The `source` contains a list of real data files:

```
data_layer  = HDF5DataLayer(name="train-data", source="data/train.txt",
batch_size=64, shuffle=true)
```

Mini-batches are formed to process the data. As the batch size increases, the variance decreases but it affects the computational performance.

Shuffling reduces the effect of ordering during the training.

Now we will proceed with defining the convolution layer:

```
conv_layer = ConvolutionLayer(name="conv1", n_filter=20, kernel=(5,5),
bottoms=[:data], tops=[:conv1])
```

- `name`: The name of the layer to identify it.

- `n_filter`: The number of convolution filters.
- `kernel`: The size of the filter.
- `bottoms`: An array to define where to get the input. (The HDF5 data layer that we defined.)
- `tops`: The output of the convolution layer.

Define more convolution layers as follows:

```
pool_layer = PoolingLayer(name="pool1", kernel=(2,2), stride=(2,2),
    bottoms=[:conv1], tops=[:pool1])
conv2_layer = ConvolutionLayer(name="conv2", n_filter=50, kernel=(5,5),
    bottoms=[:pool1], tops=[:conv2])
pool2_layer = PoolingLayer(name="pool2", kernel=(2,2), stride=(2,2),
    bottoms=[:conv2], tops=[:pool2])
```

These are two fully connected layers after convolution and pooling layers.

The computation to create the layer is an inner product between the input and the layer weights. These are also called an `InnerProductLayer`.

The layer weights are also learned, so we also give names to the two layers:

```
fc1_layer  = InnerProductLayer(name="ip1", output_dim=500,
    neuron=Neurons.ReLU(), bottoms=[:pool2], tops=[:ip1])
fc2_layer  = InnerProductLayer(name="ip2", output_dim=10,
    bottoms=[:ip1], tops=[:ip2])
```

The last inner product layer has the dimension of 10, which represents the number of classes (digits 0~9).

This is the basic structure of LeNet. To train this network, we will define a loss function by adding a loss layer:

```
loss_layer = SoftmaxLossLayer(name="loss", bottoms=[:ip2,:label])
```

We can now construct our network:

```
common_layers = [conv_layer, pool_layer, conv2_layer, pool2_layer,
    fc1_layer, fc2_layer]

net = Net("MNIST-train", backend, [data_layer, common_layers...,
loss_layer])
```

Training the neural network with Stochastic Gradient Descent is performed as follows:

```
exp_dir = "snapshots"
method = SGD()

params = make_solver_parameters(method, max_iter=10000, regu_coef=0.0005,
    mom_policy=MomPolicy.Fixed(0.9),
    lr_policy=LRPolicy.Inv(0.01, 0.0001, 0.75),
    load_from=exp_dir)

solver = Solver(method, params)
```

The parameters used are:

- `max_iter`: These are the maximum number of iterations the solver will execute to train the network
- `regu_coef`: The regularization coefficient
- `mom_policy`: The momentum policy
- `lr_policy`: The learning rate policy
- `load_from`: Here we can load the saved model from a file or a directory

Add some coffee breaks as follows:

```
setup_coffee_lounge(solver, save_into="$exp_dir/statistics.hdf5",
every_n_iter=1000)

add_coffee_break(solver, TrainingSummary(), every_n_iter=100)

add_coffee_break(solver, Snapshot(exp_dir), every_n_iter=5000)
```

Performance is checked periodically on a separate validation set so we can see the progress. The validation dataset that we have will be used as the test dataset.

To perform an evaluation, a new network is defined with the same architecture but a different data layer, which will get the input from the validation set:

```
data_layer_test = HDF5DataLayer(name="test-data", source="data/test.txt",
batch_size=100)

acc_layer = AccuracyLayer(name="test-accuracy", bottoms=[:ip2, :label])

test_net = Net("MNIST-test", backend, [data_layer_test, common_layers...,
acc_layer])
```

Add a coffee break to get the report of the validation performance, as follows:

```
add_coffee_break(solver, ValidationPerformance(test_net),
every_n_iter=1000)
```

Finally, start the training, as follows:

```
solve(solver, net)

destroy(net)
destroy(test_net)
shutdown(backend)
```

These are the two networks we created:

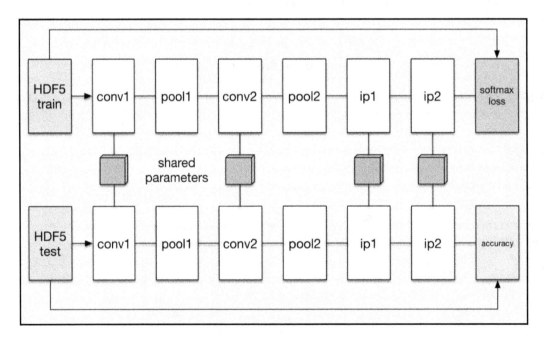

Now we run the model generated on the test data that we have. We get the following output:

```
Correct label index: 5
Label probability vector:
Float32[5.870685e-6
0.00057068263
1.5419962e-5
8.387835e-7
0.99935246
5.5915066e-6
4.284061e-5
1.2896479e-6
4.2869314e-7
4.600691e-6]
```

Summary

In this chapter, we learned about deep learning and how different it is from machine learning. Deep learning refers to a class of machine learning techniques that perform unsupervised or supervised feature extraction and pattern analysis or classification by exploiting multiple layers of non-linear information processing.

We studied deep feedforward networks, regularization, and optimizing deep learning models. We also learned how to create a neural network to classify hand-written digits using Mocha in Julia.

References

- http://docs.julialang.org/en/release-.4/manual/
- https://github.com/pluskid/Mocha.jl
- http://psych.utoronto.ca/users/reingold/courses/ai/nn.html
- https://www.microsoft.com/en-us/research/wp-content/uploads/216/2/DeepLearning-NowPublishing-Vol7-SIG-39.pdf
- http://www.deeplearningbook.org/contents/intro.html
- http://deeplearning.net/tutorial/deeplearning.pdf

Index

www.ingramcontent.com/pod-product-compliance
Lightning Source LLC
Chambersburg PA
CBHW062056050326
40690CB00016B/3116